A GUIDE TO WELSH LITERATURE

A GUIDE TO WELSH LITERATURE
VOLUME I

Edited by
A. O. H. JARMAN
and
GWILYM REES HUGHES

Christopher Davies
Swansea

© Christopher Davies (Publishers) Ltd

First published 1976 by
Christopher Davies (Publishers) Ltd
4/5 Thomas Row
Swansea. SA1 1NJ

All rights reserved. No part of this publication may be reproduced, stored in a retrieval system, or transmitted, in any form or by any means, electronic, mechanical, photocopying, recording or otherwise, without the prior permission of Christopher Davies (Publishers) Ltd

ISBN 0 7154 0124 6

*Printed in Britain by
Salesbury Press Ltd
Llandybie, Ammanford
Dyfed*

Published with the support of the
Welsh Arts Council

To Eira and Eldra

ACKNOWLEDGEMENTS

Acknowledgements are due to the University of Wales Press for permission to print Mr. Saunders Lewis's translations of *Urien Yrechwydd, Gwaith Argoed Llwyfain* and *Marwnad Owain;* to Macmillan and Co., Ltd. for permission to quote passages from Professor J. C. Clancy's translations of *Gwaith Gwên Ystrad, Dadolwch Urien, Edmyg Dinbych, Armes Prydain,* 'The War-band's Return' and 'The Wind'; to Penguin Books Ltd. for permission to print Mr. Anthony Conran's translation of *Pais Dinogad*; to J. M. Dent & Sons Ltd. for permission to quote passages from the translations of the Mabinogion by Professor Gwyn Jones and the late Professor Thomas Jones; to the National Library of Wales for permission to use illustrations from the Hendregadredd MS, Peniarth MS 28, The Black Book of Carmarthen and Mostyn MS 88; to the South Glamorgan Central Library, Cardiff, for permission to use an illustration from the Book of Aneirin; to the Archbishop of Canterbury and the Trustees of Lambeth Palace Library for permission to use a reproduction of the Red and White Dragons' fight at Vortigern's Court; to Professor E. G. Bowen for his kindness in preparing the map facing page 51; and to Mrs. Eldra Jarman for undertaking the labour of compiling the Index.

CONTENTS

Chapter		Page
I	The Historical Background of Early Welsh Verse *Ceri W. Lewis*	11
II	Taliesin *A. O. H. Jarman*	51
III	Aneirin — The Gododdin *A. O. H. Jarman*	68
IV	Saga Poetry — The Cycle of Llywarch Hen *A. O. H. Jarman*	81
V	The Later Cynfeirdd *A. O. H. Jarman*	98
VI	The Court Poets: Their Function, Status and Craft *Ceri W. Lewis*	118
VII	The Poets of the Princes *D. Myrddin Lloyd*	157
VIII	Early Prose: The Mabinogi *Glyn E. Jones*	189
IX	Tales and Romances *Brynley F. Roberts*	203
X	Historical Writing *Brynley F. Roberts*	244
XI	Functional Prose: Religion, Science, Grammar, Law *Morfydd E. Owen*	248

ILLUSTRATIONS

Facing page

The North and Wales — the geographical background of Early Welsh Verse — a newly commissioned map by Professor E. G. Bowen.	52
A page from The Book of Aneirin, Skene FAB Vol. II, p. 62	98
Frontispiece The Black Book of Carmarthen, folio. Skene FAB Vol. I.	99
Part of the Vaunting Poem of Hywel ap Owain Gwynedd. Hendregadredd ms.	188
The Red and White Dragons' fight at Vortigern's Court, see Loomis, No. 349, Lambeth, St. Alban's Chronicle, f.43, *c.* 1460.	189
Mostyn 88, p. 26, The Human Figure with signs of the Zodiac drawn on it.	266
Peniarth 28, four court officials.	267

PREFACE

This work is the first of a projected series of volumes in which it is hoped to outline the history and development of Welsh literature from its beginnings in the sixth century to the present day. Various scholars have been invited to contribute chapters on aspects of the subject in which they are specialists, and their discussions will be both descriptive and interpretative in character. The present volume deals with Welsh literature during the first seven centuries of its existence, roughly the period of Welsh independence, and surveys the poetry of the Cynfeirdd and the Gogynfeirdd and the work of prose writers from the eleventh century onwards. The end of the thirteenth century was adopted as a *terminus* for the period surveyed, but the limitation has not been applied too strictly. Some overlapping has occurred here and there between chapters by different contributors, but this was accepted as unavoidable and was not discouraged. Uniformity of interpretation was not enjoined on the contributors but a remarkable consensus of opinion has been achieved, despite the fact that much research and critical work remains to be done on early and medieval Welsh literature. Throughout the volume it has been thought important to bring out the relationship between Welsh literature and its historical and social background, both within the confines of Wales and in the broader Celtic, British or European context. Quotations from the works discussed are in nearly every instance given solely in translation, but the reader should always bear in mind that they were originally composed or written in Old or Medieval Welsh and that translation is rarely, if ever, entirely adequate. Ample bibliographies are provided at the end of each chapter in order to aid further study.

A. O. H. Jarman
Gwilym Rees Hughes

CHAPTER I

THE HISTORICAL BACKGROUND OF EARLY WELSH VERSE

CERI W. LEWIS

One outstanding feature of Welsh literature, which has aroused the interest of many distinguished scholars, is the venerable antiquity of the bardic tradition. Next to the Greeks and Romans, the Welsh, it has been claimed, have one of the oldest extant literatures in the whole of western Europe. For Welsh literature extends in an unbroken tradition, particularly in the field of poetry, from the latter half of the sixth century A.D. to the modern period. The oldest extant Welsh verse, however, belongs not to the area which is today called Wales but to regions which are now part of southern Scotland and northern England. For down to approximately the middle of the seventh century the Welsh (or Britons, as they were then called) still ruled over southern Scotland (to the south of the modern Glasgow and Edinburgh), north-west and south-west England, as well as a Wales appreciably greater in extent than the geographical area with which we are today familiar. By the middle of the sixth century, at the very latest, the old synthetic (or inflected) British tongue spoken by the people who controlled these areas had disintegrated to such an extent as to appear as a new analytic language, Welsh, and it was in this language, whose lexical, phonological and syntactical features, nevertheless, differed appreciably from those which characterize Modern Welsh, that the bards Taliesin and Aneirin composed their panegyric and elegiac verses in the second half of the century.

The synthetic British (or Brittonic) dialects, which were formerly spoken by the ancient Britons throughout the whole area lying south of the Forth and Clyde, had been introduced into this island by a series of tribal immigrations from France,

Belgium, and other parts of the Continent. These immigrations, which have been ascribed to various periods in the pre-Christian era, represented an offshoot of the Gauls who had settled in those regions in a much earlier period, and the dialects spoken by the British invaders had undergone certain phonetic changes shared by contemporary Gaulish also. These people introduced the distinctive culture which archaeologists call 'La Tène'. But there had been immigrations of people who spoke Celtic dialects before this, and it is quite possible that the Picts, who, before the foundation of the kingdom of Dálriada (mainly Argyll and its islands), ruled all Scotland north of the Antonine Wall as well as the Hebrides and the Northern Isles, represent in part the northernmost settlers from these earlier tribal movements. According to the most authoritative view, their language, Pictish, which survives only in proper names and largely undeciphered inscriptions, was probably a mixture of a non-Indo-European language spoken by the indigenous population and a Celtic language which bore some affinity to British, though it was not entirely identical with the latter.

The information which we possess concerning the organization of early British society shows that it was divided into fairly large and, from time to time, mutually hostile tribal units ruled by kings or princes, with smaller subdivisions. Every major tribal unit possessed a primitive 'capital' and, frequently, lesser towns as well; witness, on the one hand, the great hill fortresses of Iron-Age Britain, such as Maiden Castle, Dorset, which, as the excavations which have been carried out there confirm, goes back to at least *c*. 300 B.C., or, on the other hand, the lowland 'city' of Verulamium, near St. Albans, which was the tribal capital of the Catuvellauni. The urbanization of southern Britain may have reached its full development during the late second and first centuries B.C., and Yarnbury in Wiltshire, Hembury in Devon, and Carn Brea in Cornwall can all be cited as examples of the great Brythonic *oppida* which flourished on the eve of the Roman Conquest. To the east, the hill-fort area stretches across southern Britain into Sussex, and this area broadly coincides with the earliest centre of town building in Britain. Wales and the Marches constitute another area in which the construction of hill fortresses seems to have been fairly common. In Scotland, significantly, the spread of the larger hill forts is more or less confined to the predominantly Brythonic area, for the Pictish lands to the north of the Forth do not reflect a similar sequence. This urban revolution, some archaeologists have cogently argued, marked the transition from barbarism to civilization in the Celtic world. It is against this background, too, that one can best appreciate the major cultural significance of the great enclosures of Belgic Britain, such as Camulodunum, Verulamium, or Bagendon. It has further been suggested that writing, another criterion which can arguably be adopted as marking the advent of civilization, was a necessary by-product of this urban revolution, and the numismatic evidence suggests that the series of inscribed coinage current in pre-Roman Britain conforms approximately to the development suggested by the spread of the great hill fortresses.

This urban development can be associated also with an important social and political upheaval, involving the rise to power and prominence of an aristocratic military class and their *equites,* who exercised great power alongside the kings or princes. This transition, for which there is some evidence in Julius Caesar's celebrated narrative, was probably proceeding apace during the second, possibly even the third, century B.C. It is reflected in the archaeological record in the appearance of the inhumation cemeteries, which replaced the great tumulus burials of the Bronze Age. The political structure in Britain was therefore not only monarchical but also aristocratic. It was this aristocratic military caste that constituted the dominant element in native British society immediately before the Roman Conquest, and, significantly, it was this class of native *tyranni* that eventually assumed power once again after the Roman military and political organization had collapsed in the early fifth century.

In these early Celtic societies the panegyrists who were closely attached to the ruling dynasties fulfilled a vitally important function, for there is ample evidence from Classical antiquity onwards to show that these societies were not only dependent on military power and the skilful exploitation of such economic resources as they had at their command, but were also constantly sustained and inspired by an ideal, which was the cohesive bond that helped effectively to unite the tribal units and their rulers. This was the steadfast conviction that honour, immortal fame and glory, renown for the great aristocratic virtues of valour and unstinting liberality, and noble descent in the king or prince or chief were indispensable prerequisites if the society was to retain its basic stability and to flourish. It became necessary, therefore, from a very early period to nurture a distinctive class of professional propagandists who were closely attached to the individual rulers and their families and whose primary function was to sustain, and also to spread as widely as possible, the fame of their regal or aristocratic patrons by singing their praises in verse. This function originally had a profound social and religious significance, for it stemmed from the concept which prevailed in early Indo-European society that the ruler was a divine figure who combined in himself the attributes of king and priest. But even when that significance had been completely forgotten, or was no longer adequately understood, the praise-poems still continued to be a vital part of court ceremonial in Celtic societies, and the preservation of this panegyric verse was ensured by the ruling dynasties whose exploits and illustrious ancestors it extolled. It is hardly surprising, therefore, that court poets existed in many Indo-European societies: witness, for example, the Icelandic *skald* and the Anglo-Saxon *scop*. In the early Celtic societies the 'bards' constituted the class of professional propagandists who sang the praises of the ruling dynasties; these were the *bardoi* or *bardi* of the Gauls, to whom there are some interesting and explicit references in the works of the Classical writers, the *beirdd* (singular *bardd*) of Wales, and the *baird* (sing. *bard*) who sang in Ireland in the Middle Ages. Indeed, the Celtic word **bardos,* the singular noun from which both Welsh *bardd* and Irish *bard* are regularly derived, can be traced to a primitive Indo-European root the meaning of which has been convincingly established as 'a singer of praise'. And a number of important references occur in the works of some of the Classical authors to the bards or lyric poets of the continental Celts who sang 'to the accompaniment of instruments resembling lyres, sometimes a eulogy and sometimes a satire', and who extolled 'the valorous deeds of famous men . . . in heroic verse'. Obviously, these poets constituted an important and highly influential class in both war and peace.

Unfortunately, however, none of this early Celtic verse has been preserved, for originally the literature of the Celtic peoples was oral, and a tantalizingly wide chronological gap exists between, on the one hand, the comparatively early use of writing for epigraphic and, possibly, some other official purposes and, on the other hand, its general use for the composition of what is usually implied by the term 'literature'. Nevertheless, in spite of the great lacunae in the surviving evidence, there are some indisputable and significant indications which suggest that the bard in early Celtic societies still retained a number of the distinctive attributes of his primitive Indo-European precursor, who also, it would appear, sang of 'unfading glory'. Moreover, every primitive poet enjoyed immense prestige and also wielded great influence by virtue of the occult knowledge and divinatory powers that were attributed to him. To some degree, he was regarded as a shaman or magician who was able to exercise great power over things, and it was firmly believed that his verse constituted an important means to that end. The vital role which the early bard fulfilled as a 'seer' is implicit in another Irish word for a poet—*fili*, 'one who sees', a word which derives ultimately from the primitive root *u̯el-, 'to see', which occurs in the Welsh word *gweled*. This primitive root is also found in the name of the prophetess *Veleda* who is mentioned by Tacitus and is said to have given responses as an oracle to the tribe of the Bructeri. There are many passages in early Irish literature which clearly illustrate the divinatory powers which it was widely believed a poet possessed. This deep regard for the poet as one who was divinely endowed with occult powers persisted down the centuries among the Celtic peoples, to blossom eventually in eighteenth-century Ireland in the celebrated *Aisling* (or 'Vision') poetry, an exceptionally interesting corpus of verse which was fraught with deep and far-reaching political significance. A similar conception of the essential nature of poetry is implicit also in the Welsh word *awen* for poetic muse or inspiration, for it has credibly been shown that this word is semantically related to Welsh *awel*, 'breeze', both forms being derived from the primitive Indo-European root *au̯(e)-, 'to blow'. According to the testimony of Giraldus Cambrensis (1146?-1223), there were still bards in Wales in his day called *awenyddion*, that is, 'inspired poets' or 'seers', who, it was believed, were endowed with profound intuitive faculties. These bards, who obviously represented a long and ancient tradition, may well have been the originators of that distinctive type of prophetic or vaticinatory verse which became so popular in Wales as a medium for propaganda during periods of great political uncertainty or acute social stress.

Another vital function of the Celtic court bards was the preservation and codification of the dynastic genealogies. It is significant that genealogies, which must have been preserved orally, frequently in alliterative poetry, are found among the earliest extant examples of Irish verse. Nor, when we remember that most of the hereditary post-Roman British kingdoms or dynasties were founded in the period immediately following the collapse of Roman government and administration in the fifth century, can it be wholly fortuitous that the extant Welsh genealogies only begin to be reliable from about the middle of that century, a hundred years or so before the period to which the earliest Welsh poets of whom we have any knowledge are usually ascribed. There seems, on the evidence, to have been a close connection between panegyric and genealogy, and it is not unreasonable to conclude that both were preserved and transmitted orally by many generations of court bards. Unfortunately, however, little evidence has survived relating to the duties discharged by the learned classes in Celtic Britain, but it is possible to make some tentative general deductions regarding their activities from the conditions which are known to have prevailed in Ancient Gaul and Ireland. Some of the Classical authors, including Caesar, Strabo, Diodorus Siculus, and Ammianus Marcellinus, inform us that there were three important intellectual classes in the Celtic society of Ancient Gaul. These were the *bardoi* or *bardi* ('bards'), *vātes* or *manteis* ('seers', 'poets'), and *druidai* or *druides* ('druids'), who seem to have fulfilled different functions, although these are not always as clearly differentiated as one would wish. The bards, as we have already seen, were the panegyric heroic poets; the *vātes* were pre-eminently philosophers and seers; and the druids, as many scholars have emphasized, were the leading professional learned class in Gaul who, to some extent, may have fulfilled priestly and judicial functions. The druids, we are told, were responsible for the education of the young Gaulish nobility, who were required to undergo a long and arduous process of training, which could sometimes continue for sixteen, or even twenty, years. It seems, however, that their learning was never committed to writing, but was ingeniously incorporated in poetical compositions and transmitted orally from one generation to another. But after the Gauls had been converted to Christianity, the druids and the *vātes* rapidly passed from the scene, although the *bardi* were undoubtedly the precursors of the panegyric poets who flourished in the Celtic societies of Britain and Ireland.

A considerable body of evidence has survived from Irish sources which points to the existence in early Ireland of three intellectual classes bearing a broad resemblance to those of Ancient Gaul. These were the *baird* (sing. *bard*), 'bards', *druid* (sing. *druì*), 'druids', and *filid* (sing. *fili*), whose status was undeniably higher than that of the *baird,* although there were certain functions which both these classes shared. The *filid* seem to correspond to the Gaulish *vātes* or 'seers', and the superiority which they eventually gained over the druids in Ireland probably began, it has been argued, after the introduction of Christianity, a religion to which the druids, unlike the *filid,* were fundamentally opposed. The *filid,* who were organized in a fairly strict hierarchy, fulfilled both a creative and essentially learned function. On the one hand, they were expected to become highly proficient in many aspects of the traditional indigenous learning. This embraced genealogy, ancient saga, law, and the intricate rules relating to prosody and the composition of poetry, all of which was transmitted orally. On the other hand, they were required also to compose panegyric and elegiac verses extolling the qualities of the patrons to whom they were so closely attached, a task which no *fili* would conceivably have undertaken before he had mastered what were considered to be the essential elements in the great corpus of traditional lore, including a detailed knowledge of the lineage of his patron and of the royal genealogies of Ireland.

Caesar's well-known statement that the discipline of the druids was 'thought to have originated in Britain', together with the relevant evidence which has survived from Irish sources, strongly suggests that the traditional native learning of Celtic Britain was likewise preserved and cherished by a broadly similar class of lay poets and scholars who were attached to the courts of the ruling dynasties. And it seems a reasonable conclusion, which receives some confirmation from the evidence of a later period, that the official poets known as *beirdd* in Wales fulfilled the important function which was entrusted to the *filid* in Ireland. It was to this particular class that Taliesin and Aneirin belonged (see below, pp. 22-7 and Chapters II and III). 'The bards', as Mrs. Rachel Bromwich has rightly emphasized, 'were the custodians of historical records in the earliest form in which these were embodied; that is to say, the verses, orally preserved, in which the genealogies of their patrons and the leaders of their nation were contained. The mythical and legendary character of the earliest names in the genealogies shows the close affinity of these with the whole corpus of native learning which was the stock-in-trade of the poets'. The works of the bards, although they must admittedly be used with great caution, constitute therefore a very important source for the study of early British history, for some of the esoteric lore and oral traditions which they had carefully preserved and devotedly transmitted from one generation to another were eventually committed to writing in Wales in the ninth century. Traditional material of this kind probably constituted one of the sources used in the early ninth century by the Welsh monk whose name has been latinized as Nennius or Nemniuus (*fl. c.* 800 A.D.), when he was preparing the Latin compilation known as the *Historia Brittonum,* which purports to give an account of early British history from the time of Julius Caesar to approximately the end of the seventh century A.D. Moreover, Giraldus Cambrensis informs us that in twelfth-century Wales the bards had in their possession ancient manuscript books containing genealogical data, and it is incontestable that the Welsh court bards, from the late sixth century to the end of the thirteenth, were familiar with the lineage of their regal and aristocratic patrons.

It seems, therefore, to have been the practice in both Britain and Ireland for an official bard to be attached to each court, although there is some evidence to suggest that a bard could occasionally visit more than one court. This is not surprising, for certain rulers would naturally tend to acquire great renown for their bounty and unstinting hospitality. Taliesin, who may have been a native of Powys, in north-east Wales, addressed his verses not only to Cynan Garwyn, the ruler of his native province, but also to kings or princes who held sway in north Britain. His career, if it has been correctly interpreted, testifies both to the extent and to the linguistic and cultural unity of the territories which were still in his day under the authority of British kings.

As British (or Brittonic), the Celtic language of the ancestors of these rulers, was formerly spoken over so wide an area — throughout this island south of the Forth and Clyde — it may reasonably be assumed that there were appreciable dialectal differences in the various regions. Unfortunately, however, little is known of the British dialects once spoken in eastern Britain. The Roman Conquest, followed centuries later by the Anglo-Saxon invasion and settlement, have effectively obliterated the relevant evidence. In the west, on the other hand, it is possible on phonological grounds to distinguish between a West and a South-West dialect of British. The former was the parent of Primitive Welsh and the closely-related speech of Cumbria, which may be called Primitive Cumbric, while South-West British was the ancestor of Primitive Cornish and Primitive Breton, the latter being introduced by British immigrants who, as a result of intense Anglo-Saxon pressure, fled in successive waves to the Armorican peninsula from about the middle of the fifth century to the early seventh. The fact that many of these refugees, particularly during the middle and second half of the sixth century, came from Devon and Cornwall, accounts for the close relationship between Cornish and Breton, and for the various features which these two languages shared to the exclusion of Welsh. The West and South-West dialects of British probably did not begin to diverge clearly until the fifth to sixth centuries, although a few small indications of possible dialectal differentiation are faintly discernible as early as the first century A.D. It is difficult, however, to express a confident opinion on any phonological differentiation during this early period, for the direct information available for studying the history and development of British is extremely meagre, our knowledge being largely obtained by inference. Not one sentence of British has survived, nor, unfortunately, do we have any inscription written entirely in any of its dialects. Apart from the information which can be gathered from the very brief inscriptions on the coins which, as we have already seen, were occasionally minted by pre-Roman rulers, our direct knowledge of early British is confined to place-names, personal and tribal names, and a few common words, which occur in the writings of Greek and Roman historians, geographers or officials, and occasionally in various Latin inscriptions which were erected in the Roman province. Although these forms shed some light on the phonetic system of British, they provide us with hardly any information regarding its grammar and morphology. For this we must rely very largely on the science of comparative philology and comparative grammar, a study which shows that British belonged to the Celtic branch of the Indo-European family of languages. This can be supplemented by one other source which is of great importance for understanding the structure and development of British, namely the Latin words which were borrowed by the ancient Britons during the Roman occupation of Britain and which survive in the vocabulary of Welsh and in that of its sister languages, Cornish and Breton. When British eventually disintegrated and developed into the new analytic languages, Welsh, Cornish and Breton, the loan-words in general underwent the same basic phonetic developments as did the native British vocabulary itself, which had been inherited from Common Celtic and Indo-European. By comparing the Latin loan-words with the forms into which they subsequently developed and noting carefully the changes that have taken place, the philologist is able to deduce what were the major phonetic developments which ultimately transformed the dialects of British into the new analytic languages, that is, languages in which auxiliary words are the chief means of expressing grammatical relationships, to the complete or partial exclusion of inflections. Armed with this knowledge, and guided further by the information which can be gleaned from the Celtic remains on the Continent, we can trace some of the elements in the Welsh, Cornish, and Breton vocabularies back to their original forms and thus reconstruct hypothetically certain features of the parent British language.

A detailed study of this kind shows quite clearly that British was a synthetic language, that is, a language in which the grammatical relationships of words were expressed through inflections, as in Latin or Greek. The surviving evidence suggests that British was at the same stage of development as Latin, to which it bore some striking resemblances in its sound-system and morphology. As a result, the borrowing of Latin words could not have presented any serious difficulty for the ancient Britons, although there were probably a number of important differences between the two languages in matters of syntax. British obviously inherited the primitive Indo-European system of declensions for nouns, adjectives, pronouns, etc. Thus, if we take the noun *bardos as an example, a masculine noun which belonged to the -o- stems, its declension in British was probably singular accusative *bardon, genitive *bardī, dative *bardū (which later developed, through an intermediate stage, to *bardī); plural nominative *bardī, accusative *bardūs (which later developed, through an intermediate stage, to *bardīs), genitive *bardon, and possibly dative *bardobis. A noun which belonged to one of the consonantal stems was *rīx 'king' (<*rīg-s), the form from which the Welsh noun rhi, 'king, lord', is ultimately derived. Its declension in British was singular accusative *rīgan, genitive *rīgos, dative *rīgī; plural nominative *rīges, accusative *rīgās, genitive *rīgon, dative *rīgobis. There is obviously a marked resemblance between this declension and that of the cognate Latin noun rēx, rēgem, rēgis, rēgī; plural rēgēs, rēgēs, rēgum, rēgibus. There were some similarities, too, in the verbal system of both languages. The stress-accent fell regularly in British — and certainly in Late British — on the penultimate, and one important development which occurred when British disintegrated and developed into Welsh, Cornish and Breton was the loss of the unstressed final syllables. So, e.g., British *bardos > Welsh bardd, *mapos >mab, *catus >cad, *alarcos > alarch,* etc. After the loss of the old British final syllables, the accent must have fallen originally on the final syllable in Welsh words of two syllables or more. In a later period, however, the accent moved from the final syllable in Welsh to the penultimate, where it still falls regularly in words of more than one syllable. So e.g., British *abóna >* Primitive Welsh *afón > áfon;* *ụostátos >*gwastád > gwástad,* etc. The earliest Welsh poetry must therefore have been composed when the accent fell regularly on the ultimate in words of two syllables or more, a fact which obviously has a very important bearing on the rhythmic pattern of this verse.

British was probably a fairly stable language in the first century A.D., and as such it could not have been drastically dissimilar in its phonology from Common Celtic, although differences undoubtedly did exist. It was the Roman occupation that probably led first of all to the gradual disintegration of British, a phenomenon which has generally been attributed to the loss of official status and cultural prestige suffered by the language during this period, as well as to the removal, with the decline of the British noble class, of any conservative influence which may formerly have been exercised on the native inflected language, so that greater scope was provided for the spread of the more 'developed' and 'corrupt' type of British spoken by the lower orders. The Roman occupation of this island during the first century A.D. and the establishment of the Imperial province of Britain resulted in the collapse of the indigenous monarchical and aristocratic organization. The British tribal territories and their 'capitals' were adopted by the Romans as the basis for their regional administration, and gradually beneath the Roman governing class there evolved a new class of native squirearchy, who played an important role in local government and administration. These gentry were the owners of the numerous villas with rural estates, the distribution of which is more marked in the region lying south and east of a line drawn on a map of Britain from Flamborough Head to near Exeter, thus emphasizing the civil zone of the

Imperial province in the lowland south-east in contrast to the more markedly military zone in the highland north-west. Naturally, in the Lowland Zone the whole inclination of the country squirearchy would have been towards the civilization of Rome rather than to the indigenous British traditions and ideals. It is difficult to imagine how the professional bards who had been closely attached to the old British kings and military aristocracy could have flourished in such distinctly adverse circumstances, for they had obviously lost their function and British had lost its cultural status and was developing into a comparatively inferior patois. The removal of any conservative influence which may formerly have been exercised on the language by the literary *élite* and the old native learned classes must have led to an acceleration in the rate of linguistic change.

The position was somewhat different, however, in other parts of Britain. North of Hadrian's Wall the Roman occupation was brief in duration, and hence there could have been no significant upheaval in the native social organization in that region. And even within the bounds of the Imperial province the economically more backward areas of the mountainous north and west, known as the Highland Zone, were not as intensively Romanized as were the more attractive regions of south-east Britain. The villa system, with its intensive methods of agriculture, did not penetrate here to the extent which it did in the Lowland Zone, and the Roman occupation was manifestly more military in character, the region being divided into military districts which were guarded by small army garrisons. There was every opportunity, therefore, for the time-honoured Celtic customs to survive, not only in parts of Scotland in the far north, but also, to a certain extent, in Wales. It is unlikely that there would be any major linguistic breakdown in these areas, although one must not overlook the influence which may have been exerted by the more 'developed' British of the Imperial province. For the language was still spoken in the Lowland Zone of Britain during the Roman occupation, as well as in the comparatively more inaccessible regions of the highland north and west.

The withdrawal of the Roman legions in the early fifth century did not lead to an immediate disintegration of Roman life, nor did the use of Latin abruptly cease. It seems that the collapse did not begin until approximately the middle of the fifth century, when the Anglo-Saxon attacks on Britain assumed more serious proportions, resulting eventually in the conquest and occupation of south-east England by the early sixth century, and a more gradual encroachment westwards and northwards afterwards for approximately two hundred years. This must have led to the decline of organized town life, and the country gentry and their rural villas soon disappeared. Nor is it likely that Latin continued as a living speech in the regions conquered by the Anglo-Saxons, except among the clergy. According to Professor Kenneth H. Jackson, the disintegration of Roman organization in the fifth century, the social upheaval caused by the Anglo-Saxon conquest and settlement, and the removal, as a result of the elimination of the British upper classes, of those influences which had formerly tended towards linguistic conservation all acted as something of a catalyst on the phonetic developments of the preceding four centuries, when British had been slowly evolving, thus leading to a considerable acceleration in the rate of linguistic change and ultimately to the complete transformation of British into Primitive Welsh (and the closely-related Primitive Cumbric), Primitive Cornish and Primitive Breton. But it is obviously to the Lowland Zone that we must look for evidence of the great social disturbances which, it has been claimed, led to these major linguistic changes in those regions which lay outside the sphere of Anglo-Saxon influence during the early period of conquest and settlement. It has been argued that one important result of the Anglo-Saxon attacks was that refugees from south-east Britain fled in considerable numbers into the safer hill regions of the north-west and that the influence of their more 'developed' British speech was to a large degree responsible for the major linguistic breakdown that occurred in the Highland Zone in this period.

Among the various phonetic changes which ultimately transformed the Western dialect of British into Welsh the most important were: (1) a series of vowel changes; (2) a series of consonantal mutations, including lenition (or the 'soft mutation', as it is called in Welsh), the nasalization of *b, d, g,* and the spirant mutation; (3) vowel affection, a phenomenon analogous in certain respects to Germanic umlaut, whereby a short vowel in British (including the Latin loan-words) was affected by a sound in the following syllable; (4) the loss of unstressed final syllables and certain unstressed internal ones in words of more than three syllables. Undoubtedly, the most important of all these changes was the disappearance of final and unstressed internal syllables, for this inevitably resulted in the disintegration of the British case-terminations and brought about a great transformation in the whole syntactical and morphological character of the language. Welsh had recourse, therefore, to the use of prepositions, word-order or juxtaposition, and other devices to compensate for the loss of the old inflectional endings which had formerly in the parent British tongue expressed the various grammatical relationships. This is what philologists mean when they speak of a new analytic language, Welsh, developing from the ruins of the old synthetic British language. The poems which are considered to be the work of the late sixth-century bards, Taliesin and Aneirin, suggest that this process of linguistic reconstruction had been more or less completed before the date when they were composed. It must be emphasized that the phonetic changes briefly mentioned above as marking the transition of the Western dialect of British into Welsh did not all occur simultaneously, and they were gradual developments, although Professor Kenneth H. Jackson firmly believes that they were accelerated by the disturbed social conditions of the post-Roman period. Professor Jackson, who has attempted in a work of monumental scholarship to date the various sound-changes involved in the evolution of Welsh, Cornish and Breton, has suggested that the loss of the old British final syllables had been completed by about the middle of the sixth century, so that the emergence of Welsh as a new analytic language from the ruins of the synthetic parent tongue can reasonably be ascribed to the second half of that century.

Obviously, the period following the withdrawal of the Roman legions was an important and formative one in the history of Wales, as it was in the history of Britain as a whole. Between *c.* 450 and 600 A.D. the Welsh kingdoms constituted the rear of a loose and somewhat uneasy confederation of British states, extending from southern Scotland in the north to Cornwall in the south-west, which began to feel the shock of the Anglo-Saxon onslaught. Historians regard this period as the 'heroic age' of late British history—the age of St. Germanus, bishop of Auxerre, who came to Britain to combat the Pelagian heresy; of Vortigern, the *superbus tyrannus,* who is said to have invited in some of the Saxons as mercenaries to fight on behalf of the Britons against the Picts and Scots, thus unwittingly preparing the way for the *adventus Saxonum,* an action for which he was later execrated in Welsh sources; and of Ambrosius Aurelianus, described as 'almost the last of the Romans', the *dux* and *vir modestus,* who is said to have rallied the remnants of the routed Britons and led them, for a while successfully, into battle against the Saxons. It is to this period, too, that historians ascribe the enigmatic Arthur, whom R. G. Collingwood, on rather flimsy evidence, it must be admitted, regarded as a commander of a mobile field-army well trained in the use and value of heavy cavalry, and virtually the last of the Romans. A more recent study, based on the relevant archaeological evidence, depicts Arthur as the leader of the combined forces of the small kingdoms into which sub-Roman Britain had disintegrated.

In the Latin of this period the word *tyrannus* (literally, 'tyrant') can signify a usurper, and this is probably what Procopius implies when he refers to Britain as being largely under the control of 'tyrants' after the departure of the Romans.

These were typical Celtic chiefs or overlords who exercised authority by virtue of their military power, and they probably represent a resurgence of those petty Celtic chieftains who had formerly exercised authority in the Highland Zone of the north-west on behalf of the Roman administration. Notwithstanding their manifestly Celtic characteristics, these rulers still admired many aspects of Roman civilization. Their children were often given Roman names, and when they died they were commemorated by their successors in Latin inscriptions which were cut on crude stone monuments and which no doubt were partly intended to create the impression that they were worthy heirs of the civilization of Rome. Five of these 'tyrants' are the subject of a scathing diatribe in the *De Excidio et Conquestu Britanniae* ('Concerning the Ruin and Conquest of Britain'), a Latin work written about the middle of the sixth century, or possibly a little earlier, by the Welsh or Romano-British monk Gildas, who sought to charge the lay and ecclesiastical rulers of his day with sin and to saddle them with the responsibility for the ruin of Britain. He exposed the corrupt and wicked life of each of these kings, who seem to have been rulers over wide territories on the western seaboard, and he threatened each one with eternal punishment. But the 'tyrant' who figures most prominently in Gildas's scathing denunciation is Maglocunus (or Maelgwn in Welsh), ruler of Anglesey and Gwynedd in northwest Wales, who held his court on the rock of Degannwy. Maelgwn was the ancestor of the later princes of Gwynedd and, according to some sources, he died of the Yellow Plague in, or *circa,* 547. The composition of Gildas's work is therefore usually ascribed to a period before that date. In a long and eloquent passage in which Gildas mercilessly castigates this tyrant for his overweening pride and wickedness the following statement occurs:

> When the attention of thy ears has been caught, it is not the praises of God, in the tuneful voice of Christ's followers with its sweet rhythm, and the song of church melody, that are heard, but thine own praises (which are nothing); the voice of the rascally crew yelling forth, like Bacchanalian revellers, full of lies and foaming phlegm, so as to besmear everyone near them.

THE HISTORICAL BACKGROUND OF EARLY WELSH VERSE

Obviously, Gildas is here referring to the bards who sang the praises of Maelgwn in his court, and it is certainly the earliest reference to bards on Welsh soil. For Gildas, the panegyric verses of these bards, which were probably composed in Welsh, albeit in a primitive form of the language, were nothing but vain flattery. Unfortunately, however, apart from this interesting reference, nothing is known about these panegyrists: neither their names, nor even a single line of their verse, have come down to us. But it is not unreasonable to assume that these court bards were, like those who had preceded them in early Celtic societies and like those who followed them in a later period in both Wales and Ireland, members of a professional learned class entrusted with the preservation of literary, historical and genealogical knowledge and charged with the duty of upholding and spreading as widely as possible the fame and honour of their regal patron.

These bards probably knew that in Welsh tradition Maelgwn Gwynedd's great-grandfather was Cunedda Wledig, who, with eight of his sons, came to Gwynedd from the north-western province of Gododdin called Manaw and, after much slaughter, expelled the Irish who had settled there. Manaw Gododdin was a small district around the head of the Firth of Forth situated within the tribal territory of the Gododdin. There is now general agreement concerning the identification of the latter. Gododdin was the name of the country and tribe which were known in the earlier Romano-British period as the *Υotādīnī, a form which would regularly have given *Gododdin* in Welsh. According to the Greek geographer Ptolemy, who compiled in the second century A.D. a 'Geography' of the world as it was then known, the country of this tribe extended from the region around the head of the Firth of Forth as far south as the region of the Wear in Co. Durham, including Lothian and Edinburgh. In early Welsh tradition Cunedda was a figure of great importance, for a number of the Welsh dynasties of the Middle Ages trace their ancestry back to him. If we can depend on the basic details of this story, Cunedda founded a dynasty which played a decisive role in shaping the future history of Wales. Some historians have even expressed the view that Cunedda was a Duke of Britain who had been entrusted with the defence of Hadrian's Wall against the Picts and Scots. Moreover, the fact that he gave Latin names to three of his sons and that his immediate ancestors also bore Latin names has sometimes been interpreted as meaning that he was a Romanized Briton. It is also possible that he was a Christian, for the names Donatus and Marianus which were given to two of his sons have Christian associations. Much of this, however, is speculative, although tradition connects him and his family with important missionary work in Wales. There are, undeniably, some obscurities in the story, and some doubts have been expressed concerning the date of this migration from Manaw Gododdin to Gwynedd. Nor should it be overlooked that the sons and grandson referred to in Old Welsh genealogies as founding kingdoms could be eponymous creations.

The bare details relating to the migration of Cunedda and his followers occur in the *Historia Brittonum,* the compilation which the Welsh monk Nennius made *c.* 800 and a source of great importance for the early history of Wales. He is said to have been a disciple of Elfoddw, who was a bishop and, if we may depend on one tradition, a leading bishop in Gwynedd before he died in the year 809. Nennius certainly referred to Elfoddw as his *'magister'*. His work shows, however, that he was familiar with the traditions of British courts which lay far outside the confines of Gwynedd in north-west Wales. These traditions, as well as various historical materials, were used by Nennius when he was compiling the *Historia Brittonum.* Among the documents used by him was a *Genealogy of the Saxon Kings,* ascribed by some authorities to *c.* 685. Brief notes have been inserted in various places in the Northumbrian section, which gives the names of Northumbrian kings who led the invasion and conquest of substantial parts of north British territories during the second half of the sixth century. Prominent among these kings was Ida, the founder of the

THE HISTORICAL BACKGROUND OF EARLY WELSH VERSE

Northumbrian royal line, who ruled between 547 and 559. A reference to this king in the *Historia Brittonum* is followed by some interesting interpolations which must have been based on British or early Welsh traditions. First of all comes the comment:

> Then Eudeyrn (M.S. *Dutigirn*) at that time used to fight bravely against the nation of the Angles.

Nothing is known of this British king from any other extant source. This brief comment is followed by the most important interpolation of all for students of early Welsh literature:

> Then Talhaearn Tad Awen (MS. *Talhaern Tataguen)* was renowned in poetry, and Neirin and Taliessin and Bluchbard and Cian, who is called Gueinth Guaut, together at the same time were renowned in British poetry.

The period to which this comment in the *Historia Brittonum* refers is the mid sixth century, when the rulers of the northern British kingdoms were engaged in a desperate struggle against the encroaching Anglian power in Bernicia and Deira. And the expression 'British poetry' obviously means verse composed in the Welsh language, when it was at a very early stage in its development.

Unfortunately, not a single line of the poetry composed by Talhaearn (*c.* 550) has survived. But it is significant that he is mentioned on his own in the interpolation which occurs in the *Historia Brittonum,* and the interesting reference to him as *Tad Awen,* 'Father of the Muse (or of Inspiration'), suggests that he was the first in a long line of *Welsh* (as distinct from *British*) poets, so that his standing in the Welsh bardic tradition can be compared with that often assigned in English literature to Chaucer, 'the father of English poetry', as he has been called. This comparison effectively illustrates the great chronological difference in the evolution and development of the two languages. The brief comment in the *Historia Brittonum* contains everything we know of Talhaearn, Bluchbard, and Cian, although the latter must have been renowned in his day as a poet, if *Gueinth Guaut* may reasonably be taken as a scribal error for *Guenith Guaut,* i.e., *Gwenith Gwawd,* 'the Wheat of Song'.

Fortunately, however, more details have survived concerning Taliesin and Aneirin, the other two bards mentioned by Nennius, and we have two thirteenth-century manuscripts which purport to contain their works. The manuscript known as *The Book of Taliesin* (Peniarth MS. 2), now kept in the National Library of Wales, Aberystwyth, was transcribed *c.* 1275, or possibly a little later. It contains a miscellaneous collection of poems, probably compiled in the thirteenth century, and ascribed to the late sixth-century bard Taliesin. The poems belong to various periods and embrace a fairly wide range of subject matter—mythological, vaticinatory, historical and religious. But among the heterogeneous compositions attributed to Taliesin there is a small nucleus of about twelve which bear the hallmark of authenticity. These are fairly brief panegyric and elegiac poems addressed to historical figures who were Taliesin's contemporaries: to Urien, lord of Rheged, and his son, Owain, to Gwallawg ap Lleennawg, and Cynan ap Brochfael, who ruled over the kingdom of Powys in north-east Wales. Two of these rulers are mentioned by the redactor of the *Historia Brittonum,* who refers to the opposition presented to the Bernician king Hussa (585-92, or, possibly, 579-86) by four of the north British rulers, or *Gwŷr y Gogledd,* 'Men of the North'. These were Urien of Rheged, the ruler of a wide expanse of territory in north-west Britain, which extended from beyond the Solway Firth over modern Cumberland and Lancashire and, possibly, as far as Catterick; Rhydderch Hen, who ruled at Dumbarton, the capital of the British kingdom of Strathclyde; and Gwallawg and Morgant, two British princes whose territories are not clearly identified, although it is possible that Gwallawg was ruler of the British kingdom of Elmet, near Leeds. It seems that Urien Rheged was the leader of this coalition of British rulers, and he is said to have fought bravely with his sons not only against Hussa but also against Theodric of Bernicia (572-9, or, possibly, 586-93). We are further told that he succeeded in besieging his opponents for three days and nights in the island of *'Metcaud'* (Lindisfarne). But this British alliance, which had only been formed as a result of intense external pressure, soon fell apart, for while Urien was on an expedition he was treacherously murdered at the instance of Morgant, out of envy, we are told, for his acknowledged skill in battle. The poems which Taliesin addressed to Urien and to some of his contemporaries are, in general, 'stylised official tributes, [and] describe in conventional terms the splendour of the prince's establishment, his hospitality and generosity to the poet'. It may well have been praise of this sort that was lavished on Maelgwn Gwynedd by the bards whom Gildas so roundly condemned.

The manuscript called *The Book of Aneirin,* now kept in Cardiff Central Library, was transcribed *c.* 1250 and its contents are presented as a single poem, bearing the superscription *'Hwn yw e gododin. aneirin ae cant'*: 'This is the *Gododdin.* Aneirin sang it'. Approximately four-fifths of its text occurs in the orthography of the thirteenth century. The remaining fifth, however, is written in the orthography of the ninth or tenth century and preserves an earlier text, transcribed from a manuscript no longer extant, of a number of stanzas which are found in medieval orthography in other parts of the *Book of Aneirin.* This implies that at least one written text of the poem was already in existence in the ninth or tenth century, but if the poem—or part of it—is the work of Aneirin, who sang towards the end of the sixth century, a long period of oral transmission must be envisaged for the three centuries from approximately 600 to 900 A.D. The occasion for the composition of this poem, which derives its title from the territorial name of the tribe whose heroic exploits it commemorates, was a disastrous expedition made *c.* 600 by the warband of Mynyddog Mwynfawr, lord of Din Eidyn, in the neighbourhood of the modern Edinburgh. The ill-fated expedition had as its objective the recapture of the strategically-important Catraeth, which has been identified as Catterick in northern Yorkshire, from the English of Deira and Bernicia, the two Anglo-Saxon provinces which later became united in the early seventh century into the kingdom of Northumbria.

The historical allusions contained in the poems which are considered to be the authentic work of Taliesin and Aneirin blend happily with the general picture presented to us by modern scholars of the history of northern Britain in the Dark Ages, and particularly in the second half of the sixth century. It seems that the English occupation of northern England began in the previous century with the settlement of the Yorkshire Wolds, and by the end of the sixth century it is probable that all Yorkshire east of and including the Vale of York had fallen to the English, who by then were already beginning to penetrate into the Pennines. By *c.* 600 large parts of Deira were probably occupied by fairly substantial numbers of English settlers. According to Anglo-Saxon tradition, the English settlement of Bernicia began with the occupation of Bamburgh, near Lindisfarne, by Ida, ascribed by Bede to the year 547, although this may be about a decade too early. We have already seen that, according to early Welsh 'historical' tradition, which was used by Nennius when he compiled his *Historia Brittonum,* a coalition of British rulers, led by Urien, king of Rheged, fought with Ida's successors. It is quite possible that the slaying of Urien and the subsequent disintegration of the British alliance facilitated the great expansion of Bernician power under Ethelfrith, who succeeded Theodric as king in 593(?) and fused the two provinces of Deira and Bernicia into the kingdom of Northumbria in the early seventh century. The poetry of Taliesin and Aneirin fits intelligibly into this general picture, and this tends to confirm the view that poetry was composed in an early form of the Welsh language as early as the second half of the sixth century of our era. The date now generally accepted for the emergence of Welsh from the ruins of the parent British tongue gives greater significance to the important references contained in the *Historia Brittonum* to Welsh poetic tradition. For it is now generally agreed that the Welsh language had been in existence long enough and had acquired sufficient status and prestige for it to be regarded by the late sixth-century bards, Taliesin and Aneirin, as a fitting medium for the composition of their poetry. These bards are thus appropriately known in Welsh as the *Cynfeirdd,* the 'First (or Original) Poets', for they sang, in the words of Sir John Morris-Jones, 'the birth-song of the new speech'. One cannot fail to marvel, therefore, at the great verbal richness and technical accomplishment of this early verse.

It is significant, too, that the earliest Welsh verse known to us belongs to the ancient tradition of panegyric in praise of the kings and the nobility which had flourished in the early Celtic societies of Britain, Gaul and Ireland from time immemorial and had not been extinguished by four centuries of Romanization. It is equally noteworthy that nearly all the earliest examples of Welsh verse belonged originally to regions in southern Scotland, which had really been outside the boundaries of the Imperial province, for the Romans had abandoned the Antonine Wall towards the end of the second century. Indigenous Celtic traditions had every opportunity to flourish, therefore, in this region, and it has even been suggested that 'the subsequent flowering of literature in Wales may well have been encouraged by an impetus from the north'. Be that as it may, there can be no doubt that, in essence, the poems which are considered to be the authentic work of Taliesin and Aneirin belong to the centuries-old Celtic tradition of bardic verse, as, indeed, do many other Welsh poems which were composed much later, for the panegyric tradition persisted down to the modern period. Nor is it in this verse alone that one can detect the persistence of the native Celtic tradition in this island, for it has been argued that there are certain elements in the early Welsh and Irish legal codes which derive from the common cultural inheritance which the Celtic peoples shared in the centuries of their life upon the continent of Europe. All this evidence strongly suggests that the ancient British learned classes and the native nobility who had patronized them had continued in the Highland Zone of north-west Britain, albeit perhaps in an attenuated form, in spite of four centuries of Roman occupation.

The values acclaimed in this early Welsh verse—more particularly in the *Gododdin*—are those of a heroic society. The term 'heroic age' or 'heroic society' has a special connotation for students of comparative literature, for it implies a particular social setting. The society delineated by these early bards, and particularly by Aneirin, is that of a military aristocracy whose chief interest is warfare and who place great emphasis on *noblesse oblige* and heroic honour. The qualities most highly valued in the rulers of these British courts and in their noble followers were courage, fierceness and steadfastness in war, generosity, liberality and gentleness in peace. Other virtues which these rulers looked for in their followers were loyalty and gratitude, and the faithful discharge, whatever the cost, of certain services in return for the support and benefits which they had received in the past. Glory for deeds of great heroism was desired above all things, and even death was not unwelcome if it was followed by everlasting fame. The prestige of the leaders was rooted deep in their ancient aristocratic lineage and was maintained by the reputation which they acquired as intrepid warriors. To extol and enhance that prestige was, as we have seen, the basic function of the court bards, who paid much attention to personal and specific details, such as the horse which a particular warrior rode, the fine clothes he wore, or the military equipment he possessed. Some literary historians confine the term 'heroic' to epic narrative verse, but others apply it to all literature which has been composed by and for a 'heroic' society, if it reflects the features mentioned above. The heroic poems composed by Aneirin are not narrative, but are a blend of panegyric and elegy, a distinctive type which has been called 'celebration poetry'. For each verse of

THE HISTORICAL BACKGROUND OF EARLY WELSH VERSE

Aneirin's poem either celebrates the great deeds and mourns the death of one hero—occasionally more than one—or the deeds of the courageous army of Gododdin as a whole. The *Gododdin* has been described as 'the classic, and the only full-length, exposition of the ideals of the Heroic Age in Welsh literature'.

Nevertheless, some references to God and the occurrence of the expression 'in the name of the Lord of Heaven' as a conventional beginning in some of Taliesin's verses, as well as the contemptuous description of the English as 'heathen' and explicit references to Heaven, communion, altars, churches and penance in the work of Aneirin, provide us with a salutary reminder that these intrepid northern heroes of the British world were already Christians at this time. The seeds of the Christian faith may have been sown during the Roman period. But the first great mission to Scotland for which we have some information was that of St. Ninian of Whithorn in the early part of the fifth century. The results of his evangelizing efforts can be traced southwards into Cumbria as well as over southern Scotland. Evidence of his activity can also be traced as far as Skye in the west and into southern Pictland. According to Bede, it was St. Ninian's mission that was mainly responsible for the early evangelization of much of southern and eastern Scotland, and his great efforts were continued for some two hundred years by a number of worthy successors, including St. Carannoc in the mid fifth century, St. Columba, who founded his monastic house at Iona in 563 and gave Scotland a second infusion of the Faith, St. Donnan the Great, who was martyred in 618, and St. Walloch in the early eighth century. Undoubtedly, St. Ninian's monastic house at Whithorn exercised a powerful influence in Scotland, and it only lost its independence after the tide of Northumbrian conquest had engulfed Galloway, resulting in the creation of the Anglian bishopric of Whithorn in the early eighth century.

Among the notable relics of early Christianity in Scotland are the inscribed pillar stones, generally unworked and at best only roughly hewn, which were set up to mark burial sites. In general, the form of the inscription on these stones or, in some cases, the occurrence of a Christian symbol, proves beyond any reasonable doubt that the person commemorated was a Christian. Memorial stones of this kind, ranging in date from the fifth to the early seventh centuries, occur in considerable numbers in Wales and Cornwall, and to a lesser extent in Devon, the Isle of Man and the region between the Tyne and Forth. Nothing strictly analogous to these inscribed memorial stones has come to us from Roman Britain, although the existence of Christianity among some sections of the population in that period cannot be doubted. The surviving evidence suggests, therefore, that the extensive Christianization of the Celtic lands which took place during the Dark Ages was the result of a new cultural stimulus. With the weakening of the power and authority of the land-state, following the collapse of Imperial administration, the Highland Zone of Britain was drawn once again, as it had previously been during the prehistoric period, into the orbit of the great sea-based cultures which frequently embraced the western lands. The most important of these during the Dark Ages was the Christian culture which entered Wales and some of the neighbouring Celtic lands along the western sea-routes. The earliest Christian memorial stones of Wales, which have been ascribed to the period A.D. 450-650, bear inscriptions which may be in Latin, written in the Roman script, or in a very early form of Irish, engraved in Ogams, while an interesting and important series has bilingual inscriptions in Ogams and Roman capitals. The use of the Ogam script and Primitive Irish points to the existence of Irish communities and even dynasties in Wales in the fifth and later centuries. Various features in the language and lettering in this early group of stones, as well as actual allusions which occur on some of them, show that they have unmistakable cultural affinities with early Christian memorials of the western Roman empire, especially the Lyon and Vienne areas of Gaul. These stones in Wales have a marked westerly concentration, the heaviest incidence occurring in the two modern counties of Gwynedd and Dyfed. Some, however, occur far inland, in the Usk and upper Dee valleys, while others were erected on the high moorlands of Glamorgan. Significantly, there are comparatively few stones in the coastal plains of the north and south-east. It may reasonably be deduced from this evidence that Celtic Christian influences reached Wales along the western sea-routes and then penetrated inland along the remains of the Roman valley roads, which, it has been argued, continued to be used down to the early seventh century, if not later. As a result, the Gallo-Roman *peregrini* came to southeast Wales, where there is some archaeological evidence for the existence of Christianity in the Roman period, and it appears that the Celtic Church in Wales arose from a fusion of these two elements. The Gallic immigrants introduced the eremetical type of Christianity which derived from the example of St. Martin of Tours and ultimately from the early Christian Fathers in the Egyptian desert. All this evidence points to a sustained evangelizing effort from Gaul directed to Wales, as well as to Cornwall and Northumbria, where, as we have already observed, examples occur of similar Latin-inscribed stones. The general absence of these Christian monuments from the earlier Roman centres of settlement and civilization implies a sharp cultural break with the past. And the marked westerly concentration of these stones is further emphasized by the close cultural contacts which existed between these Gallic *peregrini* and the Goidelic settlers in Dyfed, north Wales, Cornwall, and the Isle of Man, as reflected in the bilingual stones, that is, those stones which are inscribed in both Latin and Ogam.

Between the fifth and eighth centuries A.D., therefore, the whole of Wales was converted to Christianity by the wandering monks and missionaries of the Celtic Church, who later came to be known as 'saints'. Inspired by the zeal and example of these missionaries, members of royal families and others devoted themselves to the religious life, the more famous among their number naturally attracting many disciples. An important aspect of the work of the Celtic 'saints', whose methods of evangelization made an indelible impression on the Welsh countryside, was the foundation of churches and monasteries which were important centres of teaching and learning, as well as refuges from a sinful world. Thus arose such famous centres as Llanilltud Fawr, Llancarfan (formerly Nantcarfan), Llandeilo or Llanbadarn. A sixth-century puritanical revival, associated with the missionary work of St. David, later affected all south Wales. It appears that this movement was carried a generation later into north Wales by St. Beuno, who in the popular mind long challenged David's strong claim, officially recognized in the twelfth century, to patronal status. Many of the sacred enclosures (Welsh *llan,* plural *llannau*), which, prefixed to the name of their founders, are thickly distributed on the map of Wales, derive from the so-called 'age of the saints', and their distribution helps to remind us of the original structure of the Church in Wales. The most distinctive feature was the *clas* or mother church serving as a focus for a group of subordinate monastic foundations united by loyalty to a common cult rather than by any organizational structure.

That the ancient Celtic literary and cultural traditions of north Britain made a deep impression on the earliest literature composed in Wales is undeniable. Indeed, it has justifiably been claimed that the 'Heroic Age of the British people in the early post-Roman period is to a large extent a Cumbric rather than a Welsh one'. In north Britain, as we have already seen, the impact of Roman civilization had been comparatively superficial, and so the indigenous Celtic literary institutions had a better opportunity to flourish there than they had in Wales, which formed a part of the Imperial province. Nor, in spite of the political reverses of the sixth and seventh centuries, which resulted in the collapse of the British kingdoms of Rheged and Gododdin and the political isolation of Wales, did literary contact between Wales and north Britain come to an abrupt end. The English penetration into the Severn valley which followed the battle of Deorham (or Dyrham), near Bath, in 577, effectively separated the Britons of Wales from those of the Dumnonian peninsula. Later, the Welsh and the Britons of Strathclyde became engaged in a bitter struggle with the encroaching English, which culminated in the English victories at Chester c. 616 and Winwaed Field in 655. The fall of the kingdom of Elmet, c. 617, removed one serious obstacle to English penetration west of the Pennines. The south-westward thrust by Ethelfrith of Bernicia, which led to the decisive English victory at Chester, undoubtedly constituted a serious threat to land communications between Wales and north Britain, although this was not the decisive factor in the separation. Communications were again open in 633-4, when Maelgwn Gwynedd's great-grandson, Cadwallon ap Cadfan, was creating havoc in Northumbria. Professor Kenneth Jackson has cogently argued that the English occupation and settlement of Cumberland, Westmorland, and Lancashire north of the Ribble can probably be ascribed to the period from about the middle to the end of the seventh century. The decisive separation of the Britons of Wales from those of the North must therefore date from that period. It was probably about this time that the Britons of Wales and northern Britain began to take the name *Cymry* (< British *Combrogī, 'people of the same region, fellow-countrymen'), singular *Cymro* (< British *Combrogos) as their particular appellation for themselves and their land; compare the first element in *Cumbraland, Cumberland*. But in spite of the political isolation of Wales, contacts between the latter and the North could still be maintained by way of the Irish Sea, which constituted an important connecting link rather than a barrier at this period. Indeed, for some considerable time after this, probably until the advent of the Norsemen in the late eighth century, some communication was maintained between north Wales and the remnants of the northern British kingdoms. Not surprisingly, therefore, a considerable body of sixth- to seventh-century north British literary tradition reached Wales, including the works of Taliesin and Aneirin, which became the foundation of the native bardic tradition, the remains of the story of Urien, the legends revolving around the battle of Arfderydd (modern Arthuret, near Longtown in Cumberland), recorded in the *Annales Cambriae* as having taken place in 573, a number of genealogies of Northern princes, and other matter of a fragmentary nature.

That the fame of the battle of Catraeth, and probably of the *Gododdin* itself, was well established in Wales *c.* 633-4, that is, within about a generation of the presumed date of Mynyddog Mwynfawr's ill-fated expedition, is proved by a reference to 'the sorrow of Catraeth, great and renowned' *(eilywed Gattraeth fawr fygedawc)* in a panegyric which was addressed, possibly by the bard Afan Ferddig, to Cadwallon ap Cadfan, king of Gwynedd, who, in alliance with Penda of Mercia, defeated and slew Edwin of Northumbria in 633 in the battle of Heathfield, known in Welsh tradition as *Meigen*. Cadwallon himself was killed in 634 in the battle of *Cantscaul* (= Hefenfelth), near Hexham, by Oswald, king of Bernicia. This poem, *Moliant Cadwallon,* 'Praise of Cadwallon', survives only in eighteenth-century copies. But the text, which has been ruthlessly modernized, reflects distinct traces of an exemplar in an orthography similar to that of *The Black Book of Carmarthen* (*c.* 1200). The vocabulary, style, formulaic patterns and metre of the poem are, however, strikingly similar to those of the *Gododdin,* and so it is quite possible that it represents a genuine fragment of a panegyric which was composed during the lifetime of Cadwallon. If the poem is the genuine work of a seventh-century Welsh bard, it was probably composed when Cadwallon ap Cadfan was at the height of his power, for it strikes a note of exultation and victory and contains no hint of the reversal of Cadwallon's fortunes. The poem has therefore been dated *c.* 633-4. Its vocabulary, style and metre show that the bards who sang in Wales in the seventh century had inherited the same Celtic literary traditions as those of the northern Britons. The same is also true of an elegy to Cynddylan ap Cyndrwyn, a Welsh king of the middle Severn valley, possibly by the bard Meigant. According to a Welsh tradition of a slightly later period, Cynddylan fought at the battle of Maserfeld (Oswestry) in 642, in which Oswald, king of Northumbria, was killed by Penda, and the elegy seems to contain references to a successful raid on a district somewhere near Lichfield in Mercia. Although this elegy has survived only in late copies, its text also shows traces of an exemplar in an orthography similar to that of *The Black Book of Carmarthen*, and once again the vocabulary, style and metre are similar to those of the *Gododdin*.

Sir Ifor Williams believed that the royal dynasty of Gwynedd, at Aberffraw, was the vital link in the chain of transmission of the early bardic poetry of north Britain to Wales. In his view, the fact that the royal dynasties of north Wales claimed descent from Cunedda Wledig, a ruler from the region of Manaw Gododdin, was pre-eminently responsible for the interest taken in Aneirin and his work in north Wales. He further believed that it was by this means that the information contained in some of the late sixth-century verse composed in north Britain became known to Nennius. This is not inherently improbable, and it may account for the renown which the battle of Catraeth had acquired in Wales *c*. 633-4. But if Aneirin's poem was known in Wales at this time, it had probably been transmitted orally, and is unlikely to have existed in a manuscript form at so early a period. The problem of manuscript transmission is a difficult one, but Professor Jackson has recently emphasized the importance of Strathclyde as an intermediate channel. For although the greater part of north Britain was subjected to the power of Northumbria during the course of the sixth and seventh centuries, the kingdom of Strathclyde, extending probably from Loch Lomond and Cunningham to Peebles and the source of the Tweed, succeeded in retaining its independence for about another 350 years. Here, it has been argued, in the court of the independent kings of Strathclyde, with its capital at Dumbarton, the traditions and stories of the 'Northern Heroic Age' were preserved and cherished. That the Britons of Strathclyde had their own bardic verse and traditions is proved by the interpolation in the *Gododdin* of two versions of a stanza from a poem celebrating the victory of the men of Strathclyde under their king, Ywain, and the death of Domhnall Brecc (or Dyfnwal Frych in Welsh), the king of the Irish kingdom of Dálriada, in west Scotland, at the battle of Strathcarron, near Falkirk, in 642. The interpolated stanza is obviously a fragment of a panegyric composed by an anonymous bard from Strathclyde on the occasion of Ywain's victory, and the fact that this poem, if we may judge from the stanza which has survived, was strikingly similar in nature to Aneirin's poem shows that verse of this kind, which had flourished in all the early Celtic societies, was being composed in Strathclyde, in southern Scotland, in the first half of the seventh century. It seems a reasonable conclusion, therefore, that it was from Strathclyde that a considerable amount of literary material from north Britain eventually reached Wales. And, significantly, when members of the Welsh professional learned class were actively compiling genealogical data, sometime between 954 and 988, with a view to buttressing the claim of Owain ap Hywel Dda to rule over much of Wales, they skilfully drew on an older collection dating from the reign of his ancestor, Rhodri Mawr (d. 877), which provided them with a number of northern genealogies, including that of the kings of Strathclyde down to Rhun, who ascended the throne in 872. It appears that members of the Welsh professional learned class took a keen interest in the traditions of north Britain in the ninth century.

Many instances can be cited of the transference southwards, to Wales, of some of the prominent figures of the Northern heroic tradition. This phenomenon can be seen in the various sagas and traditions which revolve around the names of Taliesin, Myrddin, Drystan, Gwyddno Garanhir, Urien Rheged, Llywarch Hen, and Huail mab Caw. A particularly interesting example is that of Llywarch Hen. In the genealogical tract entitled *Bonedd Gwŷr y Gogledd,* 'The Descent of the Men of the North', which is preserved in a thirteenth-century manuscript (Peniarth 45), he is established as a ruler in north Britain in the sixth century, a descendant of Coel Hen and first cousin to Urien Rheged. But towards the middle of the ninth century, during a period of great adversity for Powys, the province in north-east Wales which faced Shropshire and Cheshire, a story-teller of that region composed a cycle of tales or sagas about Llywarch and his sons, said to be twenty-four in number, and Heledd, sister of Cynddylan ap Cyndrwyn. In this cycle prose was used for narrative description, and verse of the *englyn* genre for dialogue and soliloquy. Unfortunately, the prose has not been preserved, but the *englynion* have survived as a result of being copied into *The Red Book of Hergest* (cols. 1026-49), the most valuable single manuscript collection of medieval Welsh poetry, although some *englynion* also appear in other sources, such as *The Black Book of Carmarthen*. The tales were skilfully woven around the names of Llywarch and some of his historical contemporaries in north Britain, as found in the genealogies, but these dramatic stories are located on the eastern borders of Powys (see Chapter IV). A strong but misguided tradition later arose from this cycle of tales that Llywarch himself was a poet and a native of Powys. Sir Ifor Williams, to whom we are heavily indebted for most of our knowledge of early Welsh poetry, argued cogently that the most likely place and period for the composition of this magnificent cycle was Powys in the mid ninth century, when, under constant English pressure, it was reduced to a fraction of its former extent and the last of the old native dynasty, Cyngen, who ruled over Powys from 808 to 854-5, died a pilgrim at Rome, 'whither he had been driven', in the words of Sir J. E. Lloyd, 'by old age and misfortune'. During Cyngen's reign the kingdom of Powys had suffered a severe reversal in its fortunes, for in 822 it was overrun by the English. In the preceding century Offa's Dyke, a clear symbol of Mercian supremacy, had cut off a substantial part of the kingdom of Powys. Sir Ifor Williams argued, therefore, that the political calamities which befell Powys during the late eighth and early ninth centuries provided a suitable background for the sorrowful *englynion* which are associated with the name of Llywarch Hen and ensured for their anonymous composer a ready and sympathetic audience. Unlike Taliesin and Aneirin, the poet does not refer to persons with whom he was personally acquainted, but he invests his stories of the bitter struggles of a bygone age, both in his native Powys and on the distant battlefields of north Britain, with the harrowing emotions of his own period, one of national calamity and humiliation for his native province.

Entirely different in mood and historical milieu is *Armes Prydain,* 'The Prophecy of Britain', a poem of just under 200 lines, written *c.* 930 probably by a member of a monastic community in south Wales who was bitterly opposed to the policy pursued by his king, Hywel Dda (d. 950), of recognizing the overlordship of the king of England, of living on peaceful terms with the English, and of paying tribute to the men of Wessex, called *Iwys* in the poem. This composition is therefore not so much a vaticination as an instrument of political propaganda, and the sentiments to which it gives such unambiguous expression reflect the nationalist opposition which must have existed in certain parts of south Wales in the early tenth century to the pro-English policy of Hywel Dda. But in endeavouring to incite both the political leaders and the rank and file to rise up against the traditional enemy—the English—the author, who may well have been a native of Dyfed, draws skilfully on the resources and conventions of the bardic vaticinatory tradition and exploits them for his own political purposes.

As for its immediate political background, the poem, as Sir Ifor Williams has demonstrated, must have been composed in a period when negotiations were in progress between certain of the Celtic and Norse inhabitants of the British Isles—the Irish, the Danes of Dublin, and the peoples of Wales, Scotland, Strathclyde and Cornwall (and even those of Brittany, according to the poet)—with a view to forming a pan-Celtic coalition that might resolutely oppose the aggressive policy of Athelstan, king of England, who in his royal title sometimes claimed authority over the whole of Britain. On one of his coins he appears as king of all Britain, and in many of his charters he is proudly described as 'King of the English and ruler of all Britain'. His charters also contain such imposing titles as *monarchus, basileus,* and *imperator.* The appearance during his reign of a new kind of assembly in which the bishops, ealdormen and thegns of Wessex were joined by lay and ecclesiastical magnates from every part of the land is another clear indication of his power and authority. After he had succeeded in uniting the kingdoms of Wessex and Mercia under his sway, he was in a particularly strong position to oppose the Scandinavians who had settled in York. He was able to take possession of this important northern city in 927, after the kings of Scotland and Strathclyde had been compelled to render homage to him. About this time, too, Athelstan summoned the Welsh princes to meet him at Hereford, forced them to make submission and to agree to the payment of an oppressive annual tribute of gold, silver, cattle, hounds and hawks, and fixed the Wye (in place of the Severn) as the boundary between Wales and England in the south. A policy as overtly aggressive as this inevitably led to a rising tide of opposition against him, culminating in 937 with the destruction by Athelstan at Brunanburh, somewhere in north Britain, of the combined forces of the Danes of Dublin and of the kings of Scotland and Strathclyde. Although the Welsh princes did not participate in this campaign, the coalition of Norse-Celtic forces could hardly have been achieved without a long period of detailed preliminary negotiations between the various parties involved. It seems, therefore, that *Armes Prydain* was composed while these vital discussions were in progress, and in any case before 937, for it is extremely unlikely that the formation of a strong pan-Celtic alliance could seriously have been contemplated after the decisive victory won by Athelstan at

Brunanburh. The turbulent decade from 927 to 937 in the latter's reign is therefore the most likely period for the composition of this poem. Moreover, the excessively heavy tribute which Athelstan imposed on the Welsh princes at the council of Hereford, sometime between 927 and 930, provides an appropriate background to the poet's frequent references to the contemptuous rejection by the Welsh of the English *trethau* or taxes, and Sir Ifor Williams has shown that it must be Athelstan himself who is satirically described as *mechteyrn*, that is, 'Great King' or 'Overlord'. These powerful arguments in favour of a pre-Norman Conquest date are strongly reinforced by the linguistic and metrical features of this poem, which was considered sufficiently important to be transcribed *in toto* in *The Book of Taliesin* (pp. 13-18) and hence to be attributed to the bard whose name the manuscript bears (see Chapter V).

In addition to the great interest which it naturally has for the student of Welsh literature, the poem is an historical document of considerable importance. For, quite apart from its factual content, it provides us with a rare insight into opinions and attitudes in Wales *c*. 930. The poem conveys also a great pride in the ancient glory of the Welsh (or Britons), who, after the final defeat of the Saxons and their expulsion overseas, will enter once again, we are told, into their rightful inheritance as rulers of the whole island of Britain. This theme, coupled with that of the advent of the prophesied deliverer *(y mab darogan)*, continued to haunt Welsh vaticinatory verse for many centuries, and it accounts in some measure for the attitude of the Welsh to the victory won by Henry VII, as he was to be known, on Bosworth Field on 22 August 1485 and the generally favourable reception which they gave to the Tudor monarchs. And so, by a strange twist of fate, a lingering nostalgic consciousness of the former extent of Brythonic rule in this island played some part, however small, in shaping the political destiny of Wales on the threshold of the modern age.

BIBLIOGRAPHY

J. E. Lloyd, *A History of Wales from the Earliest Times to the Edwardian Conquest* (2 vols., London, 1911; new impression, 1948); vol. I.

A. H. Williams, *An Introduction to the History of Wales* (2 vols., Cardiff, 1941-8); vol. I.

A. J. Roderick (ed.), *Wales through the Ages. Volume I: From the Earliest Times to 1485* (Llandybie, 1959), pp. 18-73.

Ralegh Radford, 'Cultural Relations of the Celtic World', *Proceedings of the Second International Congress of Celtic Studies, 1963* (Cardiff, 1966), pp. 3-27.

Nora K. Chadwick, *Celtic Britain* (London, 1963; second revised impression, 1964).

Myles Dillon and Nora K. Chadwick, *The Celtic Realms* (London, 1967).

I. Ll. Foster and G. Daniel (eds.), *Prehistoric and Early Wales* (London, 1965), chaps. vi-viii.

Sheppard Frere, *Britannia: a History of Roman Britain* (London, 1967).

Joan Liversidge, *Britain in the Roman Empire* (London, 1968).

R. G. Collingwood and J. N. L. Myers, *Roman Britain and the English Settlements* (2nd edn., Oxford, 1937).

F. M. Stenton, *Anglo-Saxon England* (2nd edn., Oxford, 1947).

Nora K. Chadwick (ed.), *Studies in Early British History* (Cambridge, 1954).

Idem, *Studies in the Early British Church* (Cambridge, 1958), chaps. i-ii.

Idem, *Celt and Saxon* (Cambridge, 1963), chaps. i and x.

Leslie Alcock, *Arthur's Britain* (London, 1971).

John Morris, *The Age of Arthur* (London, 1973).

Gordon Menzies (ed.), *Who Are the Scots? A Search for the Origins of the Scottish Nation* (London, 1971).

E. G. Bowen, *Saints, Seaways and Settlements* (Cardiff, 1969).

K. H. Jackson, *Language and History in Early Britain* (Edinburgh, 1953).

Idem, *The Gododdin* (Edinburgh, 1969).

Ceri W. Lewis, 'The Welsh Language', *The Cardiff Region*, ed. J. F. Rees (Cardiff, 1960), chap. x.

John Morris-Jones, 'Taliesin', *Y Cymmrodor*, XXVIII (1918).

Ifor Williams, *The Beginnings of Welsh Poetry*, edited by Rachel Bromwich (Cardiff, 1972).

Idem, *Canu Aneirin* (Cardiff, 1938), pp. xi-xciii.

Idem, *The Poems of Taliesin*. English Version by J. E. Caerwyn Williams (Dublin, 1968).

Idem, *Canu Llywarch Hen* (Cardiff, 1935).

Idem, *Lectures on Early Welsh Poetry* (Dublin, 1944).

Idem, *Armes Prydein: The Prophecy of Britain*. English Version by Rachel Bromwich (Dublin, 1972).

H. M. and N. K. Chadwick, *The Growth of Literature*, vol. I (Cambridge, 1932), chaps. ii-viii, and particularly pp. 37 ff.

Charles Thomas, *Britain and Ireland in Early Christian Times, A.D. 400-800* (London, 1971).
Idem, *The Early Christian Archaeology of North Britain* (Oxford, 1971).
Gerard Murphy, 'Bards and Filidh', *Eigse: A Journal of Irish Studies,* II (1940), 200-7.

CHAPTER II

TALIESIN

A. O. H. JARMAN

According to tradition, the earliest poetry that we possess in the Welsh language was composed during the latter half of the sixth century A.D. By that time, as has been shown in Chapter I, the ancient British or Brittonic language had undergone a series of changes which brought into being a speech we would recognize as Welsh, however much it differed from the modern language in vocabulary, construction and pronunciation. Nearly two hundred years had elapsed since the end of the Roman occupation and the communities which spoke the new language were developing autonomous modes of life and laying the foundations of a self-contained, indigenous literary culture. Unfortunately, we have no manuscript copies of sixth century verse written down at the time of its composition, and indeed the oldest texts that we possess of the earliest Welsh poetry are not older than the period 1250-75. There is thus a gap of some six hundred and fifty years between the manuscripts and the period during which the poems are believed to have been composed, and this has inevitably led to much controversy concerning their true dating. Cogent arguments have however been advanced by Welsh scholars in favour of accepting the poems as genuine, such as the consistency of their historical and geographical references, the archaic character of much of their language, and the fact that the texts show frequent signs of having been copied from earlier manuscripts. No doubt additions were made to the poems from time to time, and individual lines were subject to alteration or corruption, but in this chapter and the next the assumption will be made that some sixth century Welsh poetry has survived and that we possess it in texts which at least approximate to the form in which they were originally composed.

The earliest reference by name to poets composing in the Welsh language occurs in the *Historia Brittonum* or 'History of the Britons' of Nennius, a composite collection of semi-historical and mythical traditions put together close to the year 800 A.D. In this work, after a number of references to events of the mid and later sixth century, it is stated that 'at that time' five poets flourished, namely Talhaearn Tad Awen, Neirin (later to be spelt Aneirin), Taliesin, Blwchfardd and Cian. No further particulars are given. There is not a single quotation from any of the poets' works, no indication even of what was the subject-matter of their verse. Talhaearn's title of 'Father of the Muse' brings to mind Dryden's description of Chaucer as 'father of English poetry', and may perhaps be taken as suggesting that Talhaearn preceded the other four poets in point of time. Welsh tradition, however, has not preserved a single poem, or line of a poem, ascribed to Talhaearn, or to the last two poets mentioned in the list. On the other hand, the two poets who are named second and third, Aneirin and Taliesin, occupy a very different position. A large body of verse is attributed to both in medieval manuscripts and a significant nucleus, at least, of this has been widely accepted as the foundation-stone of the Welsh poetic tradition.

At this point it should be said that the earliest reference, not specifically to Welsh poets by name, but to verse composed in the Welsh language, occurs in a work written a generation or two before the period of Aneirin and Taliesin. This was the *De Excidio et Conquestu Britanniae* ('Of the Ruin and Conquest of Britain') of Gildas, a prominent ecclesiastical figure of the sixth century. It was written not later than 547 A.D and contains an eloquent denunciation of Maelgwn, king of Gwynedd in north-west Wales, who is condemned for choosing to listen, not to 'the praises of God, in the tuneful voice of Christ's followers . . . and the song of church melody', but rather to praises of himself expressed in 'the voice of the rascally crew

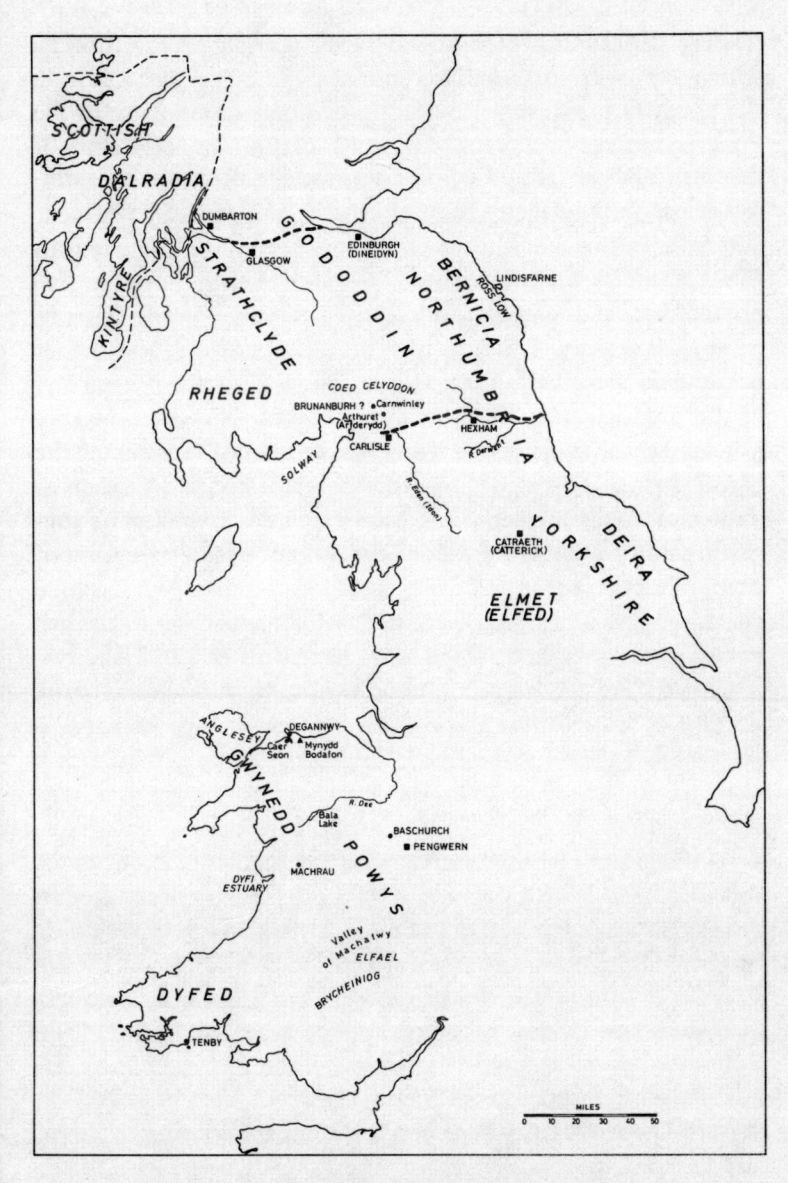

The North and Wales — the geographical background of Early Welsh Verse — a newly commissioned map by Professor E. G. Bowen.

yelling forth, like Bacchanalian revellers, full of lies and foaming phlegm, so as to besmear everyone near them'. These extravagant words refer to the bards of Maelgwn's court whose public function was to praise Maelgwn ceremonially as ruler of his kingdom. In Gildas's eyes they were to be condemned for rendering to a mere earthly monarch praises which should be offered to God alone. Neither the works nor even the names of these early bards have been preserved, although it is clear that some memory of their existence was retained, for they figure in later saga about Maelgwn's court. The language in which they composed was undoubtedly an early form of Welsh, and the words used by Gildas to condemn them make it probable that their eulogies of the king were set to music. There is in the *De Excidio* also a suggestion of what Maelgwn's bards had to say about their sovereign. Gildas refers to the king of Gwynedd as the 'island dragon' and describes him as an 'overthrower of rulers'. He furthermore declares that his power and armed might are only equalled, and perhaps exceeded, by the extent of his wickedness. He nevertheless allows, albeit reluctantly, that Maelgwn possessed a certain nobility of nature, a 'liberality in giving', which set him apart from other kings of his time. These twin attributes of the king, his strength and bravery in defending his realm and his generosity to those who expected to receive his largesse at court, are themes which are not confined to any one time or place. They were, however, a dominant element in the Welsh poetic tradition from the days of Taliesin until the later Middle Ages, and Gildas's *De Excidio* shows that they were given an equal prominence half a century before Taliesin sang. It is, of course, arguable that they were inherited from an earlier Celtic tradition of panegyric poetry of which no vestiges remain.

This chapter and the next will be concerned with poems attributed to Aneirin and Taliesin. Before this body of verse is examined attention must be drawn to one curious feature which appertains to it, namely that although its language is Welsh, it was not a product of Wales nor was its historical and geographical background Welsh. In the sixth century the areas of western Britain which spoke an early form of Welsh extended from Cornwall in the far south-west to northern England and southern Scotland. In the latter region there were three independent kingdoms, Gododdin, Rheged, and Ystrad Glud or Strathclyde. Of these, Gododdin had its centre at Edinburgh, Rheged lay around the estuary of the Solway and probably had Carlisle as its capital, while Strathclyde lay further north around the estuary of the Clyde. Here the Welsh poetic tradition had its beginning, and here was its almost exclusive historical background in its earliest phase. These kingdoms of the North maintained a precarious existence in conditions of semi-perpetual warfare, for they were surrounded by enemies on all sides, Angles to the south and east, Picts to the north, and Goidels from Ireland to the west. With Wales they had an overland connection, which seems to have continued in an intermittent form until the middle of the seventh century. By that time both Gododdin and Rheged had been over-run and conquered, but Strathclyde maintained a vigorous independence until its absorption in greater Scotland early in the eleventh century. A close association between parts of Wales and the land of Gododdin must have existed since the first half of the fifth century, when Cunedda and his 'sons' or followers are said to have migrated from the territory known as Manaw Gododdin to Gwynedd and other areas of western Wales where they dislodged recent Goidelic immigrants from Ireland and established new Brythonic ruling dynasties. Maelgwn Gwynedd was Cunedda's great-grandson. Early Welsh records and genealogical collections show a considerable knowledge of affairs in northern Britain during the sixth and early seventh centuries and much of the raw material of medieval Welsh literature is derived from these regions and reflects the ideas and some of the events of the period known as their 'heroic age'. Indeed, it was within the borders of Wales that the poems attributed to Aneirin and Taliesin were preserved and handed down to posterity after the collapse of the two kingdoms of Gododdin and Rheged.

In the foregoing paragraphs reference has several times been made to poems 'composed' in the Welsh language by the poets of the sixth century. The word has been deliberately used, for it is extremely unlikely that any of these poems were written down at the time of their composition or for a considerable time afterwards. For some centuries after the end of the Roman occupation the concept of writing meant simply the writing of Latin and the earliest scraps that we possess of written Welsh, apart from a few proper names, do not antedate the ninth century. We have therefore to envisage a situation and a period in which poetry was preserved by memory and transmitted orally from generation to generation. It is impossible to tell when Welsh poetry was first written down, but a strong case can be made for believing that this had occurred by about the middle of the ninth century. The earliest copies that we now possess, however, of the early poetry are found in manuscripts dated four hundred years later. Thus, about 1275, a collection was made in one manuscript of some sixty or more poems regarded at that time as the work of Taliesin. This *Book of Taliesin* contains a very varied and interesting assortment of poems on many different subjects, the great majority of which are not now considered to be the work of Taliesin at all but to have been composed at various periods between the ninth and the thirteenth centuries. The editorial scholarship of Sir Ifor Williams, however, has shown that twelve of the poems contained in the manuscript can be set apart from the rest and treated as genuine early material. These are known as the 'historical poems' of Taliesin and they deal with persons and events of the sixth century, almost exclusively in northern Britain. Here, it is claimed, if anywhere, is to be found the work of Taliesin and the earliest surviving poetry in the Welsh language.

For, although in Nennius's list the name of Taliesin follows that of Aneirin, it is probable that Taliesin was the earlier of the two. Of the twelve 'historical poems' the first in point of time appears to be one in praise of Cynan Garwyn, a king of Powys in north-east Wales who flourished about 580 A.D. The ascription of this poem to Taliesin may seem to be inconsistent with the statement already made that his work has as its background not Wales but northern Britain, and indeed it has been suggested by more than one critic that this particular poem is not by Taliesin but by another poet. A theory proposed by Sir Ifor Williams, however, accepts it as the work of Taliesin and argues that the poet could have been a native of Powys who commenced his career at Cynan's court and subsequently migrated to the northern court of Rheged. This view would accord well with the content of the poem, for it certainly lacks the maturity and the sense of responsibility found in Taliesin's other poems. It contains fifty short lines of five syllables (sometimes printed as twenty-five double lines) of which over two thirds are devoted to extolling Cynan's prowess in war and his conquests in Gwent, Anglesey, Dyfed and Brycheiniog. Dire threats are uttered in his name against Cornwall, and the 'wretched rulers' of all other territories are commanded to 'tremble' before him. Conquest and slaughter and the enslavement of all and sundry are lauded as admirable activities, and there is no hint of a sense of Welsh or Brythonic unity in face of a common enemy. Such an idea as this would not, indeed, have occurred to the poet, for he concludes his poem with the confident claim that 'the whole world under the sun is captive to Cynan'. The only other theme touched on by him is his gratitude for the gifts which he has received from the king—horses, mantles, bracelets, brooches and a yellow-hilted sword. No doubt, Taliesin had good reasons for praising Cynan. We may gather that the rulers of the kingdoms which bordered on Cynan's realm took a less favourable view of him and it has been caustically remarked that when Selyf, son of Cynan, faced a Northumbrian attack led by Ethelfrith in 615, not one of his neighbours was prepared to come to his aid.

Disunity among local rulers was, of course, a not uncommon feature of the life of the period. The *Historia Brittonum* of

Nennius, in a passage close to the one which refers to the five early poets, gives a list of four northern British kings who fought against the English. They were Urien, Rhydderch Hen, Gwallawg and Morgan. All these names also occur in the Welsh verse of various kinds which deals with the affairs of the North. Nennius adds, however, that Urien was killed while laying siege to the English in the island of Lindisfarne, and that his death was plotted by Morgan who was jealous of his pre-eminence in waging war. Urien was king of Rheged and is usually referred to as Urien Rheged. It was to his court that Taliesin went when he decided to leave Powys and migrate northwards. At least eleven poems have survived which may be accepted as having been composed by Taliesin after his arrival in the North. Nine of these deal with Urien, his son Owain and the affairs of the kingdom of Rheged, while the remaining two are concerned with Gwallawg, ruler of the small kingdom of Elfed or Elmet in Yorkshire. One or two references in the poems to Urien support the view that Taliesin was not a native of the North. For instance, in one line the poet tells the king that 'thee I have guarded, though I am not one of thine'. From the moment of his arrival at the court of Rheged, however, it must be presumed that Taliesin devoted his gifts to the praise of its ruler. In the poems to Urien two themes are emphasized. The first is the king's prowess in battle, his ability by defensive and offensive action to keep the enemy at bay and secure the survival of the community which he rules. The second is his commanding position at court where, amid his family and retainers, his magnanimity and generosity are made manifest to all those, including the poet, who are dependent on his patronage. This portrait of Urien has been described as Taliesin's greatest achievement. For it lay at the fountain-head of the Welsh tradition of panegyric and was echoed, developed and elaborated by Welsh poets for a thousand years. It was the mature Taliesin's contribution to the conceptual content of Welsh poetry. No doubt the raw material of the portrait was already present in the poem on Cynan Garwyn, and possibly, as we have seen, in the poems declaimed at the court of Maelgwn Gwynedd and at other courts by poets unknown to us. As well as providing a standard and an ideal for the Welsh panegyrists of the Middle Ages, Taliesin's poems may also have represented the fulfilment of an earlier tradition deriving from the Brythonic or Celtic past. This fulfilment shows itself in Taliesin's northern poems in their implicit emphasis on the king's understanding of the social implications of his position and his sense of responsibility for the well-being of the community which he rules.

Let us now look more closely at some of Taliesin's poems. Outstanding among those in praise of Urien is the one entitled, from its opening words, *Urien Yrechwydd*. It has been translated by Saunders Lewis in a rendering which follows the sense exactly and also comes close to the metrical effect of the original:

> Urien of Yrechwydd   most generous of Christian men,
> much do you give   to the people of your land;
> as you gather   so also you scatter,
> the poets of Christendom   rejoice while you stand.
> More is the gaiety   and more is the glory
> that Urien and his heirs   are for riches renowned,
> and he is the chieftain,   the paramount ruler,
> the far-flung refuge,   first of fighters found.
> The Lloegrians know it   when they count their numbers,
> death have they suffered   and many a shame,
> their homesteads a-burning,   stripped their bedding,
> and many a loss   and many a blame,
> and never a respite   from Urien of Rheged.
> Rheged's defender,   famed lord, your land's anchor,
> all that is told of you   has my acclaim.
> Intense is your spear-play   when you hear ploy of battle,
> when to battle you come   'tis a killing you can,
> fire in their houses ere day   in the lord of Yrechwydd's way,
> Yrechwydd the beautiful   and its generous clan.
> The Angles are succourless.   Around the fierce king
> are his fierce offspring.   Of those dead, of those living,
> of those yet to come,   you head the column.
> To gaze upon him   is a widespread fear;
> Gaiety clothes him,   the ribald ruler,
> gaiety clothes him   and riches abounding,
> gold king of the Northland   and of kings king.

Here we have the entire picture: Urien's eminence among his fellow-kings, his bravery, his ferocity towards the enemy, his protective function as his people's far-flung refuge and his land's anchor, his riches and his generosity, and the undoubted personal touch which speaks of his gaiety and describes him as the ribald ruler.

In the poem *Gwaith Gwên Ystrad* ('The Battle of Gwên Ystrad') Taliesin confines himself to describing a battle-scene. The description is vivid and the poet, who was probably an eyewitness, speaks in the first person. The following passage is from Clancy's translation:

> I saw savage men in war-bands;
> And after morning's fray, torn flesh.
> I saw border-crossing forces dead,
> Strong and angry the clamour one heard.
> Defending Gwên Ystrad one saw
> A thin rampart and lone weary men.
> At the ford I saw men stained with blood
> Downing arms before a grey-haired lord;
> They wished peace, for they found the way barred,
> Hands crossed, on the strand, cheeks pallid,
> Their lords wondered at Idon's rich wine;
> Waves washed the tails of their horses.

Here the 'grey-haired lord' is Urien, and the 'lone weary men' are the champions who had won a strongly contested victory for him. Those of the enemy forces—probably Picts in this case—who made their surrender with 'hands crossed' had fought to the point of exhaustion. Their fellow-warriors who did not survive had coloured the waters of the river Idon (Eden) with their blood. Another possible rendering of the last line but one would be: 'Their lords were drunk on Idon's plentiful wine',—a translation which would further heighten its savage and grotesque sarcasm. The poem continues for several more lines in a similar warlike vein and concludes with the statement that 'battle is sure to be the lot of him who is Urien's soldier'.

Probably the best-known of Taliesin's poems is *Gwaith Argoed Llwyfain* ('The Battle of Argoed Llwyfain'). This has several characteristics which differentiate it from the poet's other works. Many translations of it have been published. The following is by Anthony Conran with slight variations by Saunders Lewis:

> There was a great battle Saturday morning
> From when the sun rose until it grew dark.
> The fourfold hosts of Fflamddwyn invaded,
> Goddau and Rheged gathered in arms,
> Summoned from Argoed as far as Arfynydd—
> They might not delay by as much as a day.
>
> With a great blustering din, Fflamddwyn shouted,
> 'Have these the hostages come? Are they ready?'
> To him then Owain, scourge of the eastlands,
> 'They've not come, no! they're not, nor shall they be ready.'
> And a whelp of Coel would indeed be afflicted
> Did he have to give any man as a hostage!
>
> And Urien, lord of Erechwydd, shouted,
> 'If they would meet us now for a treaty,
> High on the hilltop let's raise our ramparts,
> Carry our faces over the shield rims,
> Raise up our spears, men, over our heads
> And set upon Fflamddwyn in the midst of his hosts
> And slaughter him, ay, and all that go with him!'
>
> There was many a corpse beside Argoed Llwyfain;
>   From warriors ravens grew red
> And with their leader a host attacked.
> For a whole year I shall sing to their triumph.

The encounter described in these lines is not known to historians nor has the enemy leader Fflamddwyn (the 'Flame-bearer') been certainly identified, though it has been suggested that he was the Bernician king Deodric who reigned 572-79 (or possibly 586-93) and who is mentioned by Nennius as one against whom Urien and his sons fought. Goddau and Rheged, Argoed and Arfynydd were British territories summoned by Urien to resist Fflamddwyn. The poem is unique among the

Taliesin poems for its dramatic quality. The actor's words are quoted directly,—Fflamddwyn's contemptuous demand for hostages, Owain's defiant rejection of this, and finally Urien's exhortation to his men to attack the enemy immediately rather than debase themselves by discussing terms. There is no description of the actual battle, apart from the bare statement that 'a host attacked' under their leader. There ensued the corpses and the ravens and the triumph which vindicated Urien's determination to fight rather than parley. It was a victory which inspired the poet to fashion a celebration poem in which, to quote Mrs. Rachel Bromwich, 'each line bears an essential relation to the whole, and barely a word is redundant.'

Such a rare symmetry is, in fact, only achieved in two Welsh poems of the early period, namely *Gwaith Argoed Llwyfain* and *Marwnad Owain* ('The Death-Song of Owain'), the poem to be noticed next. We have already met Owain, son of Urien, in the first of these two poems, which makes him respond to the enemy leader's challenge and describes him as 'scourge of the eastlands'. The phrase suggests that he was well-known for his campaigns against the Bernician invaders, who came from an easterly direction. In the Arthurian literature of the Middle Ages Owain is a figure of romance, a famous knight of Arthur's court, but this represents a legendary development of his fame and had no basis in fact. We do not know whether Owain died before or after Urien. No elegy for Urien by Taliesin exists. The date of Urien's death is not known, although the circumstances were recorded by Nennius. In *Marwnad Owain* the words *Rheged udd* ('lord' or 'prince of Rheged') are used to describe Owain, but they do not tell us whether he had succeeded Urien as king or not. The 'Death-Song' begins and ends with a prayer for Owain's soul but the prevailing theme of the poem is his ferocity towards his enemies and his skill in combating them. His generosity is also mentioned and is given a religious motivation. The reference to Fflamddwyn in the third stanza links the poem to *Gwaith Argoed Llwyfain*. The following translation is again by Conran, with slight variations by Saunders Lewis:

> God, consider the soul's need
> > Of Owain son of Urien!
> Rheged's prince, secret in loam:
> > No shallow work to praise him.
>
> A straight grave, a man much praised,
> > His whetted spear the wings of dawn:
> That lord of bright Llwyfenydd,
> > Where is his peer?
>
> Reaper of enemies; strong of grip;
> > One kind with his fathers;
> Owain, to slay Fflamddwyn,
> > Thought it no more than sleep.
>
> Sleepeth the wide host of England
> > With light in their eyes,
> And those that had not fled
> > Were braver than were wise.
>
> Owain dealt them doom
> > As the wolves devour sheep;
> That warrior, bright of harness,
> > Gave stallions for the bard.
>
> Though he hoarded wealth like a miser
> > For his soul's sake he gave it.
> God, consider the soul's need
> > Of Owain son of Urien!

The poem's most striking stanza is undoubtedly the fourth. The picture of the enemy lying open-eyed in death has been taken as an indication that Taliesin was himself familiar with the realities of the battle-scene and that his memory had retained one of his most searing impressions of the carnage. The visual paradox contained in the stanza's first couplet is matched conceptually in the third and fourth lines by the unexpected tribute to the bravery of some, at least, of Owain's adversaries. Welsh heroic verse rarely has compliments to spare for the enemy. Even here the admiration is qualified, for the daring of those who had not fled is viewed as foolhardiness and is used by the poet to emphasize Owain's superiority as a warrior.

In addition to the four poems which have been discussed, there are five others to Urien and two to Gwallawg. Some of them are textually imperfect and it is possible that parts of different poems have been joined together. In the Urien poems the portrait of the king outlined above is expanded and enlarged. Its essential features are summarized thus by Sir Ifor Williams: 'He fights for his country, he invites his men to battle and he causes such a terror in his enemies that they moan in fright. Around him there is always the sound of galloping horses or of carousal: he is always either setting out on an expedition or returning to celebrate its success. And of course he is mindful of his bard, on whom he showers gifts—of land, of gold, mead and beer, and fine raiment'. In a poem translated by Clancy under the title 'The War-band's Return' Taliesin speaks a dramatic monologue in which, having praised his patron's generosity in the standard manner, he is suddenly seized with alarm at the thought that Urien has set out on a raid from which he may not return:

> I could have no joy
> Should Urien be slain,
> So loved before he left,
> Brandishing his lance,
> And his white hair soaked,
> And a bier his fate,
> And gory his cheek
> With the stain of blood,
> A strong steadfast man,
> His wife made a widow,
> My faithful king,
> My faithful trust,
> My bulwark, my chief,
> Before savage pain.

Suddenly sounds are heard. A servant is sent to the door:

> Go, lad, to the door;
> What is that clamour?

> Is the earth shaking?
> Is the sea in flood?
> The chant grows stronger
> From marching men!

Urien has returned. Again he has conquered the enemy. Relieved from his anxiety the poet praises him jubilantly:

> Were a foe in hill,
> Urien will stab him;
> Were a foe in dale,
> Urien has pierced him;
> Were foe in mountain,
> Urien conquers him;
> Were foe on hillside,
> Urien will wound him;
> Were foe on rampart,
> Urien will smite him . . .

It is clear that Taliesin's admiration for Urien, and his attachment to him, knew no bounds. Indeed, seven of the Urien poems end with the following refrain:

> And until I die, old,
> By death's strict demand,
> I shall not be joyful
> Unless I praise Urien.

It appears, however, that on one occasion a cloud passed over their relationship. One of the poems to Urien is the earliest example in Welsh of a *Dadolwch* or reconciliation poem. It is probable that, although Taliesin had obtained an established position as the bard of Urien's court, he was not averse on occasion to visiting other courts and praising other rulers. He had, after all, begun his career at the court of Cynan Garwyn and migrated from there to Rheged. In later centuries this became normal practice for court poets in Wales. It has already been mentioned that there are two poems by Taliesin in praise of Gwallawg, king of Elmet, and one of these ends with the statement that 'he who has not seen Gwallawg has not seen a warrior'. It has been surmised that when reports reached Urien of what he took to be disloyalty on the part of his poet, he made his displeasure plain. Hence the need for Taliesin's impassioned declaration of fidelity to him and of his determination never again to seek other patrons. The following quotations are from Clancy's translation of the *Dadolwch:*

> Ruler most valiant,
> I shall not leave him.
> Urien I shall seek,
> To him I shall sing . . .
> No concern of mine,
> The princes I see:
> I go not to them;
> With them I stay not . . .
> Urien will not spurn me.
>
> Llwyfenydd's lands,
> Mine are their riches,
> Mine is their good-will,
> Mine is their bounty,
> Mine their benefits
> And their luxuries,
> Mead from drinking-horns
> And more wealth than needed
> From the best of kings,
> The kindest I've heard of.

In his poem to Cynan Garwyn Taliesin had declared that 'the whole world under the sun is captive to Cynan'. Whether Urien had been offended by this we do not know, but now we have Taliesin telling him that

> Kings of every tongue
> To you are captive;
> From you, they complain,
> They must take cover.

After expressing regret for an ill-timed jest which he had addressed to the king, the poet declares his allegiance as unequivocally as he can:

> No man loved I more
> Before I knew him.
> And now that I see
> How much will be mine,
> Save for God supreme
> I will not renounce him.

Most of Taliesin's poems are short and do not exceed about thirty-five lines. Some are in rhymed half-lines of four, five or six syllables. These are sometimes printed as in the translation quoted above of *Urien Yrechwydd*, and sometimes as in Clancy's translations of 'The War-band's Return' and the *Dadolwch*. The rhymes are sometimes maintained through a number of half-lines and would be difficult to reproduce in translation. Other poems, such as *Gwaith Gwên Ystrad* and *Gwaith Argoed Llwyfain,* are in rhymed lines of nine syllables, with variations of eight and ten. The 'Death-Song of Owain' is the earliest example of a poem in the metre of *awdl-gywydd*. The stanza which follows describes the wide host of England sleeping with light in their eyes:

> Cysgid Lloegr llydan nifer
> A lleufer yn eu llygaid,
> A rhai ni ffoynt haeach
> A oeddynt hyach no rhaid.

Each line has seven syllables and the second line rhymes with the fourth. In addition, *nifer* at the end of the first line rhymes with *lleufer* within the second, and *haeach* at the end of the third rhymes with *hyach* in the fourth. Alliteration is sometimes used as an embellishment in the various metres but there is, of course, no hint of the fully developed system of *cynghanedd* which became such an important element in Welsh versification during the Middle Ages.

In the medieval period Taliesin became known as Taliesin Ben Beirdd, 'Taliesin Chief of Poets'. By this time Talhaearn had been forgotten. Taliesin was regarded both as the first and the most eminent of the early poets, later to be called the *Cynfeirdd*. He was a founder poet and stood at the beginning of a tradition which lasted for a thousand years. As has already been indicated, however, his work must also be regarded as the maturing in some measure of a previous tradition. Otherwise there would be no adequate explanation of the taut perfection of his craftsmanship or of his disciplined control over language and metre.

BIBLIOGRAPHY

Editions:
 Ifor Williams, *Canu Taliesin,* Caerdydd, 1960.
 Ifor Williams, *The Poems of Taliesin, English Version by J. E. Caerwyn Williams,* Dublin, 1968.

Translations:
 Joseph P. Clancy, *The Earliest Welsh Poetry,* London, 1970.
 Gwyn Thomas (ed.), *Yr Aelwyd Hon,* Llandybie, 1970 (into modern Welsh).

Critical Studies:
 J. Morris-Jones, 'Taliesin', *Y Cymmrodor,* Vol. XXVIII, London, 1918.
 Ifor Williams, *The Beginnings of Welsh Poetry,* ed. by Rachel Bromwich, Cardiff, 1972.
 Ifor Williams, *Lectures on Early Welsh Poetry,* Dublin, 1944.
 I. Ll. Foster, 'The Emergence of Wales', pp. 213-35 in *Prehistoric and Early Wales,* ed. I. Ll. Foster and Glyn Daniel, London, 1965.
 Rachel Bromwich, 'The Character of the Early Welsh Tradition', pp. 83-136 in *Studies in Early British History,* ed. Nora K. Chadwick, Cambridge, 1959.
 Saunders Lewis, 'Taliesin', pp. 1-12 in *Braslun o Hanes Llenyddiaeth Gymraeg,* Caerdydd, 1932.
 Saunders Lewis, 'The Tradition of Taliesin', pp. 145-53, in *Presenting Saunders Lewis,* ed. Alun R. Jones and Gwyn Thomas, Cardiff, 1973.
 Anthony Conran, *The Penguin Book of Welsh Verse* (Introduction), Penguin Books, 1967.

CHAPTER III

ANEIRIN—THE GODODDIN

A. O. H. JARMAN

In the last chapter reference was made to the kingdom of Gododdin, which lay to the east of Rheged and had its main centre at Edinburgh. We find the name 'Gododdin' used in three senses: firstly, for the tribe or people so called; secondly, for the territory which they inhabited; and thirdly, it is the name of a long poem, attributed to Aneirin, in the form of a series of elegies for the heroes who fell at the battle of Catraeth, fought between the Gododdin and the Angles of Deira and Bernicia about the year 600 A.D. The name 'Catraeth' still survives as 'Catterick' in Yorkshire. It was a place of strategic importance in Roman times, when it was known as 'Cataracto' or 'Cataractonium'. The form *Catraeth* is derived from *cataracta*, 'waterfall', and originally was probably applied to the falls of the river Swale at Richmond. It was subsequently used for the river itself and later became the name of the town situated upon it.

History in the strict sense knows nothing of the battle of Catraeth and the poem, *Y Gododdin,* is itself virtually the only evidence that such a battle ever took place. It is however possible to use references in the poem to form a conjectural reconstruction of the background of the battle and the situation which led up to it. Catraeth was a long way from Edinburgh, but it lay in former British territory which had fallen into the hands of the advancing English. The threat from the latter to the survival of the kingdom of Gododdin was so real by the end of the sixth century that its ruler, Mynyddog Mwynfawr, decided that immediate and vigorous action was imperative. The action decided upon was an expedition against Catraeth. We gather from the poem that it was planned with some care. At his court of Dineidyn or Edinburgh, Mynyddog feasted a *gosgordd* or band of fighting men for the duration of a year. They mostly belonged to the tribe of the Gododdin but among them were included some from other parts of the Brythonic world. The preparation for battle is described in the poem as *ancwyn Mynyddog* or 'Mynyddog's feast', but it doubtless included military instruction as well as entertainment. At last the day for the attack came. The war-band of the Gododdin consisted of three hundred horsemen clad in mail, moving forward in formation and specially trained to overwhelm much larger bodies of foot-soldiers by means of planned but impetuous charges. The whole scheme nevertheless came to nought. The enemy was too numerous and too well entrenched. Mynyddog's men slew many times their own number of their foes, but ultimately the entire band fell leaving one sole survivor. Probably the enterprise was doomed from the start. It is not, however, likely that this was clear to Mynyddog when he planned it, and there are no grounds for regarding the attack as intentionally suicidal. But although victory was the aim, if it could be achieved, we gather that the members of the war-band were mentally prepared for defeat. However overwhelming the odds against them, nothing was to be allowed to deflect them from their purpose. And when we inquire into the nature of this 'purpose' we find that the poet of the *Gododdin* presents it to us, not in terms of military tactics or political manoeuvring, but on an individual and almost private plane, in terms of personal honour and fidelity to a sovereign lord. Whatever strategic calculation lay behind Mynyddog's action, the *Gododdin* as a poem knows nothing of it. Rather, the supreme aim of each individual member of the war-band is shown to be the fulfilment of his agreement to fight for his chieftain until victory or death. The term used for this in the poem is *talu medd,* the 'payment of mead'. Thus, the mead which the warrior has received from his lord in the hall during the feasting is treated as a symbol of the bond and obligation which exists between the two. The warrior is required to be 'worthy' of his mead, to 'deserve' it, and to requite his chieftain's hospitality by his prowess on the battlefield. The values acclaimed by Aneirin in the *Gododdin* are those of a heroic society in which, in the words of Professor K. Jackson, 'glory for heroic deeds is desired above all things, and death is welcome if it is followed by deathless fame'.

The *Gododdin* is the classic, and the only full-length, exposition of the ideals of the Heroic Age in Welsh literature. It is not a narrative poem and therefore does not qualify for the description 'epic', although events of epic quality lie behind it. It contains about a thousand different lines, arranged in rhyming stanzas, and is in form an elegy, or series of elegies, for the heroes who fought and fell at Catraeth. It is however much more than this. Although its prevailing tone is elegiac, it is not only a poem of lament but also of celebration. And the matter it celebrates is the matchless bravery and the unswerving loyalty of men who fought until they met their end in battle, deeming retreat before a superior enemy unthinkable and choosing death before shame. For them there could be no return to their own community, which was itself doomed partly as a result of the catastrophe at Catraeth, but in literature their poet Aneirin made them immortal. In the *Gododdin* they are praised, not in the manner of the Taliesin poems as conquerors in the field or defenders of the public weal or wise arbiters of affairs, but simply as men who fought both for their chieftain and for personal glory and who did not flinch even when they realized that the inevitable outcome of their faithfulness and of their desire for fame would be their own destruction.

Although the *Gododdin* is not a narrative poem a certain kind of time-sequence can be discerned in many of the references it contains. While there is little attempt to describe the battle of Catraeth itself, there is some delineation of its background and setting. Many of the heroes whom Mynyddog had summoned to his court were men of substance in their own localities and they joined the war-band with established reputations both for their fighting qualities and for their generosity as patrons. Thus, the poet says of Rhufawn that

> Taking the lead, he cut his way through armies,
> Five fifties fell before his blades,

but in more tranquil times,

> Rhufawn the Tall gave gold to the altar,
> And gifts and handsome largesse to the minstrel.

The court of Blaen was celebrated for its munificence:

> Blaen on his feather-cushion offered the drinking-horn
> In his opulent court;
> Blaen was supplied with drink of bragget,
> Blaen delighted in gold and purple clothing,

but on the battle-field

> Blaen raised the battle-cry and brought back booty,
> A bear in his manner, he was reluctant to retreat.

Employing sharply contrasted statements, which are a frequently occurring feature of early Welsh verse, the poet says of Erthgi:

> In his court the warrior was humble,
> Before Erthgi armies groaned.

The noble Isag is described as 'having a manner like the flowing sea for geniality and generosity and the pleasant drinking of mead'. He was nevertheless a 'wall of battle' and

> His sword echoed in the heads of mothers.

The court which was central to the theme of the *Gododdin*, however, was that of Mynyddog. There the warriors gathered and were feasted for a year:

> For a year many a minstrel was joyful.

There is no direct reference to military training. The year spent in preparation for the attack is always described as a 'feast':

> From a wine-feast and a mead-feast they attacked.

The wine and mead carry a symbolic meaning and the emphasis on the warriors' fulfilment of their 'agreement' with their chieftain,—on the 'payment' of their mead,—is constant:

> In return for mead in the hall and drink of wine
> He hurled his spears between two armies.

The agreement is sometimes mentioned without referring to the mead:

> His agreement was a purpose which was fulfilled.

Another aspect of the mead-feast appears, however, in the statement that

> They drank mead, yellow, sweet, ensnaring.

The significance of the third epithet is that, however joyful the carousal, the minstrelsy and the company of the throng crowd in Mynyddog's hall, the bond which had been forged between the warriors and their chieftain, of which the mead was the symbol, could only lead to ineluctable disaster. In the end, in order to honour their agreement, they would be required to sacrifice everything; this they did:

> The war-band of Mynyddog, famous in battle,
> They paid for their mead-feast with their lives.

Where, however, the poem describes the war-band of the Gododdin riding forth to battle, the fate which awaited them is momentarily forgotten. For the poet they were a splendid sight:

> The war-band of the Gododdin on rough-haired steeds,
> Swan-coloured horses, tightly harnessed.

And again:

> Men went to Catraeth, embattled, with a cry,
> A host of horsemen in brown armour, carrying shields,
> Spear-shafts held aloft with sharp points,
> And shining mail-shirts and swords.

The horse is almost invariably a part of the picture. The warband was first and foremost a troop of cavalry. In its opening stanza the poem mentions the 'swift thick-maned horses' ridden by the handsome youth Owain son of Marro. Of Blaen it says that

> Well-fed horses ran under him,

and Eithinyn is described as a

> Magnificent horseman before the Gododdin,
> The celebrated Eithinyn, wall of battle, bull of combat.

Many stanzas in the poem applaud the fighting qualities and bravery of the men of the Gododdin on the battle-field itself, as well as their harsh unyielding pride in face of the enemy. The very first line of the poem contrasts the youthfulness of Owain son of Marro with his strength and prowess:

> A man in might, a youth in years,

and then adds that

> He would sooner go to battle
> Than to a wedding-feast.

In another stanza an even more specific choice is indicated:

> The hero desired no father-in-law's dowry.

In other words, he himself chose death on the battle-field

rather than marriage. The same choice is viewed from another angle in yet another stanza which states that its hero Madog was

> Breathless before a maiden, but he paid his mead.

Madog was very far from being breathless in face of the enemy. The poem describes his actions on the battle-field in the following terms:

> Shattered was the front of his shield when he heard the battle-cry;
> He showed no mercy to those whom he pursued.
> He did not withdraw from battle until blood flowed.
> Like rushes he cut men down. He did not flee.

Some of the heroes are credited with a very great degree of ferocity. For instance, Neirthiad

> Made, before he would talk of peace,
> A bath of blood and death for his opponent,

and Breichiol is addressed as follows, in a couplet which recalls Taliesin's reference to 'Idon's plentiful wine':

> If the blood of the dead whom thou didst strike down were wine,
> Thou wouldst have sufficient for three or four years.

The poet then adds jocularly that

> Rapidly wouldst thou diminish thy steward's supply.

The very next line, however, dispels the levity with the entreaty:

> May Heaven's abode be thine because thou didst not flee.

In death as in life Breichiol had remained faithful to the heroic ideal. The concept of a reward in Heaven for refusing to flee, though not unknown in the Christian Middle Ages, is perhaps unexpected. In one text of this line the word for 'flee' *(thechut)* has been emended to a word meaning 'sin' *(phechut)* by the simple expedient of changing one letter. The monkish scribe who sought thus to bring the text into line with his own belief did not realize that by doing so he was undermining the primitive consistency of the ferocious stanza before him.

Nearly all the *Gododdin*'s leading themes are contained in one of its best-known stanzas:

> The warriors arose; they assembled;
> Together, with one accord, they attacked.
> Short were their lives, long their kinsmen's grief for them.
> They slew seven times their number of the English.
> By fighting they made women widows,
> Many a mother with a tear on her eyelid.

Here, in set order, we have the assembled host, the coordinated attack, the youthfulness of the warriors, their short lives, their kinsmen's sorrow, their superiority over the enemy, and the pitiless devastation wrought by their swords before they themselves fell. Some critics have thought that the last two lines of the stanza mean that the poet of the *Gododdin* was able to perceive the tragedy of war as such and to feel a certain measure of sympathy with the enemy in his sufferings. This is improbable. It is, in fact, most unlikely that an attitude as modern as this would have found any place in the mind of a sixth-century warrior poet. Aneirin is here expressing satisfaction because the men whose memory he celebrates had made women widows and had brought tears to the eyes of the mothers of the enemy.

Much of the *Gododdin* is, inevitably, pure elegy. In numerous lines and couplets, and sometimes in complete stanzas, the poet gives utterance to his personal sorrow after the loss of the heroes. He refers frequently to their early age:

> Men went to Catraeth with the dawn,
> Their ardour shortened their lives.
> Before their hair turned grey death came to them.

In the following six lines their story is summarized with classic simplicity:

> Men went to Catraeth, their host was swift,
> Fresh mead was their feast, and it was bitter,
> Three hundred men fighting under command,
> And after the shout of joy there was silence.
> Though they went to churches to do penance,
> True it is that death came to them.

In another stanza the poet names eleven members of the war-band, thus emphasizing his personal involvement in their loss:

> The war-band of Mynyddog, famous in battle,
> They paid for their mead-feast with their lives,
> Caradog and Madog, Pyll and Ieuan,
> Gwgon and Gwion, Gwyn and Cynfan,
> Peredur, armed with steel, Gwawrddur and Aeddan,
> Attackers in the fight, with shattered shields;
> And although they were slain, they slew,
> Not one returned to his homeland.

As has already been indicated, however, it would be wrong to regard the *Gododdin* merely as a poem of lament for the fallen. It is also a poem which states the heroic view that honour and renown gained through fighting the enemy, at whatever cost, are in themselves worth while and desirable. The following lines make the simple statement that the hero's aim on the field of battle was the achievement of fame:

> He slew a great host
> In order to be spoken of;
> The son of Nwython struck down
> Of the golden-torqued
> A hundred princes
> So that he might be praised.

But more usually the poet declares that the hero has sacrificed his life for the sake of fame and honour:

> The son of Sywno, —the astrologer knew it,—
> Sold his life
> For the mention of honour,

and in the stanza devoted to Breichiol he says that

> Valiant Breichiol was the talk of the world.

That fame and glory were of more importance than life is clearly implied by the line:

> Men in battle, renowned, heedless of their lives.

After the fall of the warriors the obligation to commemorate their deeds is emphasized. The poet says of Gwenabwy son of Gwenn that

> It would be wrong to leave him unremembered, great were his exploits,

and of Tudfwlch:

> His valour will live long
> And his memory among his handsome company.

Again, addressing Cynon son of Clydno Eidyn he says:

> Renowned son of Clydno, I shall sing to thee, lord,
> Praise without end or limit.

Cynon was possibly the one survivor of the battle of Catraeth, but the poet does not censure him for this. He too deserved the highest praise:

> He slew the enemy with the sharpest sword,
> Like rushes they fell by his hand.

Living and dead alike, if praise is due to the heroes, they will receive it:

> Three hundred golden-torqued warriors attacked
> Defending their land, with cruel slaughter;
> Although they were slain, they slew,
> And until the end of the world they shall be praised.

Although they have fallen the poet will make them immortal. For he claims for himself the right to apportion praise:

> The poets of the world will be the judges of brave men.

The ninety-one lines quoted above in translation will give some idea of the heroic view of the world which is expressed so vigorously and consistently in the *Gododdin*. The poem no doubt incorporates the martial ideals of the north British communities of the sixth century, but historians of the ancient world will also discern in it much that recalls the qualities attributed by classical writers to the Gauls and other Continental Celts. As has already been pointed out, the *Gododdin* is unique in Welsh literature in that it is the only work that gives the heroic view of life full and unfettered expression, undiluted by other concepts. Critics whose interest lies in the realm of ideas might find a perusal of its thousand lines monotonous. Those, however, who have an interest in language as a means of expression will find it absorbing. In stanza after stanza, in order to give utterance to what may seem to be a narrowly repetitive series of thoughts and ideas, it employs an immense variety of words, expressions, phrase and sentence formations, rhythms and metrical devices, and even of imagery. When we remember that it is the work of a poet using the language in the early dawn of its history as a literary medium, the great verbal richness of the *Gododdin* cannot fail to astonish. The poem has a linguistic vigour which is difficult to convey in translation and can only be appraised by those able to read the original text.

The *Gododdin* has been preserved in a manuscript entitled the *Book of Aneirin,* written about the middle of the thirteenth century. The manuscript contains two texts of the poem, or of parts of it, usually referred to as A and B. A is in the orthography of the thirteenth century and B in that of the ninth or tenth. Text B was copied into the *Book of Aneirin* from a manuscript source written in the Old Welsh period without much attempt being made to 'modernize' the spelling. The history of the poem between the sixth and the ninth or tenth century is obscure. We do not know when it was first written down but, as in the case of the poems of Taliesin, it is virtually certain that a period of oral transmission lasting for several generations, or even two or three centuries, must be postulated after its original composition. This allowed ample opportunity for textual alteration and corruption, and for the introduction of extraneous matter which had no connection with the *Gododdin*'s original theme. Examples of such interpolations are an *englyn* from the Llywarch Hen cycle of poems, two texts of a stanza recording a battle fought between the Britons of Strathclyde and the Goidels of Scottish Dal Riada in 642 A.D., and a very delightful cradle song by a mother to her child. There is no doubt also that it was easy to insert new stanzas on the original theme into a poem as repetitive in character as the *Gododdin*. One obvious addition of this kind is a stanza which gives the numbers of the heroes who went to Catraeth, not as three hundred, but as three hundred and sixty-three. The detection of interpolated stanzas is not, of course, always as easy as with these examples and only a very rash critic would venture to claim that the whole of the *Gododdin,* with the exception of those parts which contain obvious incongruities, is as old as the sixth century.

Assuming that the original poem was composed by Aneirin at the court of the Gododdin, shortly after the disaster at Catraeth, what was its early history and how did it come to Wales? We can only conjecture the answers to these questions. The kingdom of Gododdin did not disintegrate immediately after the battle of Catraeth, but there is reason to believe that its capital, Edinburgh, fell to the English in 638 and that the final collapse was then not long delayed. It has been suggested that Aneirin's poem was for a time preserved in Strathclyde which, with its political and religious centres at Dumbarton and Glasgow respectively, continued to maintain an independent existence for some centuries after the time we are now discussing. The occurrence of a stanza referring to an event of Strathclyde history in 642 in the text of the *Gododdin* gives support to this suggestion. Then, at some time during the seventh or eighth, or possibly the ninth century, in circumstances of which we are completely ignorant, a large body of northern material, including the *Gododdin* as well as the poems of Taliesin, various legendary themes and much genealogical information about the northern ruling families, was brought to Wales. Here it provided a foundation upon which the literary tradition of the Middle Ages was built.

BIBLIOGRAPHY

Edition:
Ifor Williams, *Canu Aneirin,* Caerdydd, 1938.

Translations:
Joseph P. Clancy (ed.), *The Earliest Welsh Poetry,* London, 1970.
Anthony Conran, *The Penguin Book of Welsh Verse,* Penguin Books, 1967.
Gwyn Thomas (ed.), *Yr Aelwyd Hon,* Llandybie, 1970 (into modern Welsh).

Critical Studies:
Ifor Williams, *The Beginnings of Welsh Poetry,* ed. by Rachel Bromwich, Cardiff, 1972.
Ifor Williams, *Lectures on Early Welsh Poetry,* Dublin, 1944.
K. H. Jackson, *The Gododdin,* Edinburgh, 1969.
A. O. H. Jarman, 'Y Delfryd Arwrol yn yr Hen Ganu', *Llên Cymru,* VIII (1965), pp. 125-49.

CHAPTER IV

SAGA POETRY—THE CYCLE OF LLYWARCH HEN

A. O. H. JARMAN

The two previous chapters have shown that the late sixth century was a period of great creative activity in Welsh poetry. Before we arrive at a comparable period we have to move forward to the ninth century. Some three or four poems, including the Strathclyde stanza which refers to the battle of 642, have been dated by scholars in the seventh century, but hitherto not a single line of a poem has been even tentatively assigned to the eighth. It is now believed, however, that a considerable body of verse, rather different in kind from that ascribed to Taliesin and Aneirin, was produced in the ninth century. This was saga poetry, most of which was set against a background in the old kingdom of Powys in central Wales and was probably the work of a poet, or of poets, living in that region. It may safely be surmised that these poets were court entertainers whose business it was to recite traditional tales or sagas before courtly audiences. Their narrative was in prose but there was clearly a practice in Wales, as in Ireland, of casting speeches, soliloquies and dialogues into verse form. The tradition was oral, as in the case of the heroic poetry, and it is possible that many of the recited tales were never written down. At some stage, however, the verse attached to the tales was deemed worthy of preservation in written form and a substantial quantity of it is found in manuscripts which are much later than the date of its composition, such as the *Black Book of Carmarthen,* written about 1200 A.D., and the *Red Book of Hergest* (*c.* 1400). Here again the lateness of the manuscripts presents us with a dating problem. Undue weight should not, however, be attached to this, for linguistic forms which are much older than the manuscripts sometimes occur in the texts.

Furthermore, three stanzas of saga poetry have been preserved which were actually written down about the middle of the ninth century (*c.* 850). These are the Juvencus *Englynion,* the earliest example we possess of a written Welsh poem. They may be quoted in the following translation by Sir Ifor Williams:

> I shall not talk even for one hour tonight,
>   My retinue is not very large,
> I and my Frank, round our cauldron.
>
> I shall not sing, I shall not laugh, I shall not jest tonight,
>   Though we drank clear mead,
> I and my Frank, round our bowl.
>
> Let no one ask me for merriment tonight,
>   Mean is my company,
> Two lords can talk; one speaks.

These stanzas were only preserved by a happy chance and are not connected with any known narrative. In all probability the speaker is a warrior chieftain who has lost his companions, possibly in battle. His only company, sitting around the cauldron at night, is his Frank or mercenary soldier, of lowly estate. With him he cannot condescend to sing or jest, or even talk. If only another 'lord', of equal rank with him, were present, there would be merriment. With his hireling he can only drink mead in silence, or at best 'speak' without expecting a reply.

The main body of saga poetry to which a ninth-century date has been given is that associated with the name of Llywarch Hen or Llywarch the Old. It is composed in the same three-line *englyn* metre as the Juvencus stanzas already quoted. The fact that these stanzas are found written in a ninth-century hand shows that this is also a feasible dating for the Llywarch Hen poems,—or at least for a substantial nucleus of them. At one time it used to be thought that Llywarch Hen himself was their author and that, like the Taliesin poems and the *Gododdin,* they date from the sixth century. As a historical figure, however, practically nothing is known of Llywarch Hen. His name occurs in northern genealogies and these show him to have been a cousin of Urien Rheged. He was in all probability a minor princeling of the late sixth century, but there are no early references to him as a poet. In the poems associated with his name he speaks in the first person and his role is that of a character in a saga. Moreover, in most of the *englynion* the scene of Llywarch's activities has been transferred from the North to Wales, and the background of the poems is the battle between the Welsh and the English for the control of the eastern border of Powys. No doubt communications were open between Rheged and Powys at the end of the sixth century, but there is no historical evidence to show whether Llywarch did in fact migrate to Wales at this time.

However, one series of stanzas, fifty-nine in all, in the Llywarch Hen cycle has a northern setting. These may be given the general title 'Llywarch and Urien'. Their subject is the death of Urien Rheged who, as we have already seen in another chapter, was killed as a result of the treachery of one of his fellow-British kings while he was laying siege to the English on the island of Lindisfarne. The evidence for this is found in the *Historia Brittonum* of Nennius and it receives what is apparently independent confirmation in one of the *englynion* which states that Urien's death occurred at Aber Lleu, a name now preserved as Ross Low on the mainland opposite the island. We have already noted that no elegy for Urien by Taliesin exists and we have no means of knowing whether such a poem was composed. The 'Llywarch and Urien' stanzas, however, constitute an elegy both for Urien and his kingdom conceived, not in the manner of a court lament immediately after the king's death, but as a sequence of saga poems issuing from the imagination of a poet working two or three centuries later. The series contains three main sections, *Pen Urien* or 'Urien's Head', *Celain Urien* or 'Urien's Corpse', and *Diffaith Aelwyd Rheged* or 'The Devastated Hearth of Rheged'. In the first two Llywarch is the speaker. He had severed Urien's head from his dead body, probably in order to prevent its desecration by the enemy, and he carries it against his side:

> I bear a head against my side,
> The head of generous Urien, he ruled a host,
> And on his white breast a black raven.
>
> My arm is out of joint, my bosom is agitated,
> My heart is broken,
> I bear a head which sustained me.

Later it appears that Urien's body, which had been left lying on the battlefield, was given burial. In *Celain Urien* the poet says:

> The slender comely body is buried today
> Beneath earth and a monument,
> Alas my hand that my lord has been struck down.
>
> The slender comely body is buried today
> Beneath earth and sand,
> Alas my hand the fate that has befallen me.

The stanzas of *Diffaith Aelwyd Rheged* mourn not only the loss of Urien but also the ruin of an entire community, and they contrast the warmth and joy of the former court of Rheged with its present desolation:

> Many a fine hound and powerful hawk
> Was fed on its floor
> Before this place became a ruin.
>
> This hearth, a pig roots it,
> It had been more accustomed to the joyful shout
> Of men, and drinking around the horns.
>
> This pillar, and the one yonder,
> It had been more accustomed around it
> To a host's cry and the distribution of gifts.

The best known of the Llywarch Hen poems is the series of *englynion* entitled 'Llywarch and his Sons'. Llywarch has now migrated from northern Britain to Powys, over which he rules and which he has defended for a considerable length of time against the English, aided by his twenty-four sons. In the course of the fighting these have fallen one by one until only a last survivor remains, Gwên. In effect, however, Llywarch has been left to defend his territories alone, for Gwên has gone to the court of his father's cousin, Urien Rheged. Then, hearing of his aged father's plight, he returns to Powys. Clearly this is not chronologically consistent with the situation in the 'Llywarch and Urien' series of stanzas discussed in the previous paragraph, but we do not insist on this kind of consistency in saga and saga poetry. There is no prose description of the meeting between Gwên and his father. Their relationship, however, is made plain in the verse account, which takes the form of a dramatic dialogue. In this, the earliest to have survived in Welsh literature, Gwên announces his arrival to his father with the words:

> My mother declares that I am thy son.

Llywarch replies:

> I know from the elation in my heart
> That we are sprung from the same stock;
> Thou hast stayed away long, Oh Gwên!

Gwên understands the last line as a reproach. He declares his intention of fighting heroically:

> My spear is sharp, flashing in the fight,
> I intend to guard the ford,
> Though I escape not, God be with thee!

Llywarch answers with an exhortation to valour. His words also carry a touch of dubiety:

> If thou escapest, I shall see thee,
> If thou art slain, I shall weep for thee,
> Lose not the honour of a man in the stress of battle.

Gwên responds by declaring again that he will bear arms manfully. In the third line of his reply, however, he strikes a note which in the poetry of that time was new and strange:

> I shall not lose the honour of a warrior
> When brave men arm for the fray,
> I shall endure hardship before I move from my post.

The idea of 'moving from one's post', for any reason whatsoever, was totally alien to the uncompromising heroic ideal we have met in the *Gododdin*. For the warriors who fought at Catraeth such a course would have been unthinkable. Llywarch's reply to his son's statement is scathing. He imputes to him the worst motives:

> The wave runs along the shore,
> Out of hand man's purpose fails,
> In battle the ready of speech seek safety in flight.

The implied charge of cowardice is manifestly unjust. Gwên's response to his father's taunt is both dignified and truthful. He will fight against the enemy but he does not promise full obedience to the demands of the heroic ideal:

> At least I can say this,
> Spears will be shattered where I shall be,
> I do not say that I shall not flee.

Llywarch replies that

> A promise not fulfilled is of no value.

But Gwên reiterates his intentions, perhaps with a little more emphasis on his determination to withstand the enemy:

> And I intend
> That my shield shall be bloodstained and shattered before I flee.

On hearing this Llywarch can contain his anger no longer. He pours forth his contempt in the bitter words:

> The horn that Urien gave thee,
> With its golden baldric around its mouth,
> Sound it if thou art hard pressed.

In his reply Gwên ignores the taunt about his life of ease at Rheged. He does not seek to deny, however, that there will be fear in his heart when he meets the enemy. But he proudly rejects the invitation to sound his horn if he needs help:

> In spite of fear of battle before the warriors of England
> I shall not degrade myself,
> I shall not awaken the maidens.

This moves Llywarch to another taunt in which he boasts of his own prowess when he was of Gwên's age:

> When I was of the age of yonder youth
> Who wears spurs of gold,
> Swiftly did I rush against the spears.

For Gwên the answer to this was not difficult. His sarcastic counter-taunt reduces the dialogue to a completely non-heroic level:

> Without doubt, a credible assertion!
> Thou livest, thy witness is dead,
> No old man was ever a weakling in his youth.

Here the exchanges between Gwên and his father end. They are followed by an elegy for Gwên, spoken by Llywarch. It becomes clear that Gwên has not only fulfilled his promises. He has done better. He has measured up to all his father's demands of him. He has gone forth to battle and has stood his ground without flinching until he fell. Llywarch now praises him unstintingly:

> Four and twenty sons had I,
> Golden-torqued, leading a host,
> Gwên was the best of them.

Even the association with Urien is now seen in a different light:

> My son was a man, a stubborn defender of his right,
> And he was nephew to Urien,
> At Rhyd Forlas Gwên was slain.

Several times Llywarch declares that Gwên has been a worthy son of his father. He takes to himself some, at least, of the credit for his bravery:

> Gwên by the Llawen kept watch last night
> With his shield on guard,
> Since he was a son of mine he did not flee.

His pride as a warrior-father had been satisfied by the death in battle of the last of his sons.

In one stanza, however, a different note is introduced:

> Gwên, I knew thy nature,
> Thy swoop was that of the eagle in the estuaries,
> Had I been fortunately born, thou wouldst have escaped.

Here we have the view, which is several times expressed in the Llywarch Hen poems, that man is born either to happiness or to ill fortune. The Welsh words used to express the concept are *mad* or *dedwydd*, with their opposites *anfad* and *diriaid*. Llywarch believes that had he himself been born *dedwydd*, Gwên would have lived. He is, however, ill-fated, and because of this he has lost all his sons. Yet another and totally different view is contained in the Elegy's two final stanzas. They read as follows:

> Four and twenty sons in Llywarch's household
> Of brave fierce warriors;
> Too much renown is evil.

> Four and twenty sons, bred of my body,
> Because of my tongue they have been slain;
> A little [renown] is good; they have been lost.

The statements made in these two stanzas are of fundamental importance for an understanding of the Llywarch Hen poems, and of the difference between them and the earlier heroic poetry. Here Llywarch is calling in question the martial ideal which has governed his life as a warrior. It is the ideal of the *Gododdin,* the pursuit of honour and renown through unyielding valour on the battle-field. He has brought up twenty-four sons to conduct their lives according to this ideal, and for its sake they have all been sacrificed. Now the enormity of his selfishness has been made manifest to him, possibly by Gwên's questionings. All his life he has used his tongue to goad men to violent action for the sake of renown, but his final mood is one of disillusionment. He concludes that no good purpose has been served. The excessive pursuit of renown is wrong. Nevertheless, a modest measure of it would be acceptable.

Several other poems of the Llywarch Hen cycle examine various aspects of this same theme. In one short series of stanzas Llywarch addresses his son Maen and exhorts him to take up arms:

> Fair Maen, when I was of thy age
> My mantle was not trodden underfoot,
> My land was not ploughed without bloodshed.

To this he adds the boast:

> I did the deed of a man although I was a youth.

The line echoes the opening words of the *Gododdin,* 'A man in might, a youth in years'. In the *Gododdin,* however, they are plain eulogy; here a reproach is intended. Maen has clearly been reluctant to bear arms. Llywarch upbraids him and charges him with cowardice. We do not know how Maen replied to his father, for no dialogue between the two exists. In the event, however, we must conclude that Llywarch's exhortations were effective and that Maen took up arms, went to battle and fell.

Another poem entitled *Mechydd ap Llywarch* deals even more specifically with the theme of cowardice. Although it is principally concerned with the exploits of Llywarch's son, Mechydd, in one section reasons, or excuses, are offered by Cynddilig, another son of Llywarch, for not going to war. Because, he says, of the falling snow, the frozen lake, the strong biting wind and the short day

> Warriors go not forth to their attack.

He is answered by an unnamed speaker (Llywarch, we presume) who rejects his excuses and declares that

> Fine is the shield on the shoulder of the brave.

He adds that

> The coward breeds many excuses

and that

> Cowardice is a poor possession for a man.

His condemnation reaches its climax in the following stanza:

> Thou art not a cleric, thou art not grey-haired, lord,
> Thou wilt not be summoned in the day of battle;
> Alas, Cynddilig, that thou wert not born a woman!

The sense of these lines seems to be that Cynddilig, though not a cleric or an old man, was excused by his fellows from participation in combat on account of his notorious and admitted cowardice. Had he been born a woman his father would have been spared the shame of avowing kinship with a coward. There is, however, a suggestion in the lines which follow that even Cynddilig was later prevailed upon to take up arms.

The problem is looked at from a different angle in yet another poem, 'The Leper of Abercuawg', which does not mention Llywarch or his sons, although it is usually included with the Llywarch Hen cycle. In his youth the leper was a daring soldier in the royal service. Now he sees warriors preparing for battle and realizes that he cannot join them. He declares:

> When warriors hasten to battle
> I shall not go; sickness prevents me.

There is naturally no censure of the leper. This is a poem of brooding over the state of mind of a fighting man whose natural inclinations have been frustrated by sickness. Indeed, throughout this whole series of poems we seem to have the work of a poet who was deeply occupied with the problem, 'Why is everyone not a hero? Why are there some who do not wish to go to war?'; and more fundamentally, 'What is the ultimate value of heroism?' For the poet of the *Gododdin* no such problem existed. The warriors of Mynyddog's warband were faced with a simple choice. It was either victory or death. There was no need to urge any of them 'not to lose the honour of a man in the stress of battle'. Not one of them ever declared that 'he did not say he would not flee'. There are a few references to fear and cowardice in the *Gododdin*. They are without exception contemptuous. One of them mentions the 'shame' of fleeing before the enemy. It was a measure of the difference between the *Gododdin* and the Llywarch Hen cycle of poems that for the unknown author of the latter this 'shame' had become a proper subject to ponder and to investigate in a work of literature. He had realized that the heroic choice offered in the *Gododdin* is not for every man. There are many moments when calculation or fear or cowardice displace heroism as factors influencing conduct. Human relations are too diverse and complicated to be shaped invariably according to the severe and unbending standards of the heroic age. The author of the Llywarch Hen poems does not confine himself to a mere academic investigation of this problem. In effect, the portrait which he gives of his central character, Llywarch, is a rejection of the whole heroic ethos. His final verdict on the heroic ideal, expressed both implicitly and sometimes explicitly, is that pride, arrogance and presumption lie at its heart and that these can only lead to ruin and destruction. In the *Gododdin* pride is a dominant and prevailing theme, pride in the assembled warriors riding forth to battle, pride in the fallen heroes who had remained steadfast until overwhelmed by the enemy, deeming posthumous fame to be of more value than life itself. It was the same sentiment that impelled Llywarch to urge all his twenty-four sons to go forth to battle and to their inevitable deaths. The concluding scene of the Llywarch Hen saga is that depicted in the twenty-one stanzas of a poem entitled 'Lament in Old Age'. Here Llywarch is a wanderer, rejected by all, deprived of his possessions, old, enfeebled, incapable. Unlike Urien, he has no sons to sustain him. Unlike the warriors of the Gododdin, he has survived his battles, to find that the pursuit of renown was an insubstantial thing:

> Before my back was bent I was bold,
> I was welcomed in the royal hall
> Of Powys, paradise of Wales.
>
> Before my back was bent I was handsome,
> My spear was first in battle, it led the attack,
> Now I am bowed, I am heavy, I am sad.
>
> I am old, I am lonely, mis-shapen, cold,
> After an honoured bed,
> I am bent double.

We have seen that in the 'Elegy for Gwên' Llywarch attributes his loss to his own overweening desire for fame and renown. In the concluding stanza of the 'Lament' he again declares that his wretched condition is due to fate:

> Sad was the fate ordained for Llywarch
> From the night he was born,
> Long toil, without respite from weariness.

Usually included with the Llywarch Hen cycle of poems, and assumed to be the work of the same poet, is a series of a

SAGA POETRY — THE CYCLE OF LLYWARCH HEN

hundred and thirteen *englynion* dealing with the saga of Heledd and her brother Cynddylan. No reference is made to Llywarch or any of his sons in this series, which is exclusively concerned with the aftermath of the devastation of Powys by the English during the reign of Cynddylan ap Cyndrwyn towards the middle of the seventh century. Cynddylan was a historical personage who flourished somewhat later than the period of Llywarch, but very little is known about him and the content of the poems which refer to him must be classed as saga rather than history. His court at Pengwern has been attacked and fired by the English, he has fallen and those of his family and household who have survived are fugitives. The series opens dramatically; Heledd, Cynddylan's sister speaks:

> Stand forth, maidens, and look upon
> The land of Cynddylan;
> The court of Pengwern is blazing,
> Woe to the young who desire rich garments.

The stanzas that follow are an elegy for Cynddylan, who is praised in the heroic manner for his prowess on the field of battle. Then Heledd utters the well-known series of *englynion* entitled *Stafell Gynddylan* ('The Hall of Cynddylan'). It may be conjectured that, having escaped from the blazing court, she has looked down on the conflagration from the surrounding hills and now has come down and stands amid the ruins. She says:

> The Hall of Cynddylan is dark tonight
> Without fire, without bed,
> I weep awhile, then I am silent.
>
> The Hall of Cynddylan is dark tonight
> Without fire, without candle,
> Save God, who will give me sanity?
>
> The Hall of Cynddylan is dark tonight
> Without fire, without songs,
> Tears wear away cheeks.

> Hall of Cynddylan, each hour I am grieved,
> Deprived of the joyful company
> That I saw on thy hearth.

She then hears two birds of prey, the Eagle of Eli and the Eagle of Pengwern, screaming at each other across the devastated plain:

> The Eagle of Eli is screaming tonight
> After feasting on blood,
> The heart's blood of fair Cynddylan.
>
> The Eagle of Eli, I hear him tonight,
> He is bloodstained, I dare not go near him,
> He is in the trees, my grief is heavy upon me.
>
> The Eagle of Eli, from his haunts
> He seeks not the fish in the estuaries,
> He demands a feast of men's blood.
>
> The Eagle of Pengwern, with grey tufted head tonight,
> Loud is his cry,
> Eager for the flesh of Cynddylan.
>
> The Eagle of Pengwern, with grey tufted head tonight,
> And talon uplifted,
> Eager for the flesh of one I love.

Other stanzas describe the 'Churches of Bassa' (Baschurch), where Cynddylan lies buried, and *Y Dref Wen* or the 'White Township', where opposing armies have constantly met and fought so that its territory has been ravaged and steeped in men's blood. Heledd then sings an elegy for her sister Ffreuer, who presumably had died during the burning of Pengwern, in which she declares that Ffreuer is happy not to have lived to see the ruin of her land and family. Ultimately, like Llywarch, Heledd becomes a homeless wanderer, half demented, brooding over a vanished past:

> I am called wild Heledd,
> Oh God! to whom will be given
> My brothers' horses and their lands?

The problem of excessive renown and overweening pride, which figures so largely in the tale of Llywarch Hen, is not discussed in the poems of the Heledd saga. Here the standard of conduct is that of the *Gododdin*. The warriors do not fall short of the heroic ideal and there is no mention of flight or retreat before the enemy. Of Cynddylan Heledd says:

> No royal prince trod on Cynddylan's domain,
> He never retreated a foot,
> His mother reared no feeble son.

In a series of stanzas referring to Caranfael, son of Cynddylan, a striking contrast is drawn:

> The unfortunate and the destitute
> And those banished from home
> Sought Caranfael as a judge.
>
> Caranfael, mirth-provoking,
> The son of Cynddylan, giver of honours,
> He was no judge, though it was sought of him.

The point made here is that Caranfael was no Urien, presiding magisterially over his people's affairs. War was his business. Entering into it light-heartedly, he was always ready to honour its heroes but had little interest in succouring its victims.

Thus, the prevailing theme of the poems associated with the Heledd saga is the death of Cynddylan and the destruction of his court and of the community which he ruled. These events are viewed after their conclusion through the eyes of his sister who had survived the catastrophe. The Heledd poems differ in one important respect from the *Gododdin*. In the latter, although the warriors have been slain, their steadfastness and valour are a source of continuing pride and satisfaction. The mood of the Heledd poems, however, is one of unrelieved despair, although some pride is expressed in the memory of Cynddylan's exploits. The subject of moral guilt is introduced in a few stanzas. In the series referring to Ffreuer Heledd uses the words,

> Through the mischance of my tongue they have been slain,

which recall Llywarch's almost identical statement in the 'Elegy on Gwên'. We do not know what this mischance was. Some specific act or attitude of selfishness on the part of Heledd and her sisters is suggested by the last *englyn* of this series (which here seems to have been misplaced):

> I and Ffreuer and Medlan,
> Though there be war on every hand
> We are not concerned; our people will not be killed.

The destruction of Pengwern seems here to be seen as a punishment of Heledd and her sisters for some manifestation of selfishness, of which no record has been preserved. This is confirmed on a more personal level by Heledd when she says in another series of stanzas:

> At the time when I lived sumptuously
> I would not rise to give help
> To a man sick of the pestilence.

We do not know the full content of the Heledd saga. It is possible that, as in the case of the saga of Llywarch Hen, its author, or the author of the poems we have been discussing, intended to use the catastrophic events of his tale to show how pride and arrogance lead to destruction.

BIBLIOGRAPHY

Edition:
Ifor Williams, *Canu Llywarch Hen,* Caerdydd, 1935.

Translations:
Joseph P. Clancy (ed.), *The Earliest Welsh Poetry,* London, 1970.
Anthony Conran, *The Penguin Book of Welsh Verse,* Penguin Books, 1967.
Gwyn Thomas (ed.), *Yr Aelwyd Hon,* Llandybie, 1970 (into modern Welsh).

Critical Studies:
Ifor Williams, *The Beginnings of Welsh Poetry,* ed. by Rachel Bromwich, Cardiff, 1972.
Ifor Williams, *Lectures on Early Welsh Poetry,* Dublin, 1944.
A. O. H. Jarman, 'Y Delfryd Arwrol yn yr Hen Ganu', *Llên Cymru,* VIII (1965) pp. 125-49.
Patrick K. Ford, *The Poetry of Llywarch Hen, Introduction, Text and Translation,* University of California, 1974.

CHAPTER V

THE LATER CYNFEIRDD

A. O. H. JARMAN

It used to be thought that a great gap lay between Taliesin and Aneirin, the *Cynfeirdd* or 'Early Poets' of the late sixth century, and the *Gogynfeirdd* who sang the praises of the medieval princes. Throughout the period 600-1100, so many critics have held, no Welsh verse was composed, or if any was, it has been irretrievably lost. This view has now been abandoned. As we have already seen, by far the greater number of the poems contained in the *Book of Taliesin* are not by Taliesin and must be dated later. We have also seen that the cycles of poems associated with Llywarch Hen, which were formerly believed to be the work of a poet of that name contemporary with Taliesin and Aneirin, are not now considered to be earlier than the ninth century. The earliest complete manuscript of Welsh verse that we possess is the *Black Book of Carmarthen* (written *c*. 1200 A.D.), which contains a collection of a large number of poems datable at various periods from the ninth century to the end of the twelfth. The authors of these poems, and of many others found in manuscripts such as the *Book of Taliesin* (*c*. 1275) and the *Red Book of Hergest* (*c*. 1400), may be described as the later *Cynfeirdd*. It should be emphasized, however, that much detailed research is still required on the poetry of this period before definite dates can be suggested for many of the poems, or before a satisfactory interpretation can be offered for a number of them. This chapter will attempt a very general survey of Welsh verse between the sixth and the twelfth centuries, but excluding both the poems discussed in Chapter IV and the work of the *Gogynfeirdd*.

Reference has already been made to a stanza found interpolated in the text of the *Gododdin* which deals with a battle

A page from The Book of Aneirin, Skene FAB Vol. II, p. 62.

Frontispiece The Black Book of Carmarthen, folio. Skene FAB Vol. I.

fought in 642 A.D. between the Britons of Strathclyde and the Goidels of Scottish Dalriada. This was the battle of Strathcarron, at which Hoan or Ywain son of Beli son of Nwython defeated and killed the Goidelic king Domnall Brecc (in Welsh, Dyfnwal Frych). The stanza reads as follows in Jackson's translation:

> I saw an array, they came from the headland,
> And splendidly they bore themselves around the conflagration.
> I saw two groups, they had come down swiftly from their town,
> They had arisen at the word of the grandson of Nwython.
> I saw great sturdy men, they came with the dawn;
> And the head of Dyfnwal Frych, ravens gnawed it.

The word translated 'headland' in the first line is *pentir,* and this may refer to the promontory of Kintyre in Domnall's territory. The stanza is remarkable for its circumstantiality. Unlike the battle of Catraeth, the encounter described in it and the main participants on both sides are known from other independent sources. This supports the view that it is a genuinely early stanza composed, possibly as a part of a longer poem, soon after the event. As far as is known, it is the only surviving fragment of literature in Welsh emanating from the kingdom of Strathclyde. In metre, style and content it has affinities with many of the stanzas of the *Gododdin*. Its subject-matter is, on the other hand, quite unrelated and it is probable that it was originally written down on a blank space in an early manuscript of the *Gododdin* and later included in the text by a scribe who was copying this manuscript. Whether this happened in Strathclyde or in Wales is too conjectural a matter to be discussed here.

In addition to the Strathclyde stanza, two other poems have been dated in the seventh century. These are *Moliant Cadwallon* ('The Praise of Cadwallon'), and *Marwnad Cynddylan* ('The Death-Song of Cynddylan'). Unfortunately they have only been preserved in very late manuscripts, and in texts which have suffered considerable corruption. Their language and orthography, however, retain a number of medieval and early features and a good case has been made for accepting them as basically genuine poems composed during the period to which their subject-matter refers. Cadwallon ap Cadfan, a descendant of Cunedda and Maelgwn, was the king of Gwynedd who in the third decade of the seventh century attempted to win back the control of North Britain from the English. In 633, in alliance with Penda of Mercia, he defeated and slew Edwin of Northumbria, but in 634 was himself killed by Oswald at Hexham. The poem *Moliant Cadwallon* deals with persons and events of this period. It describes Wales as 'Cadwallon's land' and Edwin as the 'deceitful leader' of the Bernicians. It contains verbal echoes of the *Gododdin* and in one of its lines mention is made of the 'grief of Catraeth, great and famous', a phrase which has very reasonably been understood as a reference to the disaster which had befallen Mynyddog's warband a generation earlier. There is a medieval tradition that Cadwallon had a poet called Afan Ferddig and this poem may conceivably be by him. The other poem, *Marwnad Cynddylan,* is an elegy for the king of Powys, brother of Heledd, of whom we have heard in the previous chapter. Cynddylan, though historical, is a shadowy figure and the poem contains references which are difficult to pinpoint or to relate to known events. Recalling the days when he used to visit the royal court, the poet says:

> how delightful it was
> For me when I went to Pwll and Alun,
> Fresh rushes beneath my feet till it was time to sleep,
> Feather cushions under me up to my thighs.

Now, he mourns, 'no friend remains', and

> I cannot smile, I am old, filled with longing.

The poem is ascribed to a poet called Meigant. It has seventy lines and is in a stanzaic, rhymed metre similar to that of the *Gododdin*. It therefore represents a different tradition from that of the elegiac *englynion* discussed in Chapter IV. Assuming that it was composed shortly after the death of Cynddylan, it was in existence before the saga began to evolve.

Among the interpolations in the text of the *Gododdin,* which we have already mentioned in Chapter III, is a lullaby or cradle song sung by a mother to her son Dinogad. This vivid poem of seventeen lines, which is probably unique among the modern literatures of Europe at such an early date, must have been preserved through the merest accident by its incorporation in the text from a marginal entry, as in the case of the Strathclyde stanza. We may feel gratitude to the scribe who included it in his text, while not particularly admiring his acumen in deeming it to be part of Aneirin's poem. Its subject is hunting and fishing; the mother sings to her son of his father's skill in these activities. It reads as follows in Conran's translation:

> Dinogad's smock is pied, pied —
> Made it out of marten hide,
> Whit, whit, whistle along,
> Eight slaves with you sing the song.
>
> When your dad went to hunt,
> Spear on his shoulder, cudgel in hand,
> He called his quick dogs, 'Giff, you wretch,
> Gaff, catch her, catch her, fetch, fetch!'
>
> From a coracle he'd spear
> Fish as a lion strikes a deer.
> When your dad went to the crag
> He brought down roebuck, boar and stag,
> Speckled grouse from the mountain tall,
> Fish from Derwent waterfall.
>
> Whatever your dad found with his spear,
> Boar or wild cat, fox or deer,
> Unless it flew, would never get clear.

The life described in the poem, as the reference to the 'eight slaves' shows, is that of an early community. There are several Derwents in northern Britain, but it is impossible to be certain which is referred to in the fourteenth line. Jackson suggests the

Derwent in County Durham as being within the Gododdin territory. This would mean dating the cradle song in the sixth or early seventh century, before the disappearance of the kingdom of the Gododdin. Its incorporation in the written text would have occurred considerably later.

It has already been noted in Chapter IV that, while no early Welsh verse has hitherto been dated in the eighth century, a substantial amount has been assigned to the ninth. This was, in particular, the century of saga poetry, of which the outstanding examples are the *englynion* embodying the legends of Llywarch Hen and Heledd. Two other legends which crystallized into literary form at an early date were those of Myrddin, or Merlin as he later became known internationally, and of Taliesin. The earliest forms that we possess of both these legends are in verse and it is arguable that their probable date of composition was the ninth century. Let us first consider the Myrddin legend. Basically it was a version of the wide-spread theme of the Wild Man of the Woods and variant forms of it are found in Ireland, Scotland and Brittany, as well as in Wales. In each of the different Celtic countries the Wild Man appears under different names, Suibhne Geilt in Ireland, Lailoken in Scotland, Salaün in Brittany, and Myrddin in Wales. In all its forms the simple theme of a wild man or madman living alone and miserably in the woods is found intertwined with other legendary, and sometimes historical or semi-historical, material. Indeed, there can be no doubt that it originally took shape in southern Scotland, and that from there it migrated to Wales together with all the other northern material which has already been discussed. A portion, at least, of the tale of the Scottish Lailoken, told in Latin prose, has been preserved in a late medieval manuscript. The name Lailoken was probably brought to Wales when the legend arrived from Scotland, but it was replaced by the name Myrddin when the tale of the wild man was adopted as a Welsh literary theme. The old name, however, appears in the Welsh poems in the form *llallogan,* which is used as an epithet for Myrddin without its exact meaning being clear. This underlines the close connection between the Scottish and the Welsh forms of the legend.

The Welsh legend has not been preserved in a narrative prose form. Fragments of the tale, however, are found embedded in a series of political vaticinatory poems contained in a number of medieval manuscripts such as the *Black Book of Carmarthen* and the *Red Book of Hergest.* The most important of these are the *Afallennau* ('Apple-trees'), the *Oianau* ('Greetings'), and *Cyfoesi Myrddin a Gwenddydd ei Chwaer* ('The Colloquy of Myrddin and his Sister Gwenddydd'). The content of these poems is for the most part political prophecy and deals with events of the Norman conquest of Wales. The prophecies cannot, therefore, be dated earlier than that period. They all purport, however, to be uttered by Myrddin, who speaks as a wild man living in *Coed Celyddon* or the Forest of Caledonia, and by means of this device a substantial quantity of early legendary matter is linked to later prophecy. In the *Afallennau* Myrddin declares that he has lived in the forest for fifty years, ever since he lost his reason at the battle of Arfderydd. There is evidence that this was a historical battle fought in 573 A.D., and its name still survives as Arthuret in northern Cumberland. It became the focus of a saga, of which only fragments unfortunately have been preserved, and in which the madness of Myrddin seems at one stage to have been merely a single incident. The incident, however, apparently hived off from the main saga and developed into an independent tale. This told of a battle fought between Gwenddolau, who ruled the region of Arfderydd, and Rhydderch Hael (the Rhydderch Hen of Nennius), king of Dumbarton, at which Rhydderch was victorious and Gwenddolau fell. Myrddin was a retainer of Gwenddolau and fled to the woods after his lord's downfall. The Welsh poems do not explain the exact reason for his flight, but according to the Scottish version of the legend his counterpart Lailoken saw a fearful vision in the heavens and heard a voice accusing him of having been the cause of the battle and telling him that as a punishment he would spend the rest of his days living among the beasts of the forest. As a result of his lapse into madness Myrddin acquired the gift of prophecy. Various references in the poems suggest that the tale contained other elements of which we only have an incomplete knowledge. At the commencement of each stanza of the *Afallennau* Myrddin addresses his apple-tree, which he more than once describes as growing 'hidden' in the woodlands. This may be taken to mean that it possessed the property of invisibility, which it was able to extend to Myrddin as a protection against his enemies. There are three consecutive stanzas in the poem which contain no prophecies at all and are solely concerned with the plight of Myrddin in the forest. It is reasonable to assume that in these is to be found the oldest material of the Myrddin legend in Welsh, and that they constitute, or at least represent, the original nucleus of the *Afallennau* poem. The first and third of these stanzas may be translated as follows:

> Sweet-apple tree which grows in a glade,
> Its peculiar power hides it from the men of Rhydderch;
> A crowd by its trunk, a host around it,
> It would be a treasure for them, brave men in their ranks.
> Now Gwenddydd loves me not and does not greet me
> — I am hated by Gwasawg, the supporter of Rhydderch —
> I have killed her son and her daughter.
> Death has taken everyone, why does it not call me?
> For after Gwenddolau no lord honours me,
> Mirth delights me not, no mistress visits me;
> And in the battle of Arfderydd my torque was of gold,
> Though today I am not treasured by the one of the aspect of swans.
>
> Sweet-apple tree which grows on a river bank,
> The steward, approaching it, will not succeed in obtaining its fine fruit;
> When I was in my right mind I used to have at its foot
> A fair wanton maiden, one slender and queenly.
> For ten and forty years, in the wretchedness of outlawry,
> I have been wandering with madness and madmen.
> After goodly possessions and pleasing minstrels
> Now I suffer want with madness and madmen.
> Now I sleep not, I tremble for my lord,
> My sovereign Gwenddolau, and my fellow-countrymen.
> After enduring sickness and grief in the Forest of Celyddon
> May I be received into bliss by the Lord of Hosts.

Some of the references in the above lines, such as those to Gwasawg and to Gwenddydd's son and daughter, are obscure. It is, however, probable that the tree's peculiar power not only hides it but also hides Myrddin from the men of Rhydderch. In the *Oianau* Myrddin begins each stanza with a greeting to the little pig which was his sole companion in the forest. Most of the poem consists of prophecies but it also contains a few references to the principal characters of the legend. Recalling his former lord Gwenddolau 'gathering booty from every border' Myrddin mourns him thus:

> Beneath the brown earth now he is silent,
> First of the kings of the North, greatest in generosity,

and he contrasts his own wretched lot with the luxury enjoyed by his victorious enemy:

> Little does Rhydderch Hael know tonight in his feast
> What sleeplessness I suffered last night;
> Snow up to my hips among the forest wolves,
> Icicles in my hair, spent is my splendour.

The above account of the Myrddin of Welsh tradition will no doubt seem strange and unfamiliar to those who only know Merlin the magician of Arthurian romance. The fact is, however, that in the early stages of its development the tale of Myrddin had no connection of any kind with the Arthurian legend, and that it was not until the publication in 1136 of Geoffrey of Monmouth's *Historia Regum Britanniae* ('History of the Kings of Britain') that his name was introduced into that vast complex of international literature. Geoffrey's handling of the Myrddin legend is an excellent example of a skilful medieval story-teller's readiness to take unbounded liberties with his source material. When he began to write about Myrddin he probably knew very little of him except his name, and a vague tradition that he possessed the power of prophecy. Having decided to use him as a character in his 'History' he gave his name the Latin form *Merlinus,* and attached to him a tale told by Nennius three centuries previously in his *Historia Brittonum* about a wonder-child who, by his superior wisdom, had defeated the magicians of king Vortigern's court. He then caused Merlinus to utter a lengthy and obscure series of prophecies, since known as the *Prophetiae Merlini,* and gave him a part to play in bringing about the conception of King Arthur. By doing this Geoffrey created one of the most famous characters of medieval romance. Later, however, he realized that his Merlin did not reflect the native Welsh tradition about Myrddin, for in 1148 he published a long poem, the *Vita Merlini,* in which he portrayed Merlin as a wild man of the woods. Clearly, after completing the *Historia Regum Britanniae,* Geoffrey must have learnt more about the content of the traditions represented by poems such as the *Afallennau.* He did not, however, admit that his work contained any inconsistency, let alone error, but merely made his Merlin live on in the *Vita* into a new age.

A name frequently linked with Myrddin in the Middle Ages was that of Taliesin. Sometimes, indeed, we find the two confused with each other. One difference between them was that, while there are no grounds for believing that Myrddin was a historical character, there are strong reasons for accepting Taliesin as the authentic court poet of Urien and Owain in the sixth century. After this period, however, there emerged another Taliesin, the Taliesin of legend, who was credited, like Myrddin, with possessing the gift of prophecy. Many medieval vaticinatory poems of a political character were attributed to him, although their subject-matter shows that they are manifestly late compositions. Between the sixth and the ninth centuries Taliesin was transformed in folk-memory into a legendary figure to whose name a number of well-known folk-tale themes became attached. These were combined to construct a lively tale known as *Hanes Taliesin* ('The Story of Taliesin'), which has only been preserved in late manuscripts although it shows many signs of having been originally composed in a much earlier period. The narrative part of the *Hanes* is in prose, but it also contains a number of poems not all of which are of the same date. According to Sir Ifor Williams the earliest portions of this Taliesin saga probably took literary form in the ninth century.

In *Hanes Taliesin* it is related that where Bala Lake now lies there once lived a witch named Ceridwen, wife of Tegid Foel. She was said to be learned in the books of Vergil, which in the Middle Ages meant that she was skilled in magic. Ceridwen and Tegid had a son called Morfran, who was the ugliest man in the world and was consequently nicknamed Afagddu (meaning 'utter darkness'). This son had no hope of social advancement without some powerful compensation for his disadvantage, and his mother therefore decided to make him the most learned man in the world. In that age learning would, of course, include the possession of prophetic powers. Ceridwen proceeded to boil a cauldronful of herbs with the aim of producing three drops of an essence containing a distillation of all knowledge. This 'Cauldron of Inspiration and Knowledge' required to be boiled without cease for a year and a day. Her task involved Ceridwen in continually scouring the countryside to obtain fresh supplies of herbs and while she was thus engaged she employed a young lad, Gwion Bach from Llanfair Caereinion, to keep stirring the mixture. At the end of the year Ceridwen was so weary that she sat down to rest and fell asleep, but before doing so she placed her son Morfran beside the cauldron for fear any of the liquid should splash out. As she slept Gwion pushed Morfran aside and took his place. Thereupon the mixture boiled so vigorously that three drops of the liquid burst out of the cauldron and fell on Gwion's finger. These were the drops which contained the essence of all knowledge. Gwion felt them so hot that he immediately put his finger in his mouth and swallowed the drops, becoming thereby the wisest person in the world. Realizing that Ceridwen would not allow him to usurp her son's place he made off and fled without delay.

When Ceridwen realized what had happened she set out in pursuit of Gwion, and as he saw her coming he changed himself into a hare. She however changed herself into a greyhound and pursued him to the river Dee. Reaching the river he jumped into the water and became a fish. She followed him in the form of an otter. He turned himself into a bird and she became a hawk. When she was on the point of overtaking him he saw a heap of winnowed wheat on the floor of a barn, alighted on the heap and became one of the grains. She changed herself into a black hen, found him among the grains and swallowed him, and then reassumed human form. Nine months later Gwion was born, or reborn, as a son to Ceridwen. By this time her anger against him had somewhat abated, and when she saw the newborn child she deemed him to be so beautiful that she could not bring herself to harm him. She therefore put him in a skin bag and cast him upon the waters. Two days later—to be exact, on the first of May, a significant date in Celtic folklore and mythology—the bag was found by a young prince, Elffin son of Gwyddno, in a weir between Aberystwyth and the estuary of the Dyfi. On opening the bag and seeing the child Elffin exclaimed *'Dyma dâl iesin!'* ('What a beautiful forehead!') The child, although only three days old, answered with the words *'Taliesin bid!'* ('Let it be Taliesin!') and thus acquired a name. Elffin placed Taliesin on his horse's back behind him and rode gently to his father's court but throughout the journey the child sat up sturdily and declaimed a poem. On arriving at his home Elffin told his father that he had caught a poet at the weir. When Gwyddno asked Taliesin, 'Canst thou speak, though so small?' the child replied, 'I can say more than thou canst ask'. Taliesin was then reared until he was thirteen years of age, when he was taken by Elffin to the court of Maelgwn Gwynedd at Degannwy. There he figured in a series of colourful incidents in which his superior wisdom and skill were amply displayed. Among these was the discomfiture by him of the twenty-four bards of Maelgwn's court, whom he reduced to a state of verbal impotence. This exploit recalls the defeat of

Vortigern's magicians by the wonder-child Merlin in Geoffrey of Monmouth's *Historia*.

Hanes Taliesin, thus briefly summarized, is an interesting example of the conversion of a historical sixth-century poet by a combination of folk-memory and literary invention into a wonder-child surpassing all adults in knowledge and wisdom. The theme of the wonder-child is, of course, widespread and well documented, but the circumstances of its attachment to the memory of Taliesin are obscure and cannot be explored here. The prose texts of the tale contain many late poems related to various incidents in the narrative. In the *Book of Taliesin,* on the other hand, there are a number of much earlier poems in which Taliesin boasts of his omniscience. These are not found in association with the prose narrative, but can nevertheless be made intelligible only by reference to it. As an example the following passage, translated by Sir Ifor Williams, may be quoted:

> I know why there is an echo in a hollow;
> Why silver gleams; why breath is black; why liver is bloody;
> Why a cow has horns; why a woman is affectionate;
> Why milk is white; why holly is green;
> Why a kid is bearded; why the cow-parsnip is hollow;
> Why brine is salt; why ale is bitter;
> Why the linnet is green and berries red;
> Why a cuckoo complains; why it sings;
> I know where the cuckoos of summer are in winter.
> I know what beasts there are at the bottom of the sea;
> How many spears in battle; how many drops in a shower;
> Why a river drowned Pharaoh's people;
> Why fishes have scales,
> Why a white swan has black feet.

Later, Taliesin talks of his transformations:

> I have been a blue salmon,
> I have been a dog, a stag, a roebuck on the mountain,
> A stock, a spade, an axe in the hand,
> A stallion, a bull, a buck,
> A grain which grew on a hill,
> I was reaped, and placed in an oven,

> I fell to the ground when I was being roasted
> And a hen swallowed me.
> For nine nights was I in her crop.
> I have been dead, I have been alive,
> I am Taliesin.

It is obvious that a relationship exists between parts of this quotation and some of the incidents in *Hanes Taliesin*. On the other hand, many of the details do not correspond and it is probable that the poem represents an earlier form of the tale than the one which has survived in prose. In another poem the historical and the legendary Taliesin are conflated and treated as the same person. Here Taliesin declares that he has sung before both Urien and Brochfael, king of Powys. (Brochfael was the father of Cynan Garwyn, who was praised in the poem ascribed to Taliesin which we have discussed in Chapter II.) He then states that he has come to Degannwy to engage in dispute with Maelgwn and, attaching himself to a totally different cycle of legend, he adds that he has accompanied Brân to Ireland and has sung before the sons of Llŷr in Ebyr Henfelen. It is clear that when poems of this character were composed, and later copied into manuscripts, there was little clear differentiation between traditions of a historical and of a legendary origin. The Taliesin of the Urien poems and of the *Hanes Taliesin* were seen as one and the same poet, an amalgam of panegyrist and seer. Many interpretations of the poems associated with the legendary Taliesin have been proposed. There is agreement that they contain much early medieval lore and possibly enshrine the remains of many primitive beliefs. In the past, some critics have thought that they embody survivals of druidic doctrine. There is no doubt, however, that the most satisfactory explanation of these poems is that of Sir Ifor Williams, which regards them as dramatic monologues or recitations belonging to the tradition of early medieval court entertainment. Taliesin was a character, possibly 'in a drama' as Sir Ifor Williams suggests, but certainly in a series of dramatic poems based on the legend related in *Hanes Taliesin* and suitable for declamation before an audience. We have to envisage an actor strutting forward ostentatiously, announcing that he was Taliesin, and reciting poems which told of his personal adventures and of his universal knowledge. Whether there was drama in the sense that other characters were portrayed together with Taliesin, we do not know. Possibly, as in the case of the Llywarch Hen *englynion,* the poems were used to illustrate and fill out a recited prose tale.

Nature poetry does not figure prominently as a separate *genre* in the period we are discussing. References to nature occur frequently, however, in the context of saga poetry or combined with statements of a religious, gnomic or proverbial character. These are almost invariably found in the *englyn* metre. In the following stanza, which we have already quoted from the dialogue of Llywarch and Gwên,

> The wave runs along the shore,
> Out of hand man's purpose fails,
> In a battle the ready of speech seek safety in flight,

the first line is a description of a natural scene, the second is a general gnomic statement about human frailty, while the third contains a proverbial element. All three lines are nevertheless relevant to the dialogue, for they are used to sustain Llywarch's charge of cowardice against Gwên. When he encounters the enemy, says Llywarch, Gwên will run like the wave along the shore; his purpose will fail him like that of all those who boast too readily of their brave intentions. In a similar manner the nature references in the poem on the leper of Abercuawg are relevant to the main theme of the poem, for they serve to emphasize the distress caused to the leper by his inability to go forth to battle:

> In Abercuawg cuckoos sing
> On flowering branches,
> Woe to the sick man who hears them continually.

At the commencement of the poem on Mechydd ap Llywarch there is an *englyn* of pure descriptive poetry, translated as follows by Jackson:

> Keen is the wind, bare the hill, it is difficult to find shelter,
> The ford is marred, the lake freezes,
> A man could stand on a single stalk.

Ostensibly the stanza is concerned only with the severity of winter. It leads, however, to a debate about cowardice and to the charge that 'the coward breeds many excuses', for the description of the severe weather in the opening stanza is intended as a justification for not going to war.

Another well-known series of stanzas, probably later in date than those quoted above, begins with a four-lined description of Spring. From the second *englyn* onwards the poet's thoughts turn to religion. The following is Sir Ifor Williams's rendering of four of the stanzas:

> Maytime, fairest season,
> Loud are the birds, green the groves,
> Ploughs in furrow, ox under yoke,
> Green is the sea, lands are many-coloured.
>
> When cuckoos sing on the tops of fine trees,
> Greater grows my gloom,
> Smoke smarts, sorrow cannot be hidden
> For my kinsmen have passed away.
>
> On hill, in hollow, on isles
> Of the sea, wherever one may go
> From Holy Christ there is no escape.
>
> A gift I ask which will not be denied me,
> Peace between me and God.
> May there be for me a way to the Gate of Glory,
> Christ, may I not be sad before thy throne!

Essentially this is a religious poem and the description of Spring serves to introduce its main theme. The first stanza is, however, a notable example of 'Celtic' nature poetry of the type which flourished in Ireland at an early date. Whether there is direct Irish influence here is not easy to decide. Celtic nature poetry consisted of short, bare delineations of the salient features of a scene or landscape. The descriptions were objective in character, although it is obvious that the poet enjoyed and admired the scene he was describing. It is when expression is given to religious feelings that a more personal and subjective note is introduced.

In view of the importance of panegyric in the work of Taliesin, it is strange that so little verse of this type has survived from the five centuries which separate the early *Cynfeirdd* from the *Gogynfeirdd*. We have no eulogies or elegies for such eminent royal figures of the ninth and tenth centuries as Merfyn Frych, Rhodri Mawr and Hywel Dda. It is, of course, possible that such poems were composed and subsequently lost, but we cannot fail to be struck by the fact that what the literary tradition has preserved from this period is principally saga poetry and various poems on political, religious, gnomic and many other occasional subjects. There are, however, two poems in the *Book of Taliesin* which attest the continuation of the Taliesinic tradition of panegyric. One is called *Edmyg Dinbych* ('The Praise of Tenby'), and has been dated to the period 875-900 A.D. It celebrates the pleasant natural surroundings and the social life of a court maintained by the ruling family of Dyfed on the rocky promontory at Tenby. It contains nearly seventy lines but the following two stanzas, translated by Clancy, give an idea of its quality:

> A splendid fort stands on the sea's surface:
> Mirthful at New Year's is a bright headland.
> And whenever the ocean booms its boast,
> Bards are wont to carouse over mead-cups.
> Swiftly the wave surges towards it:
> They leave the grey-green sea to the Picts.
> And may I, O God, for my prayer's sake,
> When I keep my pledge, be at peace with you.
>
> A splendid fort stands, rising high,
> Superb its pleasures, its praise far-famed.
> Splendid its bounds, stronghold of heroes,

> Withstanding the spray, long are its wings.
> Harsh sea-birds rush to the rocky peak.
> May wrath, banned, make off over the mountains,
> And Bleiddudd's be the highest bliss,
> His memory kept in mind over mead.

Bleiddudd was formerly the lord of the fort but he does not now seem to be alive, so that the poem is partly an elegy for him. The name of the present lord is not given. Among the most interesting references in the poem is one to a 'writing of Britain' *(ysgrifen Brydain)* which was kept in a 'cell' or room in the fort and was a 'chief object of care'. This was presumably a manuscript, containing either early Welsh verse or some historical material written in Welsh or Latin. The poet must have derived great pleasure from it for, referring to the place where it was kept, he says:

> Long may it remain, that cell I was wont to visit!

The other poem which attests the continuation of the tradition of panegyric is an elegy for Aeddon, lord of a court near Mynydd Bodafon in Anglesey at the other end of Wales. This can be dated early in the eleventh century and contains twenty-nine lines, several of which strike a note familiar to students of the *hengerdd* or early poetry:

> I have drunk liquor, wine and bragget, with my true brother,
> A joyous lord; he has been laid low, the end of every monarch.
> Pierced was the front of his shield: mighty, loth to flee,
>   mighty, resolute ...
> Strong at a carousal; in every assembly his will was done.

The poem also has some vivid touches of an unexpected kind, such as a complaint that after Aeddon's death his estate has been inherited by four women who do not now extend to the poet the patronage he formerly enjoyed. The latter declares that 'bitter it was that there came four bare-headed women in the dead of night' to the court, apparently after a military expedition against Caer Seon near Conwy in Eryri. They had come to Anglesey as captives, but had become favourites of their captor and were now in possession of the patrimony. Their treatment of the family bard, however, was niggardly and arrogant, and he regretfully recalls the days when Aeddon and his wife, Llywy, were in charge of affairs. Rarely does early verse give us such an intimate insight into actual human relationships.

A category of verse which exercised the skill and inventiveness of Welsh poets for many centuries was prophetic poetry, known in Welsh as *canu darogan*. This was a peculiarly Welsh phenomenon in that it reflected the national struggle for independence, and indeed the desire to recover sovereignty over lands lost to the English. Its roots went back at least as far as the account in the *Historia Brittonum* of Nennius (*c.* 800) of an encounter at Vortigern's court between a white and a red dragon, representing respectively the English and the Welsh. According to this account the red dragon was temporarily defeated by the white and then regained the supremacy, and similarly the Welsh would be overwhelmed and subjugated for a period but would finally achieve victory over the English and drive them overseas. This hope survived both the disaster of 1282 and the failure of Glyndŵr to establish an independent state at the beginning of the fifteenth century. After the Tudor victory at Bosworth Field in 1485 and the ascent of a 'Welsh' family on the throne of England it tended to fade, for it was widely believed at the time that the ancient prophecies had in substance been fulfilled.

The *Book of Taliesin* contains some ten prophetic poems, all probably to be dated in the tenth or eleventh century. One of these, *Armes Prydain* or the 'Prophecy of Britain', is outstanding in many ways. It contains just under two hundred lines and is, strictly speaking, more of an instrument of propaganda or political pressure than a vaticination. It nevertheless makes use of all the resources of the prophetic tradition and brings them to bear on the political situation about the year 930, which is the approximate date of the composition of the poem. At that time plans were afoot to form a confederacy to oppose Athelstan, the powerful king of the West Saxons, and in 937 at Brunanburh, a place of uncertain location in northern Britain, Athelstan met and utterly defeated an allied army of Scots, Strathclyde Britons and Norsemen from Ireland. No forces from Wales gave assistance to this alliance of Norse and Celtic peoples but *Armes Prydain* is the work of a partisan passionately advocating such intervention. This effectively dates it before the fateful battle, for after 937 no joint action against Athelstan was feasible. The poem makes promises of unbounded optimism. Welshmen, Bretons, Cornishmen, Strathclyde Britons, Norsemen and Scots from Ireland and Scotland are to join forces against the West Saxons under the leadership of Cynan and Cadwaladr, the two *meibion darogan* or 'sons of prophecy', who will return from past ages. The Saxons will be driven overseas to the lands whence they originally came and the island of Britain will be delivered into the possession of the Welsh. The banner of Saint David will be raised as the armies march to battle. This suggests that the *Armes* was the work of a poet from Dyfed, a dissident subject of king Hywel Dda who rejected his sovereign's conciliatory policy towards Athelstan and sought to rouse public opinion to favour a more belligerent attitude. The poem did not influence the political or military situation but it came to be held in sufficient esteem as a poetic composition to be considered worthy of preservation in its entirety and of inclusion among the works attributed to Taliesin in the thirteenth century. It is a poem of sustained vigour as the following extracts, translated by Clancy, show:

> In forest, in field, in hill, in dale,
> A candle will march for us in darkness,
> Cynan leading the charge in each assault,
> Saxons facing Britons will groan, 'Ah god!',
> Cadwaladr, sturdy pillar, with his lords,
> Total his wisdom in choosing these men.
> When their forces collapse on their beds
> In pain, blood staining foreign faces,

THE LATER CYNFEIRDD

> At the end of each challenge, great plunder,
> Saxons will rush pell-mell to Caer Wynt . . .
> The Welsh will be compelled to make war:
> With the land's swarm of men they will muster.
> Beneath blessed David's standard they will rise
> Leading Irish under a linen banner.
> And Dublin's clansmen will stand by us:
> When they come to the field they will not play false.
> They will demand what Saxons are after,
> What right have they to the land they hold,
> Whence is the wayfaring they began,
> Whence are their clans, what land were they from?
> Since Gwrtheyrn's time on us they trample:
> No right have they to our fathers' realm,
> Nor our saints' honour — why have they wronged it?
> Nor David's laws — why have they broken them?
> The Welsh will take care when they face each other
> That no foreigners leave the spot where they stand
> Till they pay sevenfold for what they did
> With certain death in return for their wrong.

The interest of such a poem is, of course, not merely literary. *Armes Prydain* is a historical document of the first importance. This is not only due to its factual content and firm dating but also to the insight it gives us into views and attitudes in Wales in the early tenth century and into the memories which were at that time retained by the Welsh from the formative period of their history as a people. In particular, it shows that a sense of national identity was highly developed in Wales at a time when in many countries such a sentiment only existed in a very rudimentary form.

Later vaticinations are found in poems such as the *Afallennau* and *Oianau,* which we have already noticed for their legendary content. In *Armes Prydain* Myrddin is mentioned as one of the authorities for the prophecy, but in the *Afallennau* and *Oianau* he speaks in the first person and each stanza, with the exception of those which are devoted exclusively to the legend, contains a separate prophecy or series of prophecies by him. Final victory is always promised to the Welsh in vague general terms, and the credibility of the prediction is usually reinforced by the circumstantiality and detail of the prophecies referring to events of the recent past. If Myrddin (or Taliesin) could be so right about these, so the inference went, why should he not be right about future events? Thus, the prophecies were propagandist poems, designed to sustain the morale of the people, and in particular of the soldiery, in the face of continuing enemy successes, and they were composed in language which was simple and comprehensible compared with the difficult diction deliberately cultivated by the court poets of the later princes. As an example, the following stanza of the *Afallennau* may be quoted:

> Sweet-apple tree with sweet branches,
> Bearing much fruit, of great value, famous, a possession of mine,
> And I prophesy before the owner of Machrau
> In the valley of Machafwy a Wednesday of blood,
> Joy to the English with bloodstained swords.
> Oh, little pig, Thursday will come,
> Joy to the Welsh in tremendous armies,
> Defending Cyminawd with swift sword-strokes,
> A slaughter of the English on ashen spears,
> And ball will be played with their heads.
> And I prophesy truth without falsehood,
> A youth will arise in the region of the South.

The first two lines of the stanza are a formula which link the prophecy to the original legend of Myrddin. The 'owner of Machrau' mentioned in the third line is Gwenwynwyn, Prince of Powys, who in 1198 sent an army to attack the English in the valley of the Machafwy in Elfael. The battle was fought on Wednesday, August 12th, and was a disaster for the Welsh. In the sixth and succeeding lines the poet promises that vengeance will come at Cyminawd. This name does not refer to a specific battle but rather to a final showdown between the Welsh and the English which was expected at some future time in an undetermined place. The youth mentioned in the last line may conceivably be Gruffudd, son of the Lord Rhys of Deheubarth, who seemed to be embarking on a promising career as successor to his eminent father during the last decade of the twelfth century, but who died in 1201. If this identification is correct, the stanza can be dated between 1198 and 1201 and may well be the work of a poet of Deheubarth who had reasons for wishing to taunt Gwenwynwyn of Powys with the failure of his over-confident military adventure at Machafwy.

This chapter has attempted to illustrate the varied character of the Welsh verse composed between the sixth and the twelfth centuries, but without making any reference to the poems of the *Gogynfeirdd,* which are the subject of a separate discussion. The treatment has been very selective, for the verse produced by the poets whom we have described as the later *Cynfeirdd* is quite voluminous and would require much more space than was available for an adequate evaluation even of its literary and non-textual aspects. It includes many poems on occasional subjects such, for example, as the Alexander legend, the Day of Judgement, the plagues of Egypt, the Miraculous Harvest, the virtues of mead and ale, and the graves of legendary heroes. A number of poems preserve scraps of primitive Celtic myth while others embody early material of the Arthurian Legend. One of these, entitled *Preiddau Annwfn* or 'The Spoils of Annwfn', uses matter from both sources. It describes an expedition led by Arthur in his ship Prydwen against Annwfn, the Celtic Otherworld, which is situated on an island and in one line of the poem is also called the 'Fortress of Glass'. One of the aims of the expedition was the capture of the cauldron of the Head of Annwfn, which was kindled by the breath of nine maidens, had pearls round its rim and would not boil the food of a coward. The description of the defences of Annwfn struck a familiar note in medieval times:

> Three hundred men stood on the wall,
> It was difficult to converse with their sentinel.

The outcome of the attack is not clear; if anything was gained, it was at great cost. The first stanza ends with the following couplet, which is used with slight variations as a refrain throughout the poem:

Three shiploads of Prydwen we went into it,
Save seven none returned from the Faery Fortress.

Let us bring our survey of the poetry of the period to an end on a light note with a quotation from a riddle poem, translated as follows by Clancy:

> Make out who this is:
> Formed before the Flood,
> Powerful creature,
> Fleshless and boneless,
> Nerveless and bloodless,
> Headless and footless,
> No older, no younger,
> Than when he began; . . .
> He's in field, he's in wood,
> Handless and footless,
> Ageless, sorrowless,
> Forever hurtless;
> And he's the same age
> As the five epochs;
> And he is older
> Than many times fifty;
> And he is as broad
> As the earth's surface;
> And he was not born,
> And he is not seen, . . .
> He springs from a nook
> Above the sea-cliff;
> He's roaring, he's hushed,
> He has no manners,
> He's savage, he's bold; . . .
> He is in hiding,
> He is on display,
> For no eye sees him;
> He is here, he is there;
> He hurls things about,
> He pays no damages,
> He makes no amends,
> And he is blameless.

The poem, undated, is found in the *Book of Taliesin*. It shows that, when Dafydd ap Gwilym came to compose his well-known *cywydd* to the Wind in the fourteenth century, neither his vigorous imaginative phrasing nor his humour were without antecedents in earlier tradition.

BIBLIOGRAPHY

Editions:
A. O. H. Jarman, *Ymddiddan Myrddin a Thaliesin,* Caerdydd, 1967.
K. Jackson, *Early Welsh Gnomic Poems,* Cardiff, 1935.
Ifor Williams, *Armes Prydein,* Caerdydd, 1955.
Ifor Williams, *Armes Prydein, The Prophecy of Britain,* English Version by Rachel Bromwich, Dublin, 1972.
Henry Lewis, *Hen Gerddi Crefyddol,* Caerdydd, 1931.

Translations:
Joseph P. Clancy, *The Earliest Welsh Poetry,* London, 1970.
Anthony Conran, *The Penguin Book of Welsh Verse,* Penguin Books, 1967.
Gwyn Thomas (ed.), *Yr Aelwyd Hon,* Llandybie, 1970 (into modern Welsh).
Translations will also be found in a number of the works listed under 'Critical Studies').

Critical Studies:
Ifor Williams, *The Beginnings of Welsh Poetry,* ed. by Rachel Bromwich, Cardiff, 1972.
Ifor Williams, *Lectures on Early Welsh Poetry,* Dublin, 1944.
A. O. H. Jarman, *The Legend of Merlin,* Cardiff, 1970.
A. O. H. Jarman, 'The Welsh Myrddin Poems', pp. 20-30 in *Arthurian Literature in the Middle Ages,* ed. by R. S. Loomis, Oxford, 1959.
Ifor Williams, *Chwedl Taliesin,* Caerdydd, 1957.
R. Geraint Gruffydd, '*Cyntefin Ceinaf Amser* o Lyfr Du Caerfyrddin', pp. 12-26 in *Ysgrifau Beirniadol, IV,* ed. by J. E. Caerwyn Williams, Dinbych, 1969.
K. Jackson, *Studies in Early Celtic Nature Poetry,* Cambridge, 1935.
K. Jackson, 'Incremental Repetition in the Early Welsh *Englyn*', *Speculum,* Vol. XVI (1941), pp. 304-21.
P. L. Henry, *The Early English and Celtic Lyric,* London, 1966.
M. E. Griffiths, *Early Vaticination in Welsh, with English Parallels,* Cardiff, 1937.
R. S. Loomis, *Wales and the Arthurian Legend,* Cardiff, 1956, pp. 131-78, '"The Spoils of Annwn", An Early Welsh Poem.'
Thomas Jones, 'The Black Book of Carmarthen "Stanzas of the Graves"', Sir John Rhŷs Memorial Lecture, *Proceedings of the British Academy,* Vol. LIII (1968), pp. 97-137.
Rachel Bromwich, 'Cantre'r Gwaelod and Ker-Is', pp. 217-41 in *The Early*

Cultures of North-West Europe, ed. by Sir Cyril Fox and Bruce Dickins, Cambridge, 1950.

Richard Barber, *The Figure of Arthur,* London, 1972, pp. 54-79, 'The Bardic Image: Names and Places'.

Pennar Davies, *Rhwng Chwedl a Chredo,* Caerdydd, 1966, pp. 67-69, 'Cristnogaeth y Cynfeirdd a'r Gogynfeirdd'.

Basil Clarke, *Life of Merlin,* Cardiff, 1973.

CHAPTER VI

THE COURT POETS: THEIR FUNCTION, STATUS AND CRAFT

CERI W. LEWIS

The poets who were attached to the courts of the independent Welsh princes during the twelfth and thirteenth centuries—the *Gogynfeirdd,* 'Rather Early Poets', as this closely-knit and manifestly esoteric school of bards is usually known in Welsh to distinguish them from the *Cynfeirdd,* 'Early (or Original) Poets'—lived and sang during an acutely critical period in the political history of medieval Wales. For during those centuries the Welsh, confronted by an enemy more powerful and, in a number of important respects, far more resourceful than any which had threatened them hitherto, became drawn into a long and frequently desperate struggle to retain their independence. In the long and chequered course of European history there have been few movements more remarkable than the sudden and widespread expansion of Norman power and influence that occurred during the latter half of the eleventh century. Between *c.* 1050 and 1100 the Normans, applying with astonishing success the special military techniques which, under daring and enterprising leadership, they had so expertly developed, rapidly spread out from their adopted homeland in north-west France and successfully extended their power and influence to lands as distantly removed from one another as England, Italy, Syria and Sicily. In the same period, too, they carried their interests to Spain, and soon after the crown of England had fallen to William the Conqueror, as a result of his victory at Hastings in 1066, the Normans were firmly entrenched on the borders of Wales, which, with the advent of the new and extremely powerful enemy, faced several centuries of far-reaching changes.

The Welsh, divided among themselves, were unable at first to offer any effective resistance to the Norman invaders. The concept of Wales as a single, united political entity was slow to develop. Although there was undeniably a distinctive pattern of *Welsh* culture and custom, the general relief pattern of the country, with its numerous valleys and mountain ranges, helped to create and to perpetuate deep divisions in its political life. On the whole, Welsh society still tended to revolve around a series of intensely local bonds and obligations, and a Welshman's primary allegiance was to his immediate family, to his particular clan, and to the ruler of one or other of the comparatively small kingdoms or princedoms into which Wales had long been divided. The country was not regarded in the Law of Hywel Dda as constituting a single united kingdom in the way in which England had come to be regarded as a unified kingdom in English law. Wales was ruled, therefore, by a plurality of kings or princes. Nor was succession to the regal office governed by a closely-defined body of rules, for although succession was confined to male heirs, no firm rule of primogeniture had been established and generally accepted. This resulted in a great deal of internal strife and political instability, which left Wales an easy prey for the powerful Norman invaders.

Not surprisingly, therefore, very extensive areas of Wales rapidly passed out of Welsh control, and by *c.* 1090-91 the whole of the country seemed in imminent danger of falling into Norman hands. But in the year 1094 a great Welsh revolt broke out in north Wales and spread rapidly to the southern parts of the country. So successful was the revolt that the Normans lost control of the more remote areas of Wales in the north and west. By their efforts the Welsh had saved themselves from complete subjection to the foreign yoke and a temporary uneasy balance was established between them and the Normans. But it was the political disorder which seriously weakened England after the death of Henry I in 1135 and the civil war which broke out between Stephen and Matilda for succession to the throne that provided the best opportunity for a powerful and more sustained Welsh resurgence, which eventually drove the Normans from the north and much of the west of the country. As a result, the Normans were largely confined to the lordships situated in the more accessible regions of the south-east and to the coastal lands of the south as far as Pembroke. This dividing line between north-west and south-east Wales broadly reflected the balance of power that had been established between the opposing forces and for the next one hundred and fifty years it roughly defined the frontier between *Pura Wallia* and the March, between Welsh and Norman Wales. Under the leadership of such able and enterprising princes as Madog ap Maredudd (d. 1160), Owain Gwynedd (d. 1170), the Lord Rhys (d. 1197), Llywelyn ab Iorwerth (d. 1240) and Llywelyn ap Gruffudd (d. 1282), the Welsh were able to postpone for over a century the final loss of Welsh independence.

The Norman incursions brought about far-reaching changes in the political, religious, social and economic life of Wales. It is their impact on the cultural life of the country, however, that is of primary interest to the literary historian. Unfortunately, even the most economically-advanced parts of Wales did not have sufficient resources in the twelfth and thirteenth centuries to produce architectural monuments of imposing grandeur or to sustain the visual arts. But the penetration of Norman influences into Wales brought the indigenous culture into enriching contact with cultural movements from outside and so rapidly ended the state of comparative isolation which had previously prevailed. It is surely significant that a considerable body of literature, including both poetry and prose, has been preserved from the post-Norman period. This contrasts sharply with the ninth and tenth centuries, for very little now remains of the literature written during that period. Nor, for that matter, has much survived from the first half of the eleventh century. That there were bards who sang the praises of their princely patrons in the period immediately prior to the coming of the Normans is beyond question. For example, the Domesday notices of Nether Went refer to a certain Berddig, the poet of king Gruffudd ap Llywelyn, who, before his untimely death in 1063, had succeeded in uniting for a while the whole of Wales, including Gwent and Glamorgan in the south-east, into a loose and uneasy political union under his sway. Berddig, who had received lands from the king in the confines of Gwent free from the payment of dues, is described in the Domesday entry as *ioculator regis*. The name of this bard occurs also among the list of witnesses to various grants recorded in the *Liber Landavensis*. But not a single line of any poem addressed to the redoubtable Gruffudd ap Llywelyn has survived. There is also a particularly interesting reference in the *Vita Sancti Gundleii,* which invariably speaks of the Welsh as Britons, to an anonymous British bard who, 'versifying in British, composed verses on his own race, and in the British speech praises concerning the manner of life of the most holy Gwynllyw and of his life's miracles'. The *Life,* which derives, it has been claimed, from the ancient *cantref* of Gwynllŵg, was compiled in the early twelfth century, but it is probably based on older material, some of which was undoubtedly of a poetical nature. But not a single line of this anonymous bard's encomiums has survived in any known source. Other examples of a similar nature can be quoted to illustrate this point.

However, with the battle of Mynydd Carn in 1081, when Trahaearn ap Caradog, the *de facto* king of Gwynedd, was crushed by the combined forces of the legitimate ruler, Gruffudd ap Cynan (d. 1137), and Rhys ap Tewdwr (d. 1093), king of Deheubarth, we find that the compositions of a long and distinguished line of court poets, who continued to sing down to the loss of Welsh independence, and indeed for some time afterwards, are carefully recorded. This practice becomes, significantly, even more marked from the period of the great Welsh resurgence in the time of Stephen. In the three major historic regions of Wales—Gwynedd, Powys and

Deheubarth—the twelfth and thirteenth centuries witnessed the flowering of the majestic court poetry of the *Gogynfeirdd,* when the stern struggle for independence reverberated in the literary sphere, resulting in a great poetic revival. It was a period when, as Sir John Edward Lloyd has so felicitously expressed it, the poets 'rising on the crest of the movement for independence, transferred the passion of the people into song and became the vanguard of a succession of Welsh poets which has continued to the present day'. It has authoritatively been shown that of the court poets who sang prior to the loss of Welsh independence and whose works are still extant the majority belonged to Gwynedd, while quite a few of the others also sang the praises of the northern princes. This distribution obviously reflects the prominent role played by the Venedotian rulers during these two centuries and the gratitude of many monks who, deeply conscious of the great debt which they owed to their princely patrons, devotedly set about perpetuating the fame and exploits of the latter by copying the many encomiums which had been addressed to them by their court poets. There are certain features in this majestic body of verse, which has been described, with considerable justification, as 'a miracle of beauty and strength', which bear some resemblance to the Irish poetry of this period. Some scholars find it hard to believe that these features which the bardic verse of both countries have in common are all to be attributed to an earlier common Celtic origin. There was undoubtedly regular intercourse between Wales and Ireland in this period and so it is by no means improbable that there were some mutual literary influences at work, some of which are reflected in the poetry of the *Gogynfeirdd.* Tradition maintains that Gruffudd ap Cynan, whose name has been linked with the literary revival mentioned above, brought poets and musicians with him when he returned in triumph to his court in Gwynedd after being in exile for some time in Ireland, and it is further maintained that he was directly responsible for introducing a number of important reforms in both these arts. This is not inherently improbable, although it must be emphasized that no authentic body of evidence has survived which substantially confirms this tradition with regard to the organization of the bards. An *eisteddfod* which is alleged to have been held by him is inadequately attested, and a statute regulating the craft and activities of the poets and musicians which bears his name, the so-called 'Statute of Gruffudd ap Cynan', can confidently be ascribed to an appreciably later period. Although it is quite impossible at this stage either to prove or to disprove this tradition convincingly, it is worth noting that some scholars and critics have detected a number of interesting analogies between Welsh and Irish institutions, metres and particular classes of poetry throughout the period which can be said to have begun with the accession of Gruffudd ap Cynan to the throne of Gwynedd. Moreover, the king's biographer informs us in *The History of Gruffudd ap Cynan* that one of Gruffudd's followers, a certain Gellan, who fell in the retreat from Aberlleiniog in 1094, was a 'harpist [and] chief-of-song'.

The fact that the flowering of the *Gogynfeirdd* poetry was contemporary with the last struggle for Welsh independence helps also to explain the major themes which recur with unfailing regularity in this splendid corpus of verse. Its chief inspiration had arisen as a result of a great national crisis which gave birth to an overwhelming sense of national consciousness. The Norman conquest of England and the very serious threat which the Norman incursions presented to the independent, but badly-organized, Welsh kingdoms gave new vigour and a more immediate significance to the heroic praise of the defending rulers of Gwynedd, Powys, and Deheubarth. Inevitably, therefore, in the verses composed by the court poets the great theme of heroic panegyric emerged once again in the twelfth and thirteenth centuries with renewed vigour and in metrical forms which became increasingly polished and ornate. Down to the loss of Welsh independence in 1282 the great classical tradition of Welsh poetry as represented by the works of the strict-metre bards was Taliesinic. Its main theme was praise of God and the saints and the king or prince. And the court poets fulfilled, as we have already seen in the first chapter in this volume, a very important function in early Celtic societies, a function which originally had a profound social and religious significance. In the stately encomiums which they ceremonially addressed to their regal or aristocratic patrons these poets portrayed an ideal which helped to sustain and unite the society to which they belonged. They practised their art, based as this was, in part, on the primitive belief in the bards' supernatural and divinatory powers, in order to instil powerfully into their patrons those virtues and qualities which were esteemed above all others and which would eventually result in stirring deeds and actions. The assumption which underlies all this poetry is that fame and honour are the supreme values. By singing of the steadfast courage and honour of his patron the court poet confirmed those virtues and ensured everlasting fame for his benefactor. As the Welsh court poet Phylip Brydydd (*fl. c.* 1220-30) declared in the verses which he addressed in the *englyn* measure to Rhys Ieuanc, 'I made fame for thee' *(Y gwneuthum it glod)*. The Welsh *pencerdd*, 'chief-of-song', and the corresponding Irish *ollam* were both firmly convinced that 'praise' is one of the few things that will never perish, and this obviously explains why the persons to whom this distinctive type of poetry was addressed longed for fame above all else: 'it was praise that he desired' *(clod a fynnai)*, as one court poet declared when speaking of his patron. And these poets regarded it as their inalienable right, after 'contemplating' long and deeply the virtues and distinctive qualities of their regal or aristocratic patrons, to confer honour and fame on the latter. In the oft-quoted words of the *Gododdin*, 'the bards of the world adjudge men of valour' *(beirdd byd barnant wŷr o galon);* or as the Irish poet proudly and confidently declared, 'No man can be famous without an *ollam*'. Nor should it be forgotten that the lament or elegy fulfilled the same basic function as the panegyric, for it, too, emphasized the virtues and qualities of the dead, who are still powerful and could contribute substantially to the well-being of the living and their descendants. The poetry of the *Gogynfeirdd* consists in the main, therefore, of panegyric and elegy, which are expressions of the same basic theme, and one searches in vain in this aristocratic body of verse for any detailed references to, or sustained comment on, the far-reaching social and economic changes which were gradually transforming the life of Wales in the twelfth and, more particularly, thirteenth centuries. The basic types of eulogy and elegy composed by both the Welsh and Irish court poets emphasize the immutable qualities which were attributed to the ideal king or chief, whose individual characteristics are never portrayed. He is, above all else, a courageous warrior and fearless cattle-raider, a valiant defender of his land and people, and a generous patron of the bards. The concept that a land's prosperity or well-being is indissolubly linked with the qualities of its ruler is a constant underlying theme in the court poetry of both countries, and there are also poems addressed to various members of the ruler's family, his wife and children, and praise poems to God and the saints.

The obverse side of panegyric in the Indo-European and Celtic tradition was obviously satire, and in both Wales and Ireland this emerges as another important function of the poet. Clearly, if eulogy could establish and fortify a man's honour and renown, satire could substantially reduce and destroy it, and societies have existed where life without honour was quite unbearable. Satire began as an extremely powerful magical malediction, and in practice it acted as a potent curse. Some notable examples have been recorded in both Welsh and Irish of the baneful effects which were brought about by satire or by the threat of it alone. We are informed in early Irish sources, for example, that a bard's satire could not only cause boils and blotches to appear on the face but was capable of making a whole countryside barren. The fourteenth-century bardic grammar which is traditionally associated with the names of Einion Offeiriad ('Einion the Priest') and Dafydd Ddu of

Hiraddug discourages the *pencerdd* from satirizing, but this may well reflect later clerical influence, another indication of the extent to which the Church had left its *imprimatur* on the bardic grammar. In any case, there is ample evidence to show that satire occurs in the works of the *Gogynfeirdd,* just as it does in the verse of the Icelandic skald. For example, Llywarch ap Llywelyn (otherwise known as Prydydd y Moch, *fl. c.* 1173-1220), the leading court poet of Gwynedd from the death of Owain Gwynedd to the rise of Llywelyn the Great to supreme power, threatened one of his minor patrons, Gruffudd ap Cynan, that if he did not dismiss the poets of markedly inferior status who were obviously his rivals, he would cause a blush to appear on Gruffudd's cheeks that would last for ever and which would be a permanent reproach to his descendants. The poet demanded that Gruffudd make an immediate choice, either to be the recipient of a poem of praise or to be subjected to a curse. The great dread which satire instilled in those against whom it was directed highlights the great value placed on panegyric, which was its exact opposite.

But it was not only to his princely patron that the Welsh court poet directed his encomiums; he also sang verses of praise to God and the saints. Rarely have men been more deeply conscious of the supernatural than in western Europe in this period, which was marked by a vivid apprehension of the invisible and of the struggle that was being constantly fought between Good and Evil. It is hardly surprising, therefore, that religion figures as another prominent theme in the poetry of the *Gogynfeirdd.* This religious verse consists of approximately twenty-six divine odes, three eulogies addressed to saints, three 'deathbed' songs, and a poem of *englynion* which portrays the signs before the day of Judgement. Most of this religious verse occurs in the Red Book of Hergest, the most valuable single manuscript collection of Welsh poetry. A few favourite themes recur again and again in this religious verse, in exactly the same way as they do in contemporary sermons. Chief among these were praise of the Trinity, and especially of the sufferings of

Christ, terror of the Last Judgement and Hell—a theme which recurs more persistently than any other—the brevity and manifest insubstantiality of human existence, devotion to the Virgin Mary and to native Celtic saints, and a contrite confession of sins. Throughout this poetry runs an intense awareness of the omnipotence of the Godhead, and the majestic sonority of much of this verse powerfully conveys this awareness. These poets were also obviously affected by the apocryphal 'harrowing of Hell' derived largely from the 'Gospel of Nicodemus'. Some of the descriptions which they give of Hell are quite terrifying and suggest that they were familiar with the religious prose of the Middle Ages, where descriptions of a similar nature are common. A knowledge of this prose probably constituted one element in the instruction imparted to young novitiates in the bardic schools. For all these bards, Christ's sufferings for the sins of humanity had a deep significance, and these sufferings are portrayed with the same stark realism as that which characterized the *Gogynfeirdd*'s descriptions of battle scenes. The poets were profoundly convinced of the fact that they were abject sinners. One variety of religious poetry found among the earlier *Gogynfeirdd* was the poem known as *marwysgafn,* that is, a death-bed song in which the poet made a contrite confession of his sins as death approached, so that he might make a good end. This type of poem derived from the same kind of tradition as that which produced the Middle English penitential lyric, and it is attested in Irish right down to the eighteenth century. Portents of the days before Judgement were also very popular in the Middle Ages, and examples are again found in Irish.

The three eulogies on saints—on St. David by Gwynfardd Brycheiniog (*fl. c.* 1175-80), on St. Tysilio by Cynddelw Brydydd Mawr (*fl. c.* 1155-1200), and on St. Cadfan by Llywelyn Fardd (*fl. c.* 1155-1200)—seem to be significant new developments in the creative literature of the period. The story of the saint and the wondrous miracles performed by him are mentioned, and the churches founded by him are celebrated by the poet. They are of interest not only to the literary critic but also to the historian, for they reflect a significant new development in this period. Disdainful at first of the native culture and hagiographical traditions of the population which they had subjugated, the Anglo-Norman conquerors eventually came to realize that, where powerful Celtic and Anglo-Norman influences met, an investigation of the origin and development of the native traditions which they encountered could be a profitable as well as an intellectually fascinating exercise. So they began gradually to explore the traditions surrounding the native saints whose names were borne by the Welsh *clas* churches and to whose festivals the Welsh people were deeply devoted. A combination of interests of this kind eventually impelled a group of Anglo-Norman monks to compile what is generally regarded as the best extant text of the *Vitae Sanctorum Wallensium,* that contained in British Museum MS. Cotton Vespasian A. XIV. This manuscript contributed to the preservation of the traditions of the Celtic Church in the west. The three poems to saints mentioned above provide us with another instructive example of that historical or pseudo-historical research into the traditions of the early Celtic Church which was one characteristic feature of the literary activity of the Anglo-Norman regime. But there was also another side to these particular antiquarian interests, for in Wales the *Vitae,* from the Latin *Life* of St. David onwards, were an expression of the Welsh Church's fight for independence and its opposition to the see of Canterbury. The claim that the seat of St. David should be granted metropolitan status is a prominent feature of the *Life,* whose author even went so far as to claim that David had formerly been archbishop of all Britain. This struggle by the Welsh Church to preserve its independence culminated in the great fight waged by Giraldus Cambrensis in the period 1176-1203. There may have been some connection between the poem to St. David and this struggle. A score of churches dedicated to the saint are mentioned in the poem, commencing with the poet's own church of Llanddewi in

Breconshire. It was in the year 1175 that Giraldus Cambrensis became archdeacon of Brecon, and so it is by no means improbable that the poem may have some connection with the long struggle to elevate St. David's to the status of a metropolitan see. The three poems to saints, however, reflect the popularity of the *Vitae Sanctorum,* and translations of some of these are to be found in Welsh. It is clear that all three poets were acquainted with the contents of some of these *Lives.*

The court poets' main function, then, was to sing praise, and in so doing they fulfilled a vital social need. In twelfth- and thirteenth-century Wales they constituted an important part of the existing political and social structure, just as they did in contemporary Ireland. They formed a closely-knit and highly trained literary class whose status, privileges and duties were defined in the Law of Hywel Dda, but not always as fully and as unambiguously as the latter-day literary historian would wish. In Wales and Ireland alike the court poet was a professional craftsman, who sometimes inherited his art from his father. Three distinct classes of bards are mentioned in the legal codes. First and highest in dignity was the *pencerdd* or chief-of-song, whose pre-eminence was symbolized by a chair in the royal court. He acquired this chair after competition with another poet. Examples of bardic controversies have come down in Welsh from the twelfth and thirteenth centuries, and seem to consist of exercises in which rival bards compete for the favours of their chosen patron. One of the most interesting of these bardic contests is the one in which Cynddelw engaged against Seisyll Bryffwrch *(fl. c.* 1155-75) for the office of chief court poet to Madog ap Maredudd, prince of Powys, who died in 1160. One is reminded also of Phylip Brydydd's contest with the *gofeirdd* or inferior poets at the court of Rhys Ieuanc. In the royal hall the *pencerdd* sat next to the *edling* or heir-apparent, and he had the right to sing two songs in the upper part of the hall *(uwch cyntedd),* one a song to God, the other a song to the king. Among the other privileges which he enjoyed was the right to instruct others in the craft of poetry. In return for all this he received various perquisites, including grants of land. Nevertheless, he was not actually one of the court officials, and although the great chiefs-of-song of the twelfth and thirteenth centuries are often found specially associated with a particular royal household, they also addressed odes to others, occasionally to rivals of the king whose praises they normally sang. Next to the *pencerdd* came the *bardd teulu*, who, as the name itself implies, was pre-eminently the bard of the king's retinue or war-band *(teulu)*. According to the legal codes, he was one of the twenty-four officers of the court, the eleventh (or, in the Venedotian version of the laws, the eighth) in dignity. According to one source, it was his duty to sing 'The Chieftainship of Britain' *(Unbeiniaeth Prydain)* to members of the king's retinue before they set out for battle. The distinction between these two grades of bards was disappearing, however, in the period of the *Gogynfeirdd*, for Cynddelw and other poets from this period sang either as *pencerdd* or as *bardd teulu*, according to the requirements of the particular occasion. The *bardd teulu*, too, enjoyed special privileges and received various perquisites that were attached to his office. Lowest in rank were the *cerddorion*, who are called *joculatores* in the Latin version, the French *jongleurs*.

There are a few indications of bardic families, the most notable example being that of Meilyr Brydydd *(fl. c.* 1100-37), the chief court poet to Gruffudd ap Cynan at Aberffraw. This bard's son, Gwalchmai ap Meilyr *(fl. c.* 1130-80), was court poet to Owain Gwynedd, the son of Gruffudd ap Cynan, and at least two, possibly three, of Gwalchmai's sons were also poets. One reason for the tendency for professions to become hereditary was their endowment with landed estates, and Sir John Edward Lloyd expressed the view that this practice explained such local names as Pentre'r-beirdd and Tre'r-beirdd. Be that as it may, another factor which undoubtedly contributed to the tendency for some professions to become hereditary was the ease with which traditional skills can be transmitted from father to son, and in this respect the family can be seen as the prototype of the school. On the whole, however, the bardic profession does not appear to have been hereditary in Wales, as it was in Ireland. It is important to remember, too, that both *pencerdd* and *bardd teulu* actually sang or chanted their poems to musical accompaniment, usually on the harp. Moreover, they fulfilled the functions of genealogists, historians and, possibly, story-tellers. In addition to eulogizing and—less frequently—satirizing, they could on occasion compose prophetic poems: a number of vaticinations have come down to us, and we are informed by Giraldus Cambrensis that there were *awenyddion*, men who fell into an inspired trance so that they might answer the questions which they had been asked.

Most of the Welsh court poets were well-born and courageous warriors, a fact which emerges clearly from many of the poems composed during this period. For example, an elegy addressed to Bleddyn Fardd (*fl. c.* 1257-85) praises the deceased not only for his ability as a bard but also for his valour and prowess on the field of battle. Even when allowance has been made for the poetic hyperbole which characterizes so much of the court poets' encomiums, it is impossible to disregard entirely the claims made by such bards as Gwalchmai ap Meilyr, Cynddelw Brydydd Mawr, Peryf ap Cedifor (*fl. c.* 1170), Prydydd y Moch and Phylip Brydydd regarding their valour and deeds on the field of battle. Some of the court poets actually made the final sacrifice in defence of their patrimony. Not surprisingly, therefore, the eulogies composed by these bards often contain substantial sections dealing with the martial exploits of their princely patrons, and many of the poets seem to take a cruel and scarcely-concealed delight in portraying the worst horrors of the conflict. They refer exultantly to 'crow on the corpse', to 'blood-stained biers and thrusting and gushing gore and gory heads a-running', to 'rigid red corpses' and 'bowels on the thorns'. This harsh realism is to be found to some extent in the verses composed by most of these poets. But it is in the work of Cynddelw Brydydd Mawr that we probably have the clearest manifestation of this delight in the terrible excesses of battle.

But it was mainly in the *Marwysgafn* or death-bed poem, referred to above, and in the *Gorhoffedd* that the Welsh court poets gave expression to their personal feelings. In the particular type of verse known as *Gorhoffedd,* a word which combined the ideas of 'boast' and 'exultant delight', the bard openly vaunted his impressive achievements in battle and his no less commendable success in love. Perhaps the two best-known examples are the *Gorhoffedd* of Gwalchmai ap Meilyr and that of Hywel ab Owain Gwynedd (*fl. c.* 1140-70), the poet-prince. These two compositions are also interesting for the light they shed on their authors' attitude to nature which, on the whole, is not a vital element in the formal and highly stylized poetry of the *Gogynfeirdd,* who generally used nature and its phenomena only as a convenient source for their similes. Moreover, the intense love of homeland to which Hywel ab Owain Gwynedd gave expression in his *Gorhoffedd* has been compared by some critics with the Irish poem 'Columcille's Greeting to Ireland', and it may be of some significance that the Welsh poet-prince had strong Irish connections through his grandfather, Gruffudd ap Cynan, and that he himself had spent some time in Ireland. There are two poems which reflect some of the elements of the *Gorhoffedd,* to wit, Cynddelw's *Rhieingerdd* to Efa, the daughter of Madog ap Maredudd, and Prydydd y Moch's *awdl* to Gwenlliant, the daughter of Hywel of Gwynllŵg. Both poems, however, have been legitimately described as 'a conventional method of eulogizing a noble lady'. Indeed, Prydydd y Moch's ode ends with the poet's intense avowal that Gwenlliant's praises will be spread far and wide 'as long as the sun rises and sets' *(hyd y daerahawd haul hyd y dwyre).*

It is in the work of Hywel ab Owain Gwynedd that we find the only examples of pure love poetry among the compositions of the earlier court poets. These love poems by the poet-prince are exquisite lyrics which are superior in both form and treatment to any love poetry composed by this particular school of bards even when, towards the end of the thirteenth century, the composition of amatory verses had become more common. Through all his love poems there runs an engaging charm and tenderness expressed in a language which is comparatively simple and pure:

> Beneath her step the rush scarce bendeth,
> The dainty white darling, so gentle her tread;
> Scarce older she seems than a maid of ten summers;
> So girlish, so comely, so perfect in seemliness.

His *rhieingerddi* contain suggestions, found also in the work of Cynddelw Brydydd Mawr, that the poet can expect a reward for praise poetry addressed to women, no less than for his praises of men. And in the complaint which he sometimes makes of failure in his love affairs he seems to set an interesting precedent for Dafydd ap Gwilym. There are, moreover, certain features in these love lyrics, and in the other poems which various *Gogynfeirdd* addressed to women, which suggest that the Welsh bards, even in the twelfth century, were familiar with some of the conventions of that influential literary movement of which the songs composed by the wandering scholar, the troubadour and the *trouvère* were the outstanding expression on the Continent. And it has been suggested that the poet-prince, helped by his special status and by his Irish connections, was the first to emancipate himself from the stringent discipline of this closely-knit school of bards and that the deeply-ingrained conservatism of other Welsh poets was not entirely proof against the new literary influence. There is a danger, however, in over-emphasizing the originality of these love lyrics in both theme and treatment. The Laws inform us that when the queen desired to hear songs in her chamber, it was the duty and privilege of the *bardd teulu* to sing to her three songs of finished art, in a voice of moderate compass, lest the hall be disturbed. These songs, which have all been lost, could hardly have all been composed on the traditional panegyric and elegiac themes which express the distinctive *ethos* of this particular school of bards. Some of them may well have been love poems, and when this type of verse was written by a great prince, the monks of a particular monastery which he had supported might well decide that the work was worth preserving. By the end of the thirteenth century, however, when the bardic discipline was manifestly less rigorous, the composition of love poetry had become more common. Written in a style and diction appreciably simpler, on the whole, than the highly stylized poems composed by the earlier court poets, these odes contain lines which provide a link with the work of Dafydd ap Gwilym. Even so, the obsolete words and archaic constructions have not been completely eradicated from these later odes, and, as Dr. Thomas Parry has observed, 'one feels that this ponderousness is rather out of keeping with the blitheness of love poetry, even when the poem affects sadness and complaint'.

That the work composed by the court poets was the product of a long and proud tradition is obvious to any one who is familiar with its contents. Welsh bardism was an old institution before the courts of the princes began to resound with the encomiums of these bards, and many of the Welsh poets who are known to have sung in the pre-Norman era were attached to the courts of kings or princes, although little of that court poetry has survived. All the Welsh court poets were deeply conscious of their dignity. In the panegyric which he addressed to Rhodri ab Owain the court poet Prydydd y Moch declared that 'my tongue is arbiter of the Britons from the North Sea to the Irish Sea, and I am rightfully undisputed among the chief bards of my noblest friends'. Cynddelw, in his famous bardic contention with Seisyll Bryffwrch, claims that he is called 'a poet of learning', and in the panegyric which he sang to Owain ap Madog the same bard proudly maintains that 'by virtue of my supreme diction, I am head of the chief bards'. They took great pride, too, in their superiority over those inferior grades of poets whom they variously called 'vain', 'petty' or 'false' bards. Cynddelw proudly claimed that he sang 'according to the canon of poets', and it was by virtue of the expertise with which they practised their difficult and esoteric craft that these poets claimed their special privileges.

A craft as difficult as that practised by the medieval Welsh court poets could only have been learned and mastered after years of instruction, and this craft must have been taught in bardic schools. It is, nevertheless, something of a misnomer to speak of 'schools', for novitiates were probably instructed by being apprenticed to a leading bard. Naturally, however, poets of outstanding ability could attract more than one pupil, and so the use of the word 'school' in this particular connection may not be entirely misleading. Unfortunately, no detailed contemporary records of the activities of these bardic schools have survived. The Laws of Hywel Dda inform us that a *pencerdd* alone had the right to be a bardic teacher, and Cynddelw in one of his poems states that 'our disciples know our lore', while in another he claims to be 'the instructor of brilliant bards'. Llygad Gŵr *(fl. c.* 1260-70) also states that he will sing the praises of his patron after the manner of a 'talented teacher'. In early days the instruction was probably imparted orally, and the fourteenth-century bardic grammar may well have been the first to have been compiled. The range of instruction was extended in later works, but the bardic craft was invariably regarded as a secret which the bardic disciples were under a strict obligation to keep. This rule was later to be severely criticized by sixteenth-century humanists. Nevertheless, however detailed the written rules contained in the grammar may have been, they could hardly have conveyed all the instruction which had been imparted orally in the bardic schools. Incomplete as it is, the grammar, if used with great caution, can shed some valuable light on the curriculum of the bardic schools of an earlier period. This can be supplemented by the information which can be drawn from the surviving poetry.

The instruction imparted to young novitiates obviously included all the rules of the poetic art relating to metres and alliteration, and no doubt examples were carefully chosen from early Welsh poetry, from the *Hengerdd* or 'Old Poetry'. It is significant that a number of the older poets, including Taliesin, Aneirin, Afan, Arofan and Morfran, are explicitly mentioned in the works of the court poets, and they crave for a muse similar to that which had inspired these early bards. The surviving works of the earliest Welsh poets were studied in great detail, and obsolete words, archaic constructions and grammatical forms were often taken from them. One bardic manual informs us that there were three things which gave amplitude to a poet,—a knowledge of stories, poetry (by which is probably meant the metrical laws and usages) and *Hengerdd*. The memorization of the numerous triad sequences which have been preserved in various manuscripts probably constituted a vital part of the professional training of the bards. It has been shown that *Trioedd Ynys Prydain,* the 'Triads of the Island of Britain', which are in effect a kind of catalogue of the names of the traditional heroes, classified in groups of three, served as a sort of index to the knowledge which the bards possessed of earlier history and legend. In Ireland, as in Wales, the bards were required to have in their repertoire a large corpus of stories and verse which preserved the traditional history and mythology of Ireland in the widest possible sense. The allusions which occur in the works of the *Gogynfeirdd,* particularly those who sang in the twelfth century, to the *hen chwedlau* seem to be firmly rooted in a detailed knowledge of the stories themselves, not merely on a superficial acquaintance with the proper names which occur in these traditional tales. From the thirteenth century onwards, however, the bards seem progressively to lose contact with this great corpus of national tradition and legend. The bard may also have been a *cyfarwydd* or story-teller, although this is by no means certain. 'Lord', said Gwydion to Pryderi, in the Fourth Branch of the Mabinogi, 'it is a custom with us that the first night after one comes to a great man, the chief bard shall have the say. I will tell a tale gladly'. And the anonymous author adds: 'Gwydion was the best teller of tales in the world'. This reference undoubtedly implies that the bards could be accomplished *cyfarwyddiaid*, whose medium was either prose or a combination of prose and verse, and it may not be altogether fanciful to imagine the early independent Welsh princes being entertained in their royal halls with tales skilfully narrated by their bards. We are given some idea of the vast amount of material at the early bard's disposal when we learn that it was part of the professional qualification of the Irish *ollam*, who corresponds broadly to the Welsh *pencerdd*, to master three hundred and fifty such tales. And there is ample evidence, from the work of Nennius (*c*. 800) onwards, to support the view that the Welsh bards and *cyfarwyddiaid* had a great wealth of traditional material at their disposal. The Welsh *cyfarwydd* can legitimately be compared with the Irish *scelaige*, 'story-teller'. But, as a number of scholars have pointed out, it is by no means certain that these entertainers were official members of the bardic order, and the statement in *Breuddwyd Rhonabwy* to the effect that 'neither bard nor *cyfarwydd* shall know [this tale] without a book' suggests that there was some kind of distinction between the two. There is no evidence to suggest that the twelfth-century *Gogynfeirdd* narrated tales in the courts of the princes, although the poetry composed by these bards proves, as we have already seen, that they were firmly acquainted with the great corpus of traditional material contained in *Trioedd Ynys Prydain*. The passage referred to in *Math* may reflect the practice of an earlier period. Whatever the final verdict may be on this particular matter, it is beyond doubt that the Welsh court poet, like the Irish *fili*, who played a prominent part in the ruler's inauguration to the kingship, would be expected to have a knowledge of the royal genealogies. In a later period, after the loss of Welsh independence, the professional bard was formally instructed in the pedigrees of the nobles and gentry, in their coats-of-arms and their estates.

It is difficult to determine precisely to what extent the traditions of the Welsh bardic schools in the later medieval period have distorted our picture of the practices followed by the court poets in the twelfth and thirteenth centuries, but the innate conservatism of the bardic tradition suggests that inferences may reasonably be drawn from the later and fuller bardic manuals as to the practices of the earlier bardic schools under the independent princes. Apparently, it took nine years in all to become a fully qualified *pencerdd,* and those bardic disciples who eventually attained the highest rank passed through the following stages: *disgybl ysbâs* ('licensed disciple') without degree, graduated *disgybl ysbâs, disgybl disgyblaidd, disgybl pencerddaidd, pencerdd* and *athro* ('teacher'). According to the evidence of a later period, the successful aspirant, on completing each stage in his training, received the appropriate degree and a licence authorizing him to practise his craft and to solicit largesse. But whether or no this is a faithful picture of the practices that were followed in the period of the *Gogynfeirdd* it is impossible to say. No villein's son was permitted to become a bardic disciple without the consent of his lord, and it is known that the court poets were often men of rank. Two prominent princes of the twelfth century, Hywel ab Owain Gwynedd (d. 1170) and Owain Cyfeiliog (d. 1197), were celebrated bards, and quite a few of the court poets, as we have already seen, were prominent warriors.

Before the loss of Welsh independence the poets were naturally subject to the dictates of native law, although the precise details relating to various aspects of their professional craft must have been determined by the bardic order itself. The same is also true of the post-Conquest period, when the nobles, including some who were of Norman extraction, assumed the role of bardic patrons formerly undertaken by the princes. One important means of asserting discipline and eradicating abuses and unfair practices was the *eisteddfod.* The earliest *eisteddfod* of which we may be absolutely certain is that recorded under the year 1176—though the term itself is not used—in

Brut y Tywysogion ('The Chronicle of the Princes'), an *eisteddfod* held at Christmas in that year by the Lord Rhys, at Cardigan. The version of the *Brut* which occurs in Peniarth MS. 20 states that

> At Christmas in that year the Lord Rhys ap Gruffudd held court in splendour at Cardigan, in the castle. And he set two kinds of contest there: one between bards and poets, another between harpists and crowders and pipers and various classes of music-craft. And he had two chairs set for the victors. And he honoured them with ample gifts. And of the harpists, a young man from Rhys's court won the victory. As between the bards, those of Gwynedd prevailed. Each of the suitors obtained from Rhys that which he sought, so that no one was refused. And that feast, before it was held, was announced for a year through all Wales and England and Scotland and Ireland and the other islands.

It is hardly likely that this competitive assembly of bards and musicians was the first to be held in Wales, for, as we have seen, the Welsh bardic order was already an old institution before this gathering took place at Cardigan castle. The Laws mention a bardic contest for a chair and describe the *pencerdd* as one who had won a chair, that is, the right to have a special seat reserved for him in the royal hall. And there are references in other sources to bardic contests. Nevertheless, this is the earliest authentic record in which the bardic institution which later came to be known as an *eisteddfod* emerges clearly into the light of history, and it is possible to detect in this record a number of those features which clearly distinguish the modern *eisteddfod*—the proclamation a year in advance, the patronage of a distinguished person, the division between poets and musicians, and the award of a chair and a prize to the victorious bard and musician. Although it is not so stated, it may reasonably be inferred from the knowledge which we have of later bardic assemblies, held in the fifteenth and sixteenth centuries, that the bardic and musical contests were not the only purpose of this festival, but that regulations pertaining to the bardic craft were also discussed and promulgated. But bardic assemblies of this kind were probably held at irregular intervals. On other occasions, to judge once again from the evidence of a later period, bardic regulations were reviewed and 'degrees' conferred during feasts at which bards assembled.

One purpose of the *eisteddfodau* and bardic codes was to prevent undesirable elements from entering the profession and usurping the bard's position. This end could also be achieved by insisting that the professional bard should undergo the rigorous system of training which has already been referred to, and this almost inevitably meant that the poetry composed by this particular class of bards would be unusually difficult. Conservative in theme and invariably conventional in treatment, archaic in diction, forms and construction, replete with compound words and adjectives which very often can only be translated into English by a whole clause, intentionally involved in syntax and abounding with stereotyped metaphors and similes, the poetry of the *Gogynfeirdd* is unquestionably the most difficult corpus of verse to have survived in Welsh and 'linguistically one of the most difficult bodies of verse in any European language'. Poetry which clearly exhibits such a highly developed technique presupposes a long and vital tradition behind it. Throughout most of the poetry composed by the *Gogynfeirdd* we can detect a conscious effort on their part to make their craft an esoteric art. For them poetry was a science and the poet himself was a trained and expert technician. Thus, in spite of all the obscurities in this verse, the rules of syntax are hardly ever broken.

It was their training which probably accounts in a very large measure for the 'backward-looking' or retrospective view of life which characterizes the compositions of the *Gogynfeirdd*. References to older poets and to the heroes of the past abound in their works. Dafydd Benfras *(fl. c.* 1220-60) began an ode addressed to Llywelyn ab Iorwerth with the earnest invocation that he might be inspired with a muse 'as mighty as ardent Myrddin's', so that he might be able

> To sing praises like Aneirin of old,
> The day he sang Gododdin.

The *Gogynfeirdd* undoubtedly regarded their sixth-century bardic predecessors as their models, and they loved to think they were following in the footsteps of the older poets. For example, Taliesin, who is assigned in Welsh tradition to the late sixth century, seems to have offended his princely patron, Urien Rheged, at one time, and with a view to re-establishing himself in the royal favour he composed a *dadolwch,* a poem seeking reconciliation and forgiveness. This is the earliest extant example of this type of poem in Welsh. Centuries later the *Gogynfeirdd* composed similar poems and they even called them by the same name. Outstanding examples from this period are the poems addressed by Cynddelw Brydydd Mawr to the Lord Rhys of Deheubarth, the poem by Elidir Sais *(fl. c.* 1195-1246) to Llywelyn ab Iorwerth, and that by Phylip Brydydd to Rhys Gryg. It is hardly surprising, therefore, that not only the main themes of the *Gogynfeirdd* but also their treatment of them should bear an unmistakable resemblance to those of Aneirin and Taliesin. There is a marked affinity in their metaphors and similes. Indeed, so conscientiously did these court poets take the works of their sixth-century predecessors as their examplars that they have been accused of attempting to rewrite their poetry. In many ways the bardic vocabulary of their predecessors had a special significance for them. For example, they frequently refer to their traditional enemy, the English, as *Brynaich,* although *Bernicia* had long since been absorbed by Northumbria, which had in its turn been swallowed up in England. Another recurring convention is that the bard's patron has no peer, he is *sans peur et sans reproche,* and in expressing this idea many of the hyperboles which are found in the works of the older bards are re-echoed by the court poets. It has been pointed out by many critics that Aneirin's *Gododdin* undoubtedly influenced the elegy on Owain Gwynedd's retinue by Cynddelw Brydydd Mawr and that it also inspired one of the most interesting poems of this period, *Hirlas Owain,* 'Owain's tall blue [drinking-horn]', by Owain Cyfeiliog, in which many expressions and phrases have been borrowed from the earlier poem. Instances of this type of conscious imitation abound in the poetry of the *Gogynfeirdd*.

Moreover, it was a fundamental principle of their verse that sound is as important as sense. According to Diodorus Siculus, the Celtic bards were essentially lyric poets who sang their verses, whether these were panegyrics or satires, to the accompaniment of musical instruments, which resembled lyres. The practice of poetry in all the Celtic lands has been deeply influenced all down the centuries by its oral origin. It is this factor which, above all else, accounts for its spontaneity, its allusiveness and special stylistic features, especially the intricate pattern of consonantal alliteration and internal rhyme known as *cynghanedd*. The primary appeal of Welsh court poetry was not to the eye but to the ear, which is 'the gateway to the heart'. This verse sought to elicit a response from the bard's sophisticated listening audience and, by appealing to a canonical corpus of mutually shared knowledge, it endeavoured to create a firm and indissoluble bond between the poet and his audience. The chime and clash of rhyme and consonantal alliteration was an essential feature in this oral verse, and phrases were sometimes included to enhance the overall metrical effect and to deepen the poetry's emotional appeal.

The long and rigorous training which the professional bards were required to undergo was ultimately intended to enable them to communicate their verses orally in an impressive and memorable manner, to attain, as Mr. Saunders Lewis has so felicitously phrased it, the melodious *aura* of their lines. Naturally, therefore, great emphasis was placed in the bardic schools on the art of versification. The Welsh court poets inherited the old metres of the *awdl* (ode), but they deemed some of these to be unworthy of poets of their exalted status and left them to poets of inferior rank. In general, the *awdlau* which the court poets sang were longer than those of the earlier poets, and are usually found in sections with different rhymes, these sections being linked together, as a rule, by alliteration or word-repetition. One *awdl* by Cynddelw Brydydd Mawr has over three hundred lines, and there are also four by the same bard which have over two hundred. It must be remembered that the *awdl* really consisted of a number of lines of particular length, each one sustaining the same rhyme. (The Welsh *awdl* 'ode' and *odl* 'rhyme' are in origin the same word). As there is obviously a limit to the number of rhymes that are possible, the *Gogynfeirdd*, whenever they desired to compose a long poem, adopted the expedient of combining various *awdlau* into one composition. The end of one *awdl* was cleverly connected with the beginning of the one which followed by the device known in Welsh as *cymeriad*, that is, repetition of the same word; or alternatively, a word was used alliterating with the one which preceded it. They also composed a series of *englynion* which were connected together by means of a single rhyme throughout, or, in the event of the rhymes being changed, by linking them with *cymeriadau*. A chain of these *englynion* eventually came in the works of these bards to serve the function of an *awdl*, a metrical development in which Cynddelw Brydydd Mawr may have played an important role. Nevertheless, the court poets do not seem to have esteemed the *englyn* as highly as the *awdl*, and they never inserted an *englyn* into an *awdl*. Professor J. Lloyd-Jones held the view that the *awdl* and *englynion* were at first intended for different audiences; that is, in his *awdl* Cynddelw is a chief-of-song *(pencerdd)*, while in his *englynion* he is a *bardd teulu*.

There are some interesting features, too, in the various embellishments which this fastidious school of bards employed to adorn their verse. Alliteration and internal rhyme similar to those found in the *Hengerdd* occur in the works of the early *Gogynfeirdd*. In Irish verse it was possible for a consonant to alliterate with its lenited, or mutated, form, as well as with itself. Alliteration of this nature occurs not only in the *Gododdin*, as Sir Ifor Williams so ably demonstrated, but also in the poetry of the *Gogynfeirdd*. This practice is well attested in link-alliteration between *englynion* and sections of *awdlau*, or in the alliteration of the end of the first line of a couplet with the beginning of the second. For example:

> kyffred a lluted a llwyr yoli *kr*eawdyr
> a llwyr *gr*euyt y grynnoï

> yt ygyfwrw enwir yn enwerys *g*oll
> yg *k*ellessric dande

In addition to full rhyme, with which all lovers of poetry are naturally familiar, there were also in early Welsh poetry two other types of rhyme—*proest*-rhyme (where the vowel or diphthong varied and the consonant remained unchanged) and 'Irish' rhyme, to use Sir Ifor Williams's phrase (where the vowel or diphthong remained unchanged and the consonant varied). The court poets used both full and *proest*-rhyme, and a few stray examples also occur in their works of 'Irish' rhyme.

It was in the poetry of the *Gogynfeirdd* that the metrical embellishment called *cynghanedd* gradually developed into a strict and regular system. Examples of consonantal alliteration and internal rhyme occur in the earliest Welsh poetry, but this was not a regular feature, for many lines occur in the *Hengerdd* which reflect none of these metrical embellishments. Nor does *cynghanedd* occur in every line of the verses composed by the earlier court poets, who obviously regarded it as an optional feature of their craft. However, Dr. Thomas Parry, by analysing in detail five poems composed by different bards from this period, has shown how *cynghanedd* gradually became more obligatory until eventually a stage is reached when the various types of *cynghanedd (croes, traws, sain,* and *llusg)* which adorn the compositions of the later *Gogynfeirdd* are on the whole similar to the types with which we are familiar today. In the well-known elegy which Gruffudd ab yr Ynad Coch sang on the death of Llywelyn ap Gruffudd in 1282 consonantal alliteration or internal rhyme (or a combination of both these metrical adornments) is a feature of every one of its lines, numbering one hundred and four in all.

The work of one of the later *Gogynfeirdd,* Casnodyn (*fl. c.* 1320-40), the earliest Glamorgan bard whose poems can be regarded as unimpeachably authentic, is of great interest in the history of Welsh metrics, for it marks a clear and definite stage in the development towards a strict system of *cynghanedd.* One interesting feature of his work is the marked predilection which he shows for the tightly-woven *cynghanedd sain.* He seems to have taken great delight in a particularly ornate variety of this type of *cynghanedd* in which rhymes and consonantal correspondences occur twice over, thus cleverly linking both parts of the line. For example:

Ll*yw* b*yw* b*erth* m*awrnerth* nyt murnyat

R*ot* ar*vot* ar*veu* ken*eu* kynnar

So strong was Casnodyn's desire to add to the metrical ornateness of his lines that he even employed four rhymes in *cynghanedd sain,* as in the following line taken from his panegyric to Gwenllïan, daughter of Cynan:

M*ein* uir*ein* r*ein* g*ein* gymraec

But lines similar to those quoted above proved to be too intricate even for this highly fastidious school of bards, so that this variety of *cynghanedd sain* never became firmly established in the strict-metre system. Nevertheless, these examples effectively illustrate the way in which the *Gogynfeirdd* deliberately aimed at increasing the difficulty of their craft by complicating their metres and indulging in metrical *tours de force.* A rhyme could be sustained for as many as fifty consecutive lines, or even more; a poet might begin many successive lines with the same letter; and, as we have already observed, the device of repeating a word or phrase, known as *cymeriad,* was skilfully used to link stanzas together. All these ornate metrical features were designed pre-eminently to emphasize and preserve the exclusiveness of the bardic profession and to safeguard the bardic craft from being corrupted by unskilled poetasters who were unworthy of their calling.

These, then, are the distinctive characteristics of the poetry composed by the *Gogynfeirdd*. It was, in essence, aristocratic verse, and its primary function was undeniably social. The hopes and aspirations, the trials and tribulations of those ordinary people who belonged to the lower strata of native Welsh society find no place in this majestic corpus of poetry. Lyrical in character and traditional in both style and treatment, its central theme was heroic panegyric and it eschewed both narrative and any attempt at detailed description. The heroes and patrons whose praises are sung by these court poets are described only in general and manifestly conventional terms, and the historical events to which some references occur in this verse are often passed over in a few, albeit memorable, phrases. To deny that this poetry has its defects, as well as its virtues, would be idle. Restricted very largely to the praise of regal patrons and conventional in its style and treatment, it may often seem uninspiringly monotonous to the modern reader who has been deeply influenced by the romantic conception of poetry and of the poet's function in society. Nor is it easy to counter the charge that the court poets were generally too intent on exhibiting the technical mastery which, after years of rigorous training, they had acquired over their medium and that, in surrendering to their fondness for metrical pyrotechnics, they often lost sight of the overall structural unity of their compositions. Unquestionably, some of their odes would benefit from the literary standpoint if they were not so long. Nevertheless, if the modern critic attempts to evaluate this verse according to the ideas held by the *Gogynfeirdd* themselves of the nature and function of poetry, he will discover that the Welsh bardic tradition has many literary gems to offer him.

That tradition experienced a major crisis in its development in the late thirteenth and early fourteenth centuries, for the Edwardian Conquest destroyed the native political superstructure on which the court poets had been for so long dependent. The bards themselves had not been reluctant to remind their princely patrons of their mutual interdependence, and they had occasionally asserted that the relationship between prince and poet bore some affinity to *carennydd,* or kinship, which constituted a bond of deep significance. There is, moreover, plenty of evidence to suggest that a number of the prominent court poets had pondered long and deeply on some of the major political issues of the period and that they had tried, though not always successfully, it must be allowed, to foster a national outlook conducive to the centralizing policy pursued by the princes of Gwynedd in the thirteenth century. In the verse which he addressed to Dafydd ab Owain Gwynedd (d. 1203), who played a leading part in the revolt against Henry II in 1165, the court poet Llywarch ap Llywelyn (Prydydd y Moch, *fl. c.* 1173-1220) anticipated the centralizing policy which was later to be pursued with such consummate skill by Llywelyn ab Iorwerth, although Dafydd ab Owain Gwynedd was never sufficiently strong to implement that policy himself. The latter was addressed, significantly, as 'lord of Aberffraw', and the solution advocated by the poet for the fratricidal strife which characterized the contemporary political life of Wales was the assertion by the prince of the authority of Aberffraw. As lord of that court, Dafydd was 'prime ruler by inherent right', and the poet reminded him that he would have to assert his authority by force, not through love and affection. It was his duty, therefore, to secure 'a strong peace' *(cadr heddwch).* Aberffraw was later held, successively, by Dafydd's younger brother, Rhodri ab Owain Gwynedd (d. 1195), and his nephew, Gruffudd ap Cynan ab Owain Gwynedd, but in spite of their comparative ineptitude, Llywarch ap Llywelyn still continued to emphasize the 'inherent right' of that court over all the people of Wales from Anglesey to Monmouth. Naturally, the rise of Llywelyn ab Iorwerth to supreme political authority was well received by this bard, who became his chief court poet. Llywarch ap Llywelyn's enlightened political outlook is clearly reflected in his impassioned appeal to the men of Powys in one of his odes, which seems to have been occasioned by Llywelyn the Great's advance towards Powys, to receive a Welsh leader who is the king of a strong people rather than be subjected to a foreigner. In several of his poems Llywarch ap Llywelyn mentioned Llywelyn ab Iorwerth's descent from the royal house of Powys as well as from the royal line of Gwynedd. The new political unity achieved by Gwynedd was seen as an 'uncovering' *(dadanhudd)* of the right order of things, which had been foretold by Myrddin.

In the following generation this new political outlook can be discerned in the work of Dafydd Benfras *(fl. c.* 1220-60), and it probably reaches its climax in the verse of Llygad Gŵr *(fl. c.* 1260-70), who sang the praises of Llywelyn ap Gruffudd when the latter was at the height of his political power from 1267 to 1277 and had been recognized constitutionally as 'Prince of Wales'. In the opinion of Dafydd Benfras, for example, Llywelyn ab Iorwerth was 'the great chieftain of fair Wales' and he is hailed as 'our common ruler'. The poet saw him as the president of a council of feudal rulers:

> Llywelyn, the ruler of rulers,
> A gentle advocate in the council of the wise.

When, later, Llywelyn ap Gruffudd ascended to the throne of Gwynedd, the feudal state had already been established in the view of the poet, and hence it was, as Mr. Myrddin Lloyd has so trenchantly observed, an inheritance into which the Venedotian prince rightfully entered. The latter was greeted by Llygad Gŵr as king of the Welsh, and it is in his poetry that we probably find the most forthright expression of the great contemporary upsurge of the Welsh national spirit. Llywelyn ap Gruffudd is seen as the head of a united Wales, the leader of Gwynedd, Powys and Deheubarth. His like had not been seen since the battle of Arfderydd; he is 'the true king of Wales' whose quarrel is with a 'foreign nation of alien speech' *(estron genedl anghyfiaith).* The poet even urges the new Arthur to annex Cornwall to his domains, and the word *Cymro* is used several times, obviously with great pride. The five odes which Llygad Gŵr addressed to Llywelyn ap Gruffudd have been described as 'the most "nationalist" poetry in Welsh before the days of [Owain] Glyndŵr'.

A number of the court poets, therefore, had grasped some of the deeper implications of the political policies pursued by the princes of Gwynedd in the thirteenth century, and if, as has sometimes been claimed, the lawyers were the 'silent executants' of Venedotian policy in this period, the court bards could on occasion be its subtlest and most effective propagandists, inasmuch as they were able to give eloquent expression in their panegyric verses to some of the ideals and aspirations that helped to formulate it. It is, therefore, hard to believe that the magnitude of the disaster of Llywelyn ap Gruffudd's death on that fateful day in December, 1282, and the beastly execution of his brother, David, by Edward I in the following year could not have been grasped by the members of an esoteric *confrérie* who, by virtue of their antecedent training and their long professional association with the ruling dynasties, had a firm understanding of the major political dilemma of their day. The utter and unrelieved despair which the court poets must have experienced in the closing years of the thirteenth century found its most poignant and eloquent expression in Gruffudd ab yr Ynad Coch's celebrated elegy on Llywelyn ap Gruffudd, which rises to a memorable climax in which the bard feels that his whole world has suddenly collapsed around him and that nature and the whole order of the universe are gravely imperilled by the political calamity of 1282 and its aftermath. The following short extract has been taken from Professor Joseph Clancy's translation:

> With Llywelyn's death, gone is my mind.
> Heart frozen in the breast with terror,
> Desire decays like dried-up branches.
> See you not the rush of wind and rain?

> See you not the oaks lash each other?
> See you not the ocean scourging the shore?
> See you not the truth is portending?
> See you not the sun hurtling the sky?
> See you not that the stars have fallen?
> Have you no belief in God, foolish men?
> See you not that the world is ending?
> Ah God, that the sea would cover the land!
> What is left us that we should linger?
> No place to flee from terror's prison,
> No place to live; wretched is living!
> No counsel, no clasp, no path left open
> One way to be freed from fear's sad strife.

This feeling of utter despair must have been experienced by many—probably by all—of Gruffudd ab yr Ynad Coch's contemporaries in the professional guild of bards. That guild had made heroic praise of the defending native rulers the basic function of its poetic activity. But in the closing years of the thirteenth century, with the loss of Welsh independence and the death of the last independent Welsh prince, the poetic activity of the professional bards seemed to have lost its *raison d'être*.

BIBLIOGRAPHY

Historical Background:
J. E. Lloyd, *A History of Wales from the Earliest Times to the Edwardian Conquest* (2 vols., London, 1911; new impression, 1948); vol. II.
A. J. Roderick (ed.), *Wales through the Ages. Volume I: From the Earliest Times to 1485* (Llandybïe, 1959), pp. 74-137 and 153-67.

Texts:
R. Morris-Jones, J. Morris-Jones and T. H. Parry-Williams (eds.), *Llawysgrif Hendregadredd* (Cardiff, 1933).
J. Gwenogvryn Evans (ed.), *The Poetry in the Red Book of Hergest* (Llanbedrog, 1909).
Henry Lewis (ed.), *Hen Gerddi Crefyddol* (Cardiff, 1931).
E. Anwyl (ed.), *The Poetry of the Gogynfeirdd from the Myvyrian Archaiology of Wales: with an Introduction to the Study of Old Welsh Poetry* (Denbigh, 1909).
Arthur Hughes and Ifor Williams (eds.), *Gemau'r Gogynfeirdd* (Pwllheli, 1910).

Translations:
  Joseph P. Clancy, *The Earliest Welsh Poetry* (London-New York, 1970).
  Anthony Conran, *The Penguin Book of Welsh Verse* (Penguin, 1967).

Critical Studies:
  T. Gwynn Jones, 'Bardism and Romance: a Study of the Welsh Literary Tradition', *The Transactions of the Honourable Society of Cymmrodorion* (1913-14), 205-310.
  Saunders Lewis, 'The Essence of Welsh Literature', *Wales,* VII, No. 27 (December, 1947), 337-41. (Now published in *Presenting Saunders Lewis,* ed. A. R. Jones and G. Thomas (Cardiff, 1973), pp. 154-8).
  W. J. Gruffydd, 'Rhagarweiniad i Farddoniaeth Cymru cyn Dafydd ap Gwilym', *Trans. Cymm.* (1937), 257-83.
  H. I. Bell, *The Nature of Poetry as conceived by the Welsh Bards.* The Taylorian Lecture, 1955 (Oxford: Clarendon Press, 1955).
  J. Lloyd-Jones, 'The Court Poets of the Welsh Princes'. The Sir John Rhŷs Memorial Lecture, *Proc. British Academy,* XXXIV (1948).
  J. E. Caerwyn Williams, 'Beirdd y Tywysogion: Arolwg', *Llên Cymru,* XI (1970-71), 3-94.
  Idem, 'The Court Poet in Medieval Ireland'. The Sir John Rhŷs Memorial Lecture, *Proc. British Academy,* LVII (1971).
  Saunders Lewis, *Braslun o Hanes Llenyddiaeth Gymraeg hyd 1535* (Caerdydd, 1932), chaps. ii and iv.
  Thomas Parry, *A History of Welsh Literature.* Translated from the Welsh by H. Idris Bell (Oxford, 1955), chap. iii.
  H. I. Bell, *The Development of Welsh Poetry* (Oxford: Clarendon Press, 1936), chap. iii.
  Gwyn Williams, *An Introduction to Welsh Poetry from the Beginnings to the Sixteenth Century* (London, 1953), chap. iv.
  T. Gwynn Jones, *Rhieingerddi'r Gogynfeirdd* (Dinbych, 1915).
  J. Vendryes, *La poésie galloise des XIIe et XIIIe siècles dans ses rapports avec la langue* (Oxford, 1930).
  T. J. Morgan, 'Arddull yr Awdl a'r Cywydd', *Trans. Cymm.* (1947), 1-38.
  Thomas Parry, 'Twf y Gynghanedd', *Trans. Cymm.* (1936), 143-60.
  John Morris-Jones, *Cerdd Dafod* (2nd edn. Oxford, 1930).

CHAPTER VII

THE POETS OF THE PRINCES

D. MYRDDIN LLOYD

The year 1160 was disastrous for Powys, the once powerful north-eastern province, the 'paradise of Wales'. Its unity was destroyed, once and for all, by the death of its powerful ruler, Madog ap Maredudd, closely followed by that of his son, Llywelyn. The foremost Powysian court poet, Cynddelw, in one of his finest poems, composed at that critical time, exclaimed: 'In the vale of Llangwm I contemplated our leader, and what I sang will be contemplated'.

In these words are exemplified three characteristic features of Welsh court poetry of the twelfth and thirteenth centuries. There is the passionate attachment to places and place-names. Not only is the poet sensitive to natural beauty, as he so often is to a marked degree, but place-names are to him evocative of his country's fortunes in which he has been deeply involved. 'Greetings to Waelest Edwy, and the court by the banks of the Dee, and that fair place like unto a strand that evokes in me longing, more and more'.

There was much pride in the Welsh way of life, and in the rights and privileges deriving from the native legal system and the pattern of society. A renewed confidence and pride had followed the rolling back of the Anglo-Norman tide. The precarious liberty thus gained had to be strenuously defended, and it needed no great insight to be agonizingly aware of how much depended on the qualities of the rulers—not only valour, but also coolness of judgement and sagacity. Panegyric had always been the prevailing mode of Celtic verse, but it is not hard to understand that then, of all times, the 'contemplation of rulers' should have acquired the significance it did, and that it should give such power and reality to so much of the cou[rt] poetry.

Not only was the poet aware of the worth of his ruler, but [he] was equally aware of his own status and that of the bardic order to which he belonged: 'And what I sang will be contemplated'. The muse (*awen*) was a divine gift bestowed on the bard as formerly on David, Prophet and King. It was he who interpreted to his community the meaning of its corporate existence. His role was as essential as that of his prince. Cyndd[elw] after offending the powerful Rhys ap Gruffudd, wore h[is] cloth as proudly as if it were the imperial toga, and re[minded] Rhys before all his court: 'You without me have no voice; I without you have nothing to say'.

Close reading of the poetry itself provides by far the best source of information on the bards, their technique, their function in society and their conception of their art. All other sources need to be tested against this extensive corpus of verse. Information can be gleaned from the Laws, the Chronicle of the Princes, the writings of Giraldus Cambrensis, the Mabinogion, the Triads, and far more so from the grammatical and metrical tracts and the so-called 'Statute' of Gruffudd ap Cynan. These tracts, however, and the 'Statute' even more so, reflect the theory and practice of a later age, and must be used with circumspection in the study of our period.

There were grades of poets. Mention is made of the *pencerdd* (the chief of song), the *bardd teulu* (a court poet of lower grade), and well below these were meaner orders such as *beirdd ysbyddaid*. The term *bardd* is used to cover all grades, and *prydydd* for a high-grade poet. Would that the work of lower orders had survived, with the 'foolish tales' scorned by Phylip Brydydd. But the *pencerdd* would not 'debase God's gift'. He saw himself in succession to the *hengerdd* (ancient song), the eulogies of the heroic age of Maelgwn Gwynedd, and of Taliesin and Aneirin. Metrical composition is defined in the Welsh *ars poetica* as consisting of 'fitting expressions adorned with exalted words, beautified with acceptable and appealing supporting words, signifying praise or dispraise'. Narrative and many exercises of the creative imagination that are generally considered as most appropriate to poetry are seldom practised, the *pencerdd* being dedicated to 'Truth' in what seems to us a narrow and restrictive sense. The *pencerdd*'s status is high, and is recognised by gifts of land, horses, cattle, raiment, a harp, gold and silver.

It is a feature of Celtic art that ornament often covers the whole surface, usually in interlacing patterns, whether it be the Book of Kells or a metal object. This aesthetic is very evident in *Gogynfeirdd* poetry, as in that of the later *cywydd* period. Not only are there end-rhymes, but the beginnings of lines are linked by sound correspondences called *cymeriad* and the body of the line is richly adorned with varying patterns of internal rhyme, and alliteration which is not confined to initials of words but extends to internal consonants, particularly those preceding or flanking stressed vowels. This highly professional poetry is made possible by long apprenticeship to an experienced poet, and the assured patronage of princes.

Metrical patterns fall into two categories—*englynion* and *awdlau*. The former, as practised by the *Gogynfeirdd*, consist of quatrains of seven-syllable lines rhyming -a, -a, -b, -ba, or with four muted final rhymes *(proest)*, the vowels matching only in length, and the final consonants being the same. The most popular *englyn* form, however, consists of thirty syllables, the main rhyme falling on any syllable from the fifth to the ninth, and repeated on the sixteenth, the twenty-third and the thirtieth. Though freer in certain respects it is a prototype of the *englyn unodl union*, the most popular of all Welsh strict metres. *Awdl* metres are generally in lines of eight or nine syllables in monorhyming sequences that can be quite long. Variety is achieved by such devices as altering the position of the main rhyme and inserting sequences of internal rhymes. Changes of rhythm can be effected by thus varying the rhyme scheme and by the treatment of stresses.

The earliest surviving manuscripts to contain the bulk of the poetry date from the fifteenth century. They are the Hendregadredd MS., in the National Library of Wales, and the *Red Book of Hergest,* in the Bodleian Library. A few poems occur in earlier manuscripts, such as the thirteenth-century *Black Book of Carmarthen,* and Peniarth 3, both in the National Library of Wales.

The establishment of firm Welsh rule in Gwynedd by Gruffudd ap Cynan after long years of bitter struggle heralded a new age and new confidence. It was felt worthwhile to build in stone and to plant gardens. Much reorganization took place, and it would be strange indeed if the bardic order were not placed on a new footing. What was later described as the 'Statute of Gruffudd ap Cynan' reflects the thought and practices of subsequent times, just as what passed for the 'Laws of Hywel' contain a good deal that was formulated later than his day, yet the ascription of the Laws and the 'Statute' to these respective rulers cannot be without some significance.

With the establishment of a dynasty of princes in Gwynedd came a dynasty of bards, the line of Meilyr Brydydd. The earliest of the three extant poems ascribed to Meilyr is a 'prognostication' after the event following the battle of Mynydd Carn (1081), in which the death of Gruffudd's opponents is lamented, and detestation expressed for the 'Scots' (i.e. Irish) who had fought with Gruffudd on his return from exile in Ireland. However, if this early poem is his, Meilyr in the course of fifty years had not only changed his allegiance, but he no longer composed plaintive verse in the vaticinatory tradition held to derive from Myrddin. His majestic elegy to Gruffudd ap Cynan (1137) set the pattern, though not without antecedents, for the main body of court poetry addressed to the Welsh princes throughout the twelfth and thirteenth centuries. This stately elegy consists of four long monorhyming sequences of nine-syllable lines closely knit into a pattern, not only of final rhymes, but by much internal rhyming and alliteration, and *cymeriad.* The effect of these devices is to produce a smooth flow of words, and a sombre stateliness. Later poets were to show considerable development in the technique, greater variety was introduced to avoid monotony and to produce different effects, but the basic constituents are all found in Meilyr's elegy.

Gruffudd's life is seen as a continuation of an ancient struggle. There is harking back to Taliesin. Whereas later poets liken the princes also to the heroes of classical antiquity, especially those of the Trojan War, to Biblical heroes, to those of the *matière de France* and increasingly to Arthur and his knights, Meilyr invariably turns to men of Gruffudd's own line of ancestry, through Rhodri Mawr, back to Urien and the leaders of the old North. The Kingdom of Bernicia had long been absorbed in Northumbria, and Northumbria in a united Saxon England, and by Gruffudd's day into Norman England with a French-speaking upper crust. Yet, for Meilyr the struggle was still the same, the enemy was the *Brynaich* (Bernicians), and Gruffudd's mission was to '*gwared Bedydd*', to succour the 'baptized world', or Christendom, as though the Anglo-French aggressors were worshippers of Thor and Woden! Throughout the period of Welsh rule the bards were to promulgate this conception of history. In reality Welsh fought Welsh as often as they fought the English, marriages and military accommodations with Norman lords and the English royal line were common, Gruffudd ap Cynan left money to the church at Chester and his biographer claims he was a good neighbour to the English King, but on all this the poets were to maintain an eloquent silence. Irish-born and half Hiberno-Scandinavian Gruffudd was represented as meaningful for his day by fulfilling in his generation the role of Urien and other heroes of the heroic age. The elegy rings with echoes of Taliesin and Aneirin in vocabulary, poetic technique and allusions. Giraldus Cambrensis informs us that the Welsh of his day could not forget they had once ruled the whole island, and Gruffudd, whose sway extended only over Gwynedd, is still described as '*Prydain briawd*' (the possessor of Britain), but on the other hand the conception of the unity of *Wales*, from

Port Skewet (near Chepstow) to the gates of Chester is maintained, and the claim of the prince of Aberffraw to overlordship.

The princely qualities extolled are valour and generosity. Gruffudd was *'mur cadau'*, a bulwark or wall of defence in battle, and a provider of feastings where mead flowed, and where poets and harpists practised their age-old art. The two qualities, valour and generosity, were, as in *Cynfeirdd* poetry, welded together in lines of sharp antithesis: *'Cnoynt frain friwgig o lid llawrydd'* (Ravens chewed mangled flesh from the fury of the free-handed one). Sudden allusions take the place of detailed accounts of battles: 'At Gwern Gwygid each thrust into the other, the blood of men dripped, ashwood (spears) was bent, and from his battles new tales were borne.' At most there are pictures extending over some four lines: 'The King of England came with a host, he came but did not return any richer in cattle; we in Snowdonia had our herds of horses; he did not break into the pastures.' The poet who sang Gruffudd's praise thus was not one of the *manfeirdd*, the petty rhymers whom he scorned; he reclined next to his lord at feastings, was entrusted to go on his errands, and the relationship between them was like unto *carennydd*, or kinship, a very firm bond in the whole structure of Welsh society.

Taliesin's poems were quite short, and swift in movement, and the *Gododdin* is stanzaic, each 'stanza' devoted to a named individual member of the war-band, and creating its effect with a few rapid 'brushstrokes', but with Meilyr's long elegy, although all is woven into a network of sound correspondences, the movement is slow and stately; the basic unit is the single line of nine syllables, but the effect is gradual and accumulative, line on line like a course on course of firmly laid brickwork. Although this technique will be varied and modified by his successors, the perfection of the individual line thus practised by Meilyr was pursued by the *Gogynfeirdd* to a greater degree than ever before or since by Welsh poets.

Relations between prince and *pencerdd*, a chief court bard, were not always smooth. 'Weary am I of the service of rulers, blessed are they, monks in churches' was to be the heart-cry of one of Meilyr's own grandsons, and several intercessionary poems *(dadolwch)*, pleading for restitution to favour, were composed. Similarly, towards the close of their lives, some composed a 'death-couch poem', pleading for the forgiveness of the heavenly Ruler. Meilyr's *marwysgafn* is a poignant lyrical appeal. The metrical variations of line length and rhyming pattern, with repeated internal rhyme, convey the feeling of earnest persistency: '*Gwledig gwlad orfod, goruchel wenrod, gwrda gwna gymod, rhyngod a mi';* (Head ruler, holding mastery over his domain, the supremely high and holy (or bright) sphere, Lord, make Thou reconciliation between Thee and me.) For the eulogizing of 'perishable' rulers he has had much gold and silk, but now when his tongue is halting, as his silence approaches, he, Meilyr the *'Prydydd',* is a pilgrim on his way to Peter, who desires to await the call in the holy soil of the isle of Bardsey, 'the monastery by which the full tide flows, island of adorable Mary, eternal refuge with its graveyard held in the bosom of the salt sea.'

Boasting poems were common in early medieval Europe. The most delightful of all Welsh poems in this vein is the *Gorhoffedd* of Gwalchmai, son of Meilyr. Rapidly alternating in flashing phrases are his unabashed vaunting of prowess in battle in the cause of Owain Gwynedd, his keen delight in nature conveyed in vivid glimpses, and his passionate love of fair ladies. The Welsh relied in warfare on rapid mobility and intimate acquaintance with their terrain, and Gwalchmai is seen on his spirited charger speeding with observant eye over the land he loved to defend. The note is struck in the opening lines: 'Quickly-rising sun, summer hurrying on, sweet the chatter of birds in the balmy weather. I am the splendid one, fearless in battle, a lion in the van, sweeping is my fury. A night have I spent closely guarding the border, by the babbling fords of Dygen Freiddin.' His eye is caught by the lush greenery of young grass, the sparkle of running water, and he hears the 'nightingale singing her wonted song'. In that inland region by the Severn his mind flies back to his native Mona where bright-feathered seagulls play on the wave as on a bed. He is a long way from Anglesey, and in May his thoughts wander far for the love of a young Caerwys maiden, but in Owain's cause, 'the destroyer of our bondage,' the English scatter before his sword-blade. '*Although* Llywy is of the hue of snow on trees, when there was action by Chester, I poured out blood.'

Much of the imagery of *Gogynfeirdd* poetry is conventional, but in this poem all is sharp, fresh, vivid and animated. The sheer beauty of all Wales on a lovely day in May passes before his eyes. He is fascinated by the restless splendour of waves on a shore, apple blossom, and proud trees in their fresh coats. He cherishes the names of streams: 'Ogfanw, Cegin and Clawedog,' and of places throughout Wales where he has fought, been in love, or been thrilled by their beauty. However, he is never distracted from his loyalty to Owain, the 'uncoverer' (a legal term) of the claims and glories of his ancestors, and who by inherent right should hold sway from his native Anglesey to faraway Gwent—where the girls are mad about him, Gwalchmai, whom they have never seen!

'After excess of love, deep-seated hatred is usual.' So sang Gwalchmai in another poem to Owain composed in a very different vein. In a series of monorhyming sequences, Owain is addressed in each under the name of an ancestor: 'I address the generous one of the stock of Gruffudd ... of Yago ... of Rhodri ... of proud Rhun' (a link with the heroic age) '... and of Eneas' (the evoking of the Trojan legend and the strong sense it conveyed of national destiny). Rapid references to Owain's exploits in the field are touched upon in this swiftly moving eulogy, but at one point there is the nearest approach by any of the *Gogynfeirdd* to a detailed description of a battle, a sea-fight on Menai—'Three fleets approaching to test him severely, Irish, Vikings, Normans, and a thousand war-cries on the slopes of Moelfre.' There is furious conflict and slaughter, and the whole animated description is clinched in a hyperbole: 'No ebb tide on Menai for the blood colouring the salt sea.' But there is now a rift. They were both very proud men, and Gwalchmai does not demean himself to belittle Owain. He acknowledges the munificence of his gifts in the past, and confesses that his coldness hurts like being in prison.

We do not know what caused the rift, or whether there ever was a reconciliation, but there is no extant elegy to Owain by Gwalchmai. A eulogy and an elegy of his to Madog ap Maredudd, ruler of Powys (died 1160), have survived. Although Madog is extolled for the conventional qualities, freshness of imagery is still evident: 'No more do you hoard gold than meadow-sweet, and it is no easier to evade your retribution than to find a sandless beach!' 'To love God of inexhaustible trustworthiness': so begins the elegy, but as for Madog, 'A friend I had, whom I no longer have. The love of man has no sure splendour. I loved the ruler of Powys, and today for me his going is hard to bear.' He was the 'roof-tree' of Powys; the fall of enemy towers, joy at feastings, and many keen moments during peace and war are conjured up in a rapid succession of succinct phrases, but now it is a beginning of Lent.

Did Gwalchmai then return to the court of Owain Gwynedd? It is doubtful. In a sad little poem styled the 'Dream of Gwalchmai' he describes himself as grey and dejected after the deaths of Madog, of his own son Goronwy (who served as we know from another poem in Owain Gwynedd's *teulu*—a household troop of picked young warriors) and of Genilles who was to him precious as gold (presumably his wife). His gift of achieving freshness of imagery, however, has not deserted him and in the 'Dream' he is worn down on the 'grindstone of anxiety'. Yet he still pleads for the Divine impulse granted to David the Prophet, the gift of poetry, but now he sees that the really 'well born' are those who are moved by the love of God to spend their means on feeding the hungry, clothing the naked and providing the sick with a bed, a home, and a hearth.

Gwalchmai lived however to sing the prowess of Dafydd and

Rhodri, two of Owain Gwynedd's quarrelsome sons. Relations continue to be prickly at times, for the poet confesses to Dafydd that he was not 'precious' in the eyes of Rhodri, but later with a touch of his old vigour and forceful expression he assures Rhodri of his loyalty: 'If I should deserve it through treachery, may there be no-one sharing a common tongue with me except Cain alone!'

A large corpus of Cynddelw Brydydd Mawr's verse has survived, and his name is the one that most readily comes to mind when one thinks of twelfth-century Welsh court poetry. Much of his work does not immediately offer what men of our age seek from poetry. Long eulogies in a diction archaic even in his own day, high-sounding compound words closely woven together, with a terse economy of syntax, often with little of that freshness of imagery and warmth that appeals to us in Gwalchmai, all this has to be faced. Much of the verse strikes us as sheer rhetoric, but it should be remembered that it was meant to be declaimed, chanted to harp music, on a public occasion. But this is not the full story. There are poems that reveal very different qualities, and when it is least expected he can surprise us with sheer lyricism, quiet meditation, or deep-felt tensions, scorn, affection, or even psychological insight expressed with all the resources of his bardic skill.

Cynddelw was a native of Powys whose earliest compositions are those of a court poet at Mathrafal during the prosperous years preceding the death of Madog ap Maredudd (1160). These early poems provide glimpses, all too rare, of the delights and courtesies of the chase, of rich pasture land, fine horses and deer, joyous feastings and bards held in honour. As became a Powys poet, Cynddelw was a master of the *englyn* in more than one of its varied patterns, and in fact favoured more and more the thirty-syllable kind that in his hands came ever closer to the *englyn unodl union,* a form that has retained its extreme popularity to our own day. He also made extensive use of *awdl* metres in the tradition of Taliesin as maintained by Meilyr and Gwalchmai, and sang eulogies and elegies to

Madog in both styles.

In a contest in *englyn* metre, Cynddelw and Seisyllt Bryffwrch fought for the office of *pencerdd* at the court of Madog. From Seisyllt's abusive words we learn that Cynddelw could claim no bardic ancestry, but fortunately for Welsh poetry this disability was not considered decisive, and it certainly did not weaken his faith in himself and his own 'God-given' talent. 'And I, you poets, in, and you out!' Thus he taunts inferior bards at a New Year feast where the bustle was like the 'noise of a chattering wave on a beach around a seagull's feet'.

Darker days were soon to follow the death of Madog. It became painfully evident what that strong ruler had been: 'A firm anchor in a deep sea—barren and vicious' (the word *diffaith* conveys both meanings). Cynddelw then composed in *englyn* metres an elegy that, to modern taste, is his finest poem. The nine opening *englynion* are evocative of days of triumph and prosperity—Maes y Croesau, Maestref, Mathrafal, these place-names all recall happy memories, brisk action, magnificent horses breaking the rich turf with their hooves and prancing in January, Madog a bulwark against aggression. A change of metre follows to break between the joy that has been and the sorrow to follow—a complimentary *englyn* of a different pattern to Llywelyn ap Madog, the hope of Powys. Then a return to the former metre and the evocation of a place-name—Cynwyd—where things had looked ominous, where there had been cause for deliberation, where proud warriors had their shields battered, and where the host of Powys was scattered. 'No-one was left alive with two coats.' 'The death of Madog, great my grief; the slaying of Llywelyn—a complete inundation.' Change of mood is again marked by change of metre. Place-names are now laden with nostalgia, and there follow *englynion* where rhyme is muted—as in some of Wilfred Owen's poems, final consonants are repeated but not the vowels—a powerful device for conveying a sense of loss. In the two final *englynion* of the normal *unodl* type the poet moves from a grim picture of glutted birds of prey battening on the

Powysian dead to indignation at the mean advantage taken by Gwynedd to occupy the vale of Edeirnion, but it will never do, for 'it is idle to think of possessing anything of this world that comes not from God'.

Although Cynddelw, as far as we know, was the first poet of all Wales in that he sang at the courts of Powys, Gwynedd and the South, his poems on Powysian themes are numerous and date from various periods of his life. He sang to the *gwelygorddau,* or kindred groups of warriors stemming from the heroes of the past, and to the privileges of Powys-men derived from their prowess at the great victory of Meigen (A.D. 633). There are several poems to rulers of various parts of splintered Powys following the death of Madog, but of greater appeal today is the *Rhieingerdd,* the complimentary poem to Efa *(Eve),* daughter of Madog, and the poem to Tysilio and the church of Meifod, situated near Mathrafal.

The *Rhieingerdd* is a fast-moving poem in monorhyming sequences of nine-syllable lines with the usual variation of a ten-syllable line and its change in rhyme pattern. The love-lorn poet is addressing his horse, 'the lively spirited one', and pouring into its ear his praises of Eve. The device of 'likening' *(dyfalu),* later to be brought to perfection by Dafydd ap Gwilym, is here found, though sparingly used: Eve is of the hue of dawn, like gleaming white snow on the heights of Epynt, or the foam around an oar, like the bright fragments of foam dashed by the ninth wave. Like the foam on a curving wave is the brightness of her breast alongside her bracelet. But the amorous poet has seen even more, he has seen the exquisite curve of her side, 'and whoever has not seen that has not seen beauty!' She speaks the attractive cultivated Welsh of the court in the valley where the poet is hurrying to visit her. The court ladies are all of a flutter, through glass windows they watch for him like a row of bright seagulls. Tall, golden-haired Eve is refined, and her bard is losing sleep!

The lengthy poem to Tysilio, consisting of nine monorhyming sequences of eight-syllable lines, is one of three poems by the *Gogynfeirdd* to Welsh saints and churches dedicated to them; the others, to be mentioned later, being to David and to Cadfan. Following the opening invocation to the Deity, who is the 'stronghold of peace', the joy and tranquillity of heaven are described as reflected in Meifod. The life, legends and temptations of Tysilio are mentioned in brief allusions. Son though he was of Brochfael, ruler of Powys, he 'hated the love of cruelty'. Cynddelw speaks of his own love for Meifod, the burial place of kings. Humility (which did not come to him easily) and pride jostle each other: not only pride in the church of Meifod, its *clas,* its crozier of gold and its vessels, but in his own poetic gift, for the creator of heaven and earth who had fashioned him of the four elements had also made him a poet of standing. Meifod is praised in lyrical terms, but there are also glimpses of other churches associated with Tysilio in various parts of Wales, including 'Mona where the clover comes down to the water's edge'.

Among the eulogies of Powysian rulers there is an *awdl* to Owain Cyfeiliog, one of the finest Welsh poets of his day, but of his muse there is not a word. He is praised as a ruler, a bestower of largesse, and a warrior. Of all the Welsh princes, Owain alone turned a deaf ear to the appeals of Archbishop Baldwin and Giraldus Cambrensis to support the Third Crusade. Cynddelw approves of his being 'opposed to oppressive war for Rome—for the court in London'. In the tradition of the *Cynfeirdd* there is savage exultation over ruthlessness in battle, alongside warm appreciation of the graces of courtly living in the hall: 'In Owain's court there is civility and refuge; drink without stint or refusal and no-one in want.' Owain is also acclaimed in a chain of *englynion* for his forays and carousals: 'By the Long Hill, the tall, powerful eagle; by Severn the delightful smile of men.'

However, after the break-up of Powys in 1160, the fate of Wales depended on Owain Gwynedd. The whole power and heady rhetoric of Cynddelw's verse is poured into a series of eulogies of Owain. No longer the patient building of line on line, but great surges held together by long repetitions of initial phrases. Carnage is portrayed with unsparing realism: 'I saw bloodstained corpses—their laying out was left to the wolves; I saw after battle entrails on thorns.' Reference is made to 'Owain's ravens,' and the sixth-century Owain ab Urien and the twelfth-century Owain Gwynedd are thus fused into one as in the eyes of the poet their mission is one. The rapidity of Owain Gwynedd's movement is conveyed through rapid juxtaposition of place-names—Rhuddlan, Pembroke, Pennardd—a technique that is to be developed by two major poets of the next century as we shall see.

When Owain died in 1170 Cynddelw rose to the occasion in eight long monorhyming sequences of great eloquence and energy. The fourth sequence can be taken as typical. Owain is the New Year's gift of all the bards, the life of the needy, the shepherd of Mona. Cynddelw has been honoured with splendid cattle, and he will sound his patron's praise far and wide. Paradoxically he prays that God will bring to His peace him who was so thrustful in war, and references to Owain's decisive victories at Maescarnedd and elsewhere are enforced by several heavily alliterated lines of pounding rhythm *(carn* having the meaning of a horse's hoof). The tempo then changes to convey the spirit of Owain's generosity: 'He gave me red gold and honour. May the Trinity grant him mercy'. The sequence closes with an enumeration of the qualities of the ideal ruler as exemplified in Owain: 'Gentle towards the gentle in the peaceful countryside, rough towards the rough at the clash of arms; sweet towards the sweet at the recounting of his greatness, bitter towards the bitter when strife is sought . . .'

Fratricidal strife broke out at Owain's death, resulting almost immediately in the death of Prince Hywel, perhaps the finest Welsh poet of his day. Again, there is no mention of Hywel's poetry in Cynddelw's eulogy although it is one of his longer poems. A great warrior had been lost: 'At the scattering, the sowing of iron (i.e. the hurling of spears), when he puts on courage, he can be heard.' The spirit and turmoil of war are powerfully conveyed in describing the fall of a tower at Cynfael: 'Noise like a crashing wave, the crackle of flames echoed from the hillside, and fragments of foam showering around.'

Pre-eminence over all Wales was to pass to Rhys ap Gruffudd. It would appear that Cynddelw had fallen out of favour with this southern prince. In an intercessionary panegyric he achieves a smoothness of perfection, the fruit of long experience and of mastery over his medium. He treats with disdain the hostility of the court: 'You court silencers, get me silence. Be silent you poets, you are about to hear a poet!' Soon the full significance of Rhys's reign is unfolded. Without faltering he runs through the gamut of praise in the approved manner, 'with the splendid authority of poetic art'. Rhys had turned the tide of Norman advance, and Cynddelw goes to the heart of the matter by proclaiming that he had restored the *Majesty of the South*. He had restored prestige to the Welsh language and tradition. Resurgence of pride in Welsh was a consequence of Rhys's success. It needed a poet of the highest order to express the new age adequately in verse; Rhys and Cynddelw had need of each other, and it was ridiculous that there should be coldness between them.

Two long odes to God are ascribed to Cynddelw, although there is a conflict of manuscript authority in the case of the more interesting of them. The other is a homily of typical medieval piety, ornate in style, but Cynddelw knows well the effect of an arresting simple sentence coming between involved constructions: e.g. *'Daioni fy Rhi a'm rhydda'* (It is the goodness of my Lord that will liberate me). The *Gogynfeirdd* were deeply divided on the sanctity of internal boundaries within Wales. For Cynddelw and some of his successors, as we shall see, these had a divine sanction, and he refers to the Deity as 'Lord of *all* boundaries'. 'We have been warned. Once there was Arthur... Julius Caesar has been... Brân ap Llŷr... performing feats in lands beyond his border, in battle, in conflict ... there was great Hercules... Alexander, ruler of the world, restless even unto the signs of the heavens—why do we not see, plagued with affliction, that all overreaching is destruction, ... the rejection of the Supreme Lord of all Scripture is a perverse misdoing.'

Cynddelw's deathbed poem is in striking contrast to Meilyr's. He did not feel that his tongue was halting, and it is in fact his last eulogy, composed with undiminished power. He begins with a paean of praise to the Creator of all things—morning and evening, streams, woodland and meadow, and 'true measure', fruit, grass and mountain heather. Then follow appeals for mercy: 'I am a foolish exile who has strayed from the blessed land,' and with great power of language he pleads before the 'King of Heaven' for admission to his 'glorious domain'. A crescendo of praise of Christ for his redeeming work, and then even in a petitionary poem he still finds room for pride in his poetic talent which he has always venerated as God's gift. The poem then builds up to an outburst of praise of God under several of His attributes, and he appeals to the 'Dawn of all Light' not to abandon him to that 'black loveless host'.

Where we get a glimpse of Cynddelw other than as a public figure is in three anguished *englynion* on the death of his son. Very seldom in medieval Welsh poetry do we see so far into a mind tortured by a private grief. He is cruelly torn between faith and despair. One moment he sees his son among the shining ones of the heavenly realm, succoured by God, but then: 'The world is a dreadful place without you, Dygynnelw—and God with you!' (Here surely more is meant than a mere farewell.) He is a broken man, he clutches for comfort at the thought, to which a later poet returns in his country's dark hour in 1282, that our griefs are precious in the eyes of God, but falls back into despair on which note the poem ends: 'A hidden grave—a lovely ending for Cynddelw.'

Two of the twelfth-century princes were themselves poets, composing for their own delight, and with a freshness seldom found among the professional bards. Owain Cyfeiliog, closely related to the three most powerful Welsh rulers of his day, held sway over the strategically-placed Cyfeiliog whence he could and did, descend in forays into the rich lowlands and hill country of the Severn border. Intelligent, known in the English court for his ready wit, and commended by Giraldus Cambrensis for the good government of his province, he was an intrepid warrior. In his joyous poem, *Hirlas Owain* (Owain's long blue drinking horn) he and his choice band of household troops are carousing after a successful raid on the Severn lowlands. Most of the 'stanzas' begin with the words 'Fill up, cupbearer', who is then ordered to pass the horn around to Rhys . . . to Ywain, Ednyfed, Tudur, Goronwy and the others. Brisk allusions are made to the day's adventures, and character sketches drawn with a few deft strokes. Cynfelyn is seen 'sublimely drunk from the foaming mead'. Echoes of the *Gododdin* ring through the poem, but the occasion is a happy one save for the loss of Moreiddig 'who will be greatly missed'. There is a startling example of that keen awareness of the natural scene which is such a marked feature of much Welsh and Irish medieval poetry. The war-band is hastening home from the skirmish: 'Sweat poured from all as they were returning, and lo! the Long Hill and the hollow were full of sun!'

Knowledge of the terrain was essential to the training of young warriors, and in a chain of englynion to Owain Cyfeiliog's *teulu* (household troops) are named in topographical order many places in northern and mid Wales. It is asked, 'Where shall we go from Forden?' One is sent ahead: 'Go, young man, quickly, and say we have reached Kerry . . . Arwystli . . . Penweddig . . .', and thence northward to Anglesey, and completing the circle eastward and southward. The tone is brisk and light-hearted: 'Go, young man, and speak to no-one, unless it be my lady-love. Make speed on a slender piebald mount, say we have reached Llannerch'.

Hywel ab Owain Gwynedd, the other prince-poet, could well express the excitement of battle: 'When ravens were gleeful, when blood gushed forth . . .', yet he is remembered rather for the sheer joy and bright flashing imagery of his nature and love poetry. He delights in summer when hills are well trodden, the apple trees adorned in white, and he sets out with gleaming white shield, but his mind soon turns to the fair *petite,* shapely in her youthfulness, and so refined that never a word comes from her mouth that is indelicate: 'O how confused I have become through the foolishness of love!' His modest fair lady is slender and fair, white in her purple dress, and he loves her for her demureness, her seemliness, her beauty, and her cultivated Welsh quietly spoken. In his *Gorhoffedd* he enthuses over the things he loves: the white-foaming wave flowing angrily past the homesteads, his lord, habitations, seashore and mountain, the stronghold, trees, meadows, waters and valleys, the white seagulls and the lovely ladies, soldiers and their fine steeds, clover-covered fields, but also the far-extending wild places. Again he sees the Merioneth seashore 'where a white arm was my pillow'.

In the second half of the *Gorhoffedd,* which may be a separate poem, Hywel sets out to sing the praises of his lady-loves, referring to them by name: Gwenllïan of the hue of summer, fair Gwerfyl, beautiful Gwladys whom he will praise while gorse is yellow, bright laughing Lleucu (whose husband does not laugh), lovely Nest of the hue of apple-blossom, Enerys, Hunydd and Hawis—yes he has had eight, and he could tell more, but 'teeth are good for biting the tongue!' Here and in a short poem by Cynddelw, that medieval stock figure, the jealous husband, who was later to become, if we can believe him, such a bane in the life of Dafydd ap Gwilym, makes his earliest appearances in extant Welsh poetry.

The Celtic custom of fosterage created a strong bond between foster-brothers. Natural brothers were often brought up as strangers, and the practice of gavelkind frequently led to dispute and jealousy. Hywel was reared in a family of warriors, that of Cedifor the Irishman, whose seven sons stood by their foster-brother to the death at Pentraeth (1170). One of the three survivors, Peryf ap Cedifor, in two chains of *englynion* gives vent to their virulent hatred of the sons of Cristina, Dafydd and Rhodri. These *englynion* provide an insight into family relationships, and Peryf was master of the arresting opening line: 'While we were seven, three sevens dared not challenge us.'

Gwynfardd Brycheiniog is the earliest and best court poet hailing from South Wales within the period covered in this chapter. The Lord Rhys had long been gathering strength and, after 1172, his authority, under Henry II, as 'Justice' extended all over South Wales. He held the King's favour until his death in 1189, when Rhys broke out again into campaigns of conquest rivalling those of his early years. Whether in peace or war, patriotic feeling ran high, and pride in the language was strong. Gwynfardd's two poems reflect this new confidence. His eulogy of Rhys in fifty lines of monorhyme has an impressive cumulative effect. 'Many battles for many strongholds before achieving peace' is a fitting comment. Resounding words are woven into a well-ordered pattern, and the poem achieves a climax where the extent of Rhys's authority and influence is symbolized by weaving together into its metrical pattern place-names, from Tren (the Tern in 'Shropshire') to Aber Taradr well beyond the eastern extremity of Gwent to places in the North around the Dee and the Severn: 'How delightful it is to take in Wales from end to end, exerting authority over Port Skewet and serving at feastings at Porth Wygyr in Anglesey.'

A vigorous ecclesiastical policy grew out of the Welsh resurgence. Giraldus's arduous but unsuccessful fight for the establishment of St. David's as a metropolitan see was an expression of the new spirit. Rhys on the one hand made much of the long religious traditions of Wales, and of St. David in particular, but at the same time he, like other Welsh princes, lavishly patronized the Cistercians, a new and vital element in the religious life of Europe. The long-term effect of this policy on Welsh culture was incalculable. Gwynfardd Brycheiniog's great poem to Dewi is fully in keeping with his patron's policy.

There is a shrewd remark towards the end, when the saints from far and wide gather together to pay their respects to Dewi, and among them are the saints of Anjou (Plantagenet propagandists please copy!). Whoever would praise Dewi, let him do so boldly in *good* Welsh, for Dewi is worthy of *learned* Welsh. We are reminded what the love of Dewi entails—the restraining of anger, avoiding theft, love of the Mass and care for those in need. The poet enthuses over St. David's and the pilgrims; among them the clergy, men of high degree, women and maidens, the learned. 'These', says Gwynfardd, 'are they whom I love, and I am one of them'. Churches dedicated to Dewi are named, including Henfynyw 'in its fields of clover and well-acorned trees'. Loyal as he is to Rhys he reminds us that the cult of Dewi implies 'loving God more than rulers', and he concludes with a mention of the gentleness of Dewi, and a plea for Divine mercy. Of all the many Welsh poems to the saints, Gwynfardd Brycheiniog's 'In praise of Dewi' is the finest.

Powys after the death of Madog ap Maredudd (1160), Gwynedd after Owain Gwynedd (1170) and the South after Rhys (1197) broke up into smaller and weaker units, often at loggerheads with each other, and it was a time of foreboding, but the very end of the century saw the meteoric rise of Llywelyn the Great. It meant riding roughshod over the rights of kinsmen and ignoring the sanctity of boundaries, but by consummate skill in diplomacy and war he bound most of Wales into a closer feudal unity than ever before, a process culminating in the recognition of his grandson, Llywelyn the Last, as 'Princeps Wallie'. The stakes were high and it is not strange that the court poets concentrate intensely on the pursuit of the Gwynedd policy, although they differ widely in their attitude towards it. Apart from religious poetry there is far less of other kinds, and nature and love themes figure but little. References to preaching, and more detailed references to Scriptural tales are among the signs suggesting the influence of the friars.

Forthrightness and moral fervour are marked features of Elidir Sais, or the 'Englishman'—so described possibly as a consequence of long exile in England. He did not approve of Llywelyn's ousting of his uncles, Rhodri and Dafydd. In a bitter elegy to Rhodri (died 1195), after an invocation to Mary and referring to what Christ was able to do with 'five loaves and the fishes', he laments the fate of 'Britain', lacking a just possessor now that Rhodri is lost. 'Would to God he could come again to put down aggressors.' Similarly in a religious poem of later date he compares to the conquest of Jerusalem by 'Syladin' the removal of Dafydd from his lands, and is appalled at Gwynedd remaining silent. Llywelyn could not have been pleased, and the tone of an intercessionary poem by Elidir could hardly have mollified him. The poem, which is not without its obscurities, opens with gnomic sayings, but Elidir then confesses his grief after the honourable brothers, pleads that he is unaccustomed to life as a wanderer, and beseeches Llywelyn, whose anger he describes as terrible, not to drive him from his wide and extensive territories. He offers counsel *('Cysul a roddaf*—a traditional gambit): 'Think what you do when you commit aggression over a border, bringing everyone down to his knees. Be a supporter of the weak, be just and gentle to those of rightful descent, let there be mercy within your strongholds of stone, and the love of God.' It does not appear that Llywelyn relented, and Elidir probably endured a long exile. A body of religious verse is attributed to him: 'I shall be God's poet as long as I am a man.' He refers to religious books it does not do to question, and 'there is much God will do for puny man'. Bearing the probable cause of his vicissitudes in mind, one feels there is more than mere orthodoxy in his cry that 'of all sins, the worst is pride'.

Elidir had long to wait but he rises to his full height in a poem following the death of Llywelyn in 1240. The metre chosen helps to secure the powerful onrushing effect. With God what counts is 'truth and civilized peace and genuine mercy. Woe to those whose trust, if they do wrong, is in the treacherous world that passes away.' 'I have seen Llywelyn, his hosts drawn from all parts of Wales; I have seen the leaders of Gwynedd and the

South, pillars of war bivouacked together; I have seen men in battle and spirited horses, and wine, a following of people and jousting. I have seen hosts, daily carousals, and success upon success. *That* has all vanished like the drop of your hand, all have to leave this passing world ... Let everyone ask himself while there is time what he really wants, what he dreads.' The true ideal is 'tranquil joy and a faith that prevails'. Christ will appear at the last day displaying his wounds, the marks of the scourgings, the nails, his blood and his Cross, and will ask, 'This is what I have done, what have you done?'

It is good to know Elidir came home after long exile. In 1246, he stood in awe by the grave of Ednyfed Fychan, seneschal of Gwynedd, a man of power in his day: 'Above the fresh grave of Ednyfed have I been; my tears streaming'.

It was Giraldus Cambrensis who said of the Welsh how fortunate they would be if they had but one prince, and he a good one. Of all the court poets who applauded the *Machtpolitik* of the House of Gwynedd the most forthright was Llywarch ap Llywelyn, or Prydydd y Moch. He stressed as no poet had done before the 'inherent right' of whoever ruled Aberffraw to suzerainty over all Wales, and the duty of all local rulers to submit to him. Dafydd ab Owain had a precarious hold over Aberffraw for a year or so, and Llywarch reminds him it was not love that had made him what he was, 'but spears piercing their way from his hand, and a red blade in the hand of a warrior, ferocity, the clash of arms, the fury of the sword and the smashing of skulls.' Thus did he establish a *'cadr heddwch'* (a strong peace). It was not always well, however, between Dafydd and Llywarch, but the poet was so sure of his status that he did not resort to a plea for forgiveness, but to very plain speaking, standing on the dignity of the poetic art over which he claimed mastery. 'You, ruler of the West, should do well by me; to insult me is to cast aspersions on my art. Better am I to you than many horses and their riders journeying afar on your errands.' This gives an interesting sidelight on the influence that a *pencerdd* claimed he exerted in the community, and on the relationship between ruler and court poet. Llywarch was later to confront even Llywelyn the Great with the bold and succinct phrase, 'Me—Llywarch; You—Llywelyn'.

When Rhodri came to rule from Aberffraw, his 'inherent right' was proclaimed by Llywarch, but he rises to his full height in acclaiming the rise of Llywelyn to his great power. He met the charge of overreaching by Llywelyn with the assertion that presumption is on the part of anyone who withstood the claims of Aberffraw's ruler. He invites the men of Powys to consider who he is, and asks them which is better, a 'Frenchman' or a generous Welshman. The concept that Welshness requires allegiance to the one prince is taking shape. Those who cried 'Peace, peace,' are reminded of Llywelyn's achievement: 'Tonight, wherever you look there is peace'.

Technically the *Canu Bychan* (the Short Poem) is the most interesting of the eulogies by Llywarch to Llywelyn. The onrushing metre is that of Elidir Sais's great poem, but how different are the sentiments. The widespread power and extreme mobility of Llywelyn's host throughout Wales are excitingly conveyed by the sudden juxtaposition of place-names from far distant parts of the country: 'In the court of Aberffraw patronizing the poetic art, in Carmarthen a myriad spears. In Degannwy, in Swansea, powerfully marching on Kidwelly, in Caernarfon songs of praises, and in Chester my hero has been. In Shrewsbury . . . in pleasant Cardigan, in fierce Ellesmere, in famed St. Clears, in courtly Brecon, in Montgomery with his household troops in Kerry, in restless Haverfordwest, in beautifully situated Rhuddlan on Teifi . . . in Rhuddlan in Tegeingl, holding court at Mold . . .'

In a poem to Rhys Gryg, who held sway under Llywelyn, as Llywarch is at pains to mention, the place-names of the South are similarly recalled to mind, and there is the same reminder that the path of war had led to peace. 'In turbulent Swansea, the towers are broken, and today there surely is peace.'

It was a commonplace for a eulogy or elegy to begin with an invocation to the Deity, but there is one such poem where the pious introduction is extended to become the greater part of the poem, and the traditionally praised qualities of the ruler are given a minor place. It is the elegy of Gruffudd ap Gwrgenau to Gruffudd ap Cynan ab Owain Gwynedd (d. 1200). Gruffudd, a poet of no mean merit, had evidently pondered much over the teachings of the Church, and the elegy opens with a magnificent line, where the effect is caused not only by splendour of imagery, but by a most effective contrast between consonant repetition and the variation of long vowels and diphthongs: *'Gŵr a gynneil y lloer yn ei llawnedd'* (He who supports the moon in its full phase). It is, however, in his one other extant poem that Gruffudd achieves the perfection of his art. It is a chain of six *englynion* arranged like the 'stanzas' of the *Gododdin* to express with great poignancy the loss of fallen comrades, each mentioned by name, and then in the last *englyn* a sudden change to muted rhyme *(proest)*. One friend alone is left, and he will die. The thud of the half-rhyming heavily accented monosyllables—*'grym', —'drwm',* prepares one for the utter desolation of the final line: *'Oddyna/ni bydd dda/ddim'* (Henceforth, there will be value in—*nothing).*

Llywelyn Fardd is credited with eulogistic verse in *englyn* and *awdl* metres addressed to several rulers, and with a few religious poems including one on a well-worn medieval theme, 'Signs before Doomsday'. Horror at the brittleness of life is powerfully conveyed in an elegy to a Cedifor who presumably had lived in a place where the poet was known in his youth, for he anticipates Goronwy Owen by five centuries in exclaiming of his former acquaintances: 'There is none where a hundred have been'. Llywelyn's masterpiece, however, is his long poem nominally in praise of St. Cadfan, but in fact to the church of Tywyn, Merioneth, and its *clas* of resident clergy whose hospitality the poet had enjoyed. It is a eulogy of civilized life as seen at Tywyn under the abbot Morfran. Like St. David's it is a seat of 'faith, religion, trust, and communion', in the image delineated by God himself. The limewashed church is in 'a valley without tension, without false religion, where the Cross and the offerings and the trees are well kept, by the sea and the shore and the high mountains'. Strife and warfare it is spared, and within the context of true Christian devotion there is room for civilized living 'where there are fine things, and poets, and versifying, tranquillity and mead in vessels, fine conversation and admirable men without dishonour or hardness'. Fifteenth-century Welsh poets are also much given to conviviality in Cistercian houses, but the balance is altogether different, a whole dimension lost, and the sociability not seen so clearly within a framework where the religious life is a reality.

Much of the finest religious poetry of their day was composed by two sons of Gwalchmai, Einion and Meilyr. Einion is the only Welsh poet after Taliesin and Myrddin to become a figure in Welsh folklore. He saw the rise of Llywelyn as the 'swirl of a great windstorm in a surly February'. The finest poem to a woman by a Welsh court poet after Hywel ab Owain Gwynedd is Einion's elegy to Nest. There are several examples of *Gogynfeirdd* elegies opening with lines of natural description, and the relevance or otherwise of these lines can vary. Einion is most effective in the contrast he feels. It is Maytime, the lovely colour of the groves, the chatter of birds, the calm of the sea and the gentle breezes are at utter variance with the poet's mood. He is sad and shedding salt tears, having lost the 'candle of Cadfan's church in her silken robe, a woman without deceit. The red soil covers her in silence who had been so light-hearted and sportive. No living man can feel as I do; anguished am I like Pryderi; no remedy do I know. This is no idle talk, a low hidden shroud torments me. Never was anyone so dear to me as she', and he finds it difficult to believe that even God himself would want to be separated from her.

Einion's religious poetry is imbued with the same simple sincerity and delicacy. He yearns for purity—'a few sins are too many'—and dwells feelingly on the sufferings of Christ. He would go on pilgrimage over the Alps to the Holy Land, and would end his days in Bardsey, an island 'surrounded by the foam like the fringe of a dress'. He would eschew 'crooked words, vain passion, lust of women, the planning of warfare, and other causes of woe'. His praises of God in verse he would wish to be like prayers. A crescendo in a divine poem presents a series of things men find delightful, such as 'mead and the feastings of a victorious ruler, a long bright summer, a well-fed horse in April, the play of spears and the waving of banners', but more delightful in the end he finds the cultivated praise of God springing from the heart. 'His bard I will be', sang his brother Meilyr, and all his extant work is in praise of God. He sees God's people as one *clas* (the ecclesiastical 'familia') or as one *teulu* (family), and in a poem attributed to him, but also to his father, he refers to 'the Trinity, a Unity to which I am akin.'

Madog ap Gwallter, a Franciscan, can hardly be described as a court poet, but he had mastered their technique and adapted it to his purpose. The leonine hexameters he wrote under the name *'Frater Walensis Madocus Edeirnianensis'* express strong patriotic sentiments, but the three Welsh poems are very different. A native of Llanfihangel Glyn Myfyr, then considered part of Edeirnion, he composed a chain of *englynion* to the Archangel Michael, patron of his parish, dwelling mainly on his encounter with the 'serpent': 'With your long lance, now in the keen battle, break the teeth of Babel's ruler. Never has it been more needed, Michael, such is the guile of that unseen monster'. His *awdl* to God reveals the same dread of the power of evil. He likens the soul of man to a beleaguered city whose walls are crumbling like dry soil, and he calls on the five senses to act as watchmen. The *imago Dei* is not lost, but is heavily overlaid with sin, and Madog urges men to consider the dignity of their origin. He would flee from being 'splashed' by the mud of this world, and defends his fugitive attitude by reminding us that the world itself is fugitive.

Madog is best known for his Nativity poem, the earliest in Welsh. He tells the story (and that in itself is unusual in the Welsh poetic tradition) in the *rhupunt* metre. In less skilful hands the slow staccato movement with the heavily loaded rhyme-scheme can easily become wearisome, but Madog charms by a freshness and simplicity reminiscent of the well-known paintings of the early Franciscans: 'No greater marvel will ever be, lips can't express it . . . the mighty little giant, strong, powerful, frail, with pale cheeks . . . his chair a little heap of hay'. The Kings arrive: 'To the house they go, without door or frame, windy doorways. His mother seated on the ground, her precious breast to His lips. A man they see, in a God they believe, it is well that they believe'. The simplicity of diction is rendered more effective by being set in a complex metrical pattern, the whole conveying a feeling of wonder and adoration.

Cynddelw held the poets of the southern courts in low esteem, and he would have thought no better of their successors if we are to judge by the numerous chains of depressingly conventional *englynion* and the few *awdlau* by Phylip Brydydd and Y Prydydd Bychan that have survived. The interest of Y Prydydd Bychan's work is mainly for historical reasons. Even in the days of Welsh rule it appears that the status of the *pencerdd* could be insecure in the southern courts. Precedence was given at feastings in Llanbadarn Fawr, for instance, to low-grade poets with 'their many foolish tales'. (Would that more of these tales had survived, for then the Mabinogion would not be such an isolated feature in Welsh literature.) The *Hengerdd* of Taliesin is ever new, and Y Prydydd Bychan takes his stand with him and with the poets of Maelgwn Gwynedd, and would sing only 'truth'. (How Gildas would have lifted an eyebrow!)

Dafydd Benfras was the leading court poet of Llywelyn the Great at the height of his power. He lived on to lament the deaths of his sons, Dafydd and Gruffudd, and to celebrate the heyday of Llywelyn the Last, but was spared the final *débâcle*. Whilst consciously modelling himself on Cynddelw and Llywarch, he and the younger Bleddyn Fardd brought to fruition the new smoothness of line and the simplification of diction. The *pencerdd,* we are told in the grammatical tracts, was called upon to sing the praises of God and then of the prince. It would seem that a few 'token' lines of divine praise were often 'got over' quickly before launching on the real business of the day, but not so in a poem by Dafydd Benfras where about half the poem is given to a realistic description of the Harrowing of Hell. Somewhat comically to our way of thinking, after establishing this precedent the poet suddenly turns to the one whom, after Christ, he calls the 'second best', and applauds his 'harrowing' as far as the Shropshire Tern. The directness of style he has mastered served him in good stead during the violent swings of fortune that followed the death of Llywelyn ab Iorwerth, the 'great head of Wales and its *orderliness'*. The 'spirit of the world is in confusion' after his going. The calamitous death of Gruffudd left the land leaderless, and the poet is driven in on himself in keen soul-searching. He must have been reflecting a mood that many felt: 'Let us give more heed to the preaching. We have all been guilty of *hubris* and overreaching. There is no doubt we have all been too aggressive, and Christ has now made us too sad'.

In an elegy to Llywelyn and his two sons, an ironic twist is given to the Maytime gambit: 'It is May, the stream is getting lower and lower.' He lived however to see the rise of the last Llywelyn, a glorious *'dadanhudd'* while it lasted, drawing its meaning as the culmination of an ancient struggle, and the 'Bernicians' had again to be prevented from 'crashing through Offa's Dyke!' His model for his triumphant ode to Llywelyn's success is based on Llywarch's *Canu Bychan,* only the place-names are arranged this time in topographical sequence, Llywelyn taking possession of region by region in turn like the advance of a mighty wave.

Like Cynddelw he sang the praises not only of rulers but of the leading men under them, men who formed a rising class. As Cynddelw had sung to Rhiryd Flaidd, so did Dafydd Benfras lament the death of Gruffudd, son of Ednyfed Fychan. The princes were 'liquidated' in 1282-83, but the continuing of patronage of the bards, and the perpetuation of their art and their ideals, were assured by men of this class, together with

Cistercian abbots, who assumed the role of leadership.

For a century and a half since the rise of Gruffudd ap Cynan, the Welsh in spite of all temporary reverses of fortune had experienced a growing self-realization as a people. The success of the House of Gwynedd was shaping a new outlook, and by 1267 the unity of Wales was recognized by the English crown in the title of *Princeps Wallie*. For a decade the culmination of long political advance seemed to have been achieved, and the poet who celebrated this culmination was Llygad Gŵr, of Hendwr in Edeirnion. His five *awdlau* to Llywelyn the Last are a magnificent expression of that prince's achievement, and the mood it engendered. He had united the three provinces and claimed the allegiance of all Welshmen, and had stood up for them 'against a foreign nation of alien speech'. The unity of Wales, based on one language and the hard-fought-for welding together into one principality under a prince of their own blood and speech was what Llywelyn had attained, and Llygad Gŵr's stirring verse is the finest expression we have of the elation and outlook of that brief decade.

The age-old scruples were however still causing heartburning in some quarters. Llywelyn was forced to incarcerate his own brother, Owain Goch, for long years. Two poems by Hywel Foel ap Griffri have survived. One has the arresting opening line *'Gŵr/ysydd yn nhŵr/yn hir westi'* (A man who is in the tower, long a guest). The many years of captivity are felt in the long vowels, and the irony of *'gwesti'* (guest, or even a one night's guest) is biting. Hywel upbraids Llywelyn: 'Why does not brother forgive brother? It pertains only to God to dispossess a man'.

The final calamity wrung from two poets of no mean stature their finest work. Bleddyn Fardd was oppressed by the feeling that the lamps were all going out. He had lived to see the loss of the six—Llywelyn the Great, his two sons and three grandsons, and he realized it was the end of the world he knew. 'The men of Gwynedd, woe is me for their loss; alas, they are all dying.' Then there comes to his mind a vaticinatory poem attributed to Myrddin (Merlin), 'Woe to the birch tree in the Vale of Wye; its branches fall—each one, every two.' Thus are conveyed awe, inevitability and the sense of doom. Bewilderment at the death of Owain Goch is likened to that of Eve on being ejected from the Garden. In the elegy to the three sons of Gruffudd symbolic use is made of a nature description with which the poem opens. It is winter-time, and there is a cold film of frost over Snowdonia now. His is the only thirteenth-century death-couch poem that has survived. Before leaving this world, which is like a dream, he pleads for forgiveness, and in the description of the hell he would avoid, he draws, surely, on the hell he has known, 'where there is great sorrow, with no-one to intercede for us, where our foes extol falsehood, and where there is suffering without respite'.

The elegy to Llywelyn is undoubtedly Bleddyn's greatest poem: moving, brilliantly thought out, and where every word is weighed and wonderfully set in the pattern. In the invocation with which the poem begins, Christ is addressed as he who bore the greatest pain. It is to common manhood and the community of suffering that the poet appeals: 'What I have to say refers to a *man.*' In the hour of confusion he appeals for steadiness: '*A bortho ofid bid bwyllocaf*' (He who bears grief let him be the most restrained). He finds consolation in the thought that Christ came into the world so that Adam's children should not suffer the pains of hell. In referring to the vicarious sufferings of Christ, he declares that Llywelyn also was killed for 'us'. Is it not the implication that vicarious suffering by a man of his quality is never in vain? The reference to Priam would, to people familiar with the Trojan legend, offer the hope that a seemingly final calamity could be a new beginning. It is a courageous poem, and artistically perfect, for form and content are most skilfully matched.

The better-known and far longer elegy to Llywelyn by Gruffudd ab yr Ynad Goch (Son of the Red Judge,) is the most powerful expression in the language of dismay and unrelieved black despair. It is at the same time a miracle of art. The one main rhyme, - *aw,* - *aw,* - *aw,* like an unending wail occurs ninety-four times. Several surges of grief are expressed in the repetition of emotive initial words over a series of lines: 'Many a streaming tear coursing down cheeks, many a blood-stained side gashed, many a widow bewailing him, many a fatherless son, many a ruined homestead in the track of the conflagration, many an anguished cry as after Camlan . . .' The disturbances of nature are more than mere pathetic fallacy for it was an age-old folk belief of great power that 'these signs forerun the death and fall of kings'. 'Do you not see the track of the wind and the rain, do you not see oak striking oak, do you not see the sea shrivelling up the land, do you not see truth trimming itself, do you not see how the stars are fallen? Why do you not believe in God, you crazy people? Do you not see that the world is withered; would to God that the sea come over the land; why are we left to linger?'

Several religious poems of great descriptive power and eloquence are also attributed to Gruffudd ab yr Ynad Coch. They are marked by the same directness of statement and smooth mastery of a complicated metrical pattern as the Elegy, and by intense moral earnestness: 'If man only thought of the intensity of pain in His hands from the nails tearing his flesh, he would not commit sin or hanker after it'. Unsparing realism in describing the fate of the damned is enforced by grim irony: 'The fair long and disastrous, the oven of darkness, and each one with eyes fixed on his paws'—that is, crouching in fear and with all vestige of humanity lost. It is small wonder that the poet exclaims: 'May I not be an accuser; may I not be a fomenter of strife, may I not be unlovable, a *honer* of falsehood'—putting a sharp edge on it to one's own destruction.

BIBLIOGRAPHY

Text:
  Llawysgrif Hendregadredd, Cardiff, 1933.
  The Poetry in the Red Book of Hergest (reproduced and edited by J.

Gwenogvryn Evans), Llanbedrog, 1911.

Hen Gerddi Crefyddol, edited by Henry Lewis, Cardiff, 1931.

The Myvyrian Archaiology of Wales, Vol. I, London, 1801; Second edition (in one volume), Denbigh, 1870.

The Poetry of the Gogynfeirdd from The Myvyrian . . . Edited by Edward Anwyl, Denbigh, 1902.

Translations:

Joseph P. Clancy, *The Earliest Welsh Poetry,* London, Macmillan, 1970.

Anthony Conran, *The Penguin Book of Welsh Verse,* 1967.

D. M. and E. M. Lloyd, *A Book of Wales,* London, Collins, 1953 and later editions. (Contains poems by several of the *Gogynfeirdd,* and passages from medieval manuscripts on the 'Bardic Functions' and 'How to praise each thing.')

Critical Works in English:

Articles on 'Welsh Literature' in recent editions of the *Encyclopaedia Britannica* (W. J. Gruffydd and Thomas Jones) and in *Chambers' Encyclopaedia* (Thomas Jones).

T. Gwynn Jones, 'Bardism and Romance', *Transactions of the Honourable Society of Cymmrodorion,* Session 1913-14.

H. Idris Bell, *The Development of Welsh Poetry,* Clarendon, 1936.

Thomas Parry, *A History of Welsh Literature,* translated by H. Idris Bell, Clarendon, 1955.

J. Lloyd-Jones, 'The Court Poets of the Welsh Princes', *Proceedings of the British Academy,* 1948.

Gwyn Williams, *An Introduction to Welsh Poetry,* Faber, 1953.

D. M. Lloyd, 'Some Metrical Features in Gogynfeirdd Poetry,' *Studia Celtica,* III (1968), 39.

Critical Works in Welsh:

The most recent and comprehensive study is by Professor J. E. Caerwyn Williams, 'Beirdd y Tywysogion: Arolwg,' *Llên Cymru,* Vol. XI, Jan-July 1970 (to be continued).

Part of the Vaunting Poem of Hywel ap Owain Gwynedd. Hendregadredd ms.

The Red and White Dragons' fight at Vortigern's Court, see Loomis, No. 349, Lambeth, St. Alban's Chronicle, f.43, c. 1460.

CHAPTER VIII

EARLY PROSE: THE MABINOGI

GLYN E. JONES

The literary tradition of Wales, as has already been shown in several of the preceding chapters, was from the earliest times an oral one. The poems, tales, sagas and historical traditions were all transmitted by means of the spoken word for centuries by a professional class of poets and story-tellers, known as *cyfarwyddiaid*. Only a portion of this literature has been preserved in manuscript form, and practically none of the early prose as opposed to the poetry. For example, of the popular prose-verse sagas in which the narrative itself was composed in prose, the dialogue and monologue in verse, only some of the verse portions have survived in manuscripts. The earliest examples of these are the ninth century *englynion* found in the Juvencus manuscript in the Cambridge University Library. These stanzas are probably the remnants of a lost prose-verse saga. The probable existence of an early oral prose literature should be borne in mind when we come to study the earliest prose literature which has been preserved in manuscripts, for we find that this literature is mature and sophisticated and obviously springs from a long and developed tradition of composition in prose.

Yet, the earliest extant texts written in the Welsh language are not literary at all, but are of a highly practical nature. The oldest surviving text written in Welsh is the eighth century *Surexit*-memorandum in the Book of St. Chad, a MS. of the Gospels, now in the Cathedral Library, Lichfield, but originally kept at Llandeilo Fawr, Carmarthenshire. It is a short text in Old Welsh (as the language of the period 800-1100 is known) and Latin, telling of a lawsuit over land. It is probably a copy of an earlier original. Apart from a number of glosses in Old Welsh from the ninth to the eleventh centuries, there are two other main texts, the Computus Fragment and *Braint Teilo*. The Computus Fragment is a piece of some twenty-three lines in Old Welsh, dealing with the calendar. It is preserved in a MS. in the Cambridge University Library, and was probably written in the first quarter of the tenth century. *Braint Teilo,* found in the twelfth-century manuscript known as *Llyfr Llandaf* ('The Book of Llandaf'), is a document stating the bishopric of Llandaf's rather dubious claims to certain rights and immunities. Linguistically it is a text of some interest since it is an example of prose from the period of transition from Old to Medieval Welsh. It is dated late eleventh or early twelfth century. It was probably within the same period that the greatest treasure of our prose literature was composed. This is the collection of tales known as *Pedair Cainc y Mabinogi,* and it is with these tales that we shall be concerned for the remainder of this chapter.

Pedair Cainc y Mabinogi ('The Four Branches of the Mabinogi') survive complete in two manuscripts only, *Llyfr Gwyn Rhydderch* ('The White Book of Rhydderch') and *Llyfr Coch Hergest* ('The Red Book of Hergest'), with fragments of the Second and Third Branches only in one other manuscript—Peniarth MS. 6. The dates of the portions of these three manuscripts in which these tales occur extend from *c.* 1225 to *c.* 1425. The tales are given their title from a colophon at the end of each of the branches, which has a formula to the effect: 'Thus ends this branch *(cainc)* of the *mabinogi';* hence, they are collectively known as *Pedair Cainc y Mabinogi.* The individual branches are commonly referred to as *Mabinogi Pwyll, Mabinogi Branwen, Mabinogi Manawydan* and *Mabinogi Math.* These tales, and others not really associated with them, have been known to the public under the title *The Mabinogion* since they were published under that title in Lady Charlotte Guest's celebrated edition (1838-49), but the form *'mabynnogyon',* occurring only in *Mabinogi Pwyll,* is almost certainly a scribal error for *mabinogi.* The term originally meant 'youth', then 'a tale of youth', and finally simply a 'tale' or 'story'. Thus *cainc o'r mabinogi* means a branch, part or portion of the whole story.

These tales were composed at a much earlier date than that of the manuscripts in which they survive. The late Sir Ifor Williams, on orthographic and linguistic evidence, placed their composition in the latter half of the eleventh century. A more recent study of the whole question of their date of composition, by Dr. T. M. Charles-Edwards, with special attention to some aspects of the society depicted in these tales,—some of which are quite archaic, as the evidence of the legal terminology and institutions shows (particularly in *Mabinogi Pwyll*),—has forcibly argued for a date of composition between 1050 and 1120.

A brief outline of the content of these tales will give us some idea of the nature of the material that they contain. *Mabinogi Pwyll:* (i) The story of an adventure Pwyll, lord of Dyfed, had in Annwfn (the Otherworld), after which he was called Pwyll, lord of Annwfn. (ii) The meeting of Pwyll and Rhiannon at Gorsedd Arberth, and their subsequent marriage. (iii) Rhiannon gives birth to Pryderi, who is stolen from her bedside. She is blamed for his disappearance and punished. (iv) The restoration of Pryderi to his parents. *Mabinogi Branwen:* (i) Branwen is given in marriage to Matholwch, king of Ireland. Her enraged half-brother, Efnisien, mutilates Matholwch's horses. Matholwch is given a magic cauldron in recompense. (ii) In Ireland, Branwen is punished for the insult to Matholwch. (iii) Bendigeidfran, her brother, sails to Ireland with his armies to avenge her. Only seven men, Pryderi among them, and Branwen survive the battle and return with Bendigeidfran's severed head. (iv) Branwen dies, and the seven survivors spend a period feasting in Harlech and Gwales, but on opening a forbidden door have to leave and go to bury Bendigeidfran's head in London. *Mabinogi Manawydan:* (i) Manawydan fab Llŷr marries Rhiannon, Pryderi's mother. (ii) Enchantment falls on Dyfed and Manawydan and Pryderi spend a period in England. On their return to Dyfed, Pryderi and Rhiannon become entrapped in a magic fortress which vanishes. (iii) Manawydan succeeds in lifting the enchantment and freeing Pryderi and Rhiannon. *Mabinogi Math:* (i) Math, lord of Gwynedd, can only live with his feet in a maiden's lap, except when he is involved in war. Gilfaethwy, son of Dôn, falls in love with the maiden, Goewin. (ii) Gwydion, Gilfaethwy's brother, tricks Pryderi into exchanging his swine (which had come from Annwfn) for enchanted horses and dogs. Pryderi pursues them to Gwynedd, and while Math musters Gwynedd, Gilfaethwy rapes Goewin. (iii) The death of Pryderi. (iv) The story of Lleu Llaw Gyffes, whose mother swore he would never have a name, bear arms, or obtain a wife from among mortals. Gwydion and Math revoke all three destinies. (v) The betrayal of Lleu by his wife Blodeuwedd and her lover.

Clearly, there is here a fusion of a mass of different tales, themes and traditions. Stemming from Gwent, Dyfed and Gwynedd, the stories themselves are tales of wonder and of magic, one marvellous event following swiftly upon the other. From the *Gorsedd* (mound) of Arberth (modern Narberth in Pembrokeshire) no nobleman departs without either receiving wounds or seeing a marvel; here Pwyll meets Rhiannon on her magic steed, and after an ascent of this mound, as *Mabinogi Manawydan* tells us, a mist falls upon Dyfed, leaving Pryderi and Manawydan and their wives in a land of desolation. Other themes are the cauldron given to Matholwch, *y pair dadeni* ('cauldron of resuscitation'), which restored life to those killed in battle, but not their speech; the enchanted fortress into which Pryderi was led by a strange white boar; the witchcraft of Gwydion who, with Math, created a wife for Lleu Llaw Gyffes from the flowers of the oak, the broom and the meadow-sweet. A number of familiar international motifs are immediately apparent, such as *The Calumniated Wife, The Forbidden Door* and *The Unfaithful Wife,* to mention but three.

The tales are set in an aristocratic milieu. The manners, habits and customs are those of the court. The pastimes are hunting, feasting and carousing and entertainment by the traditional *cyfarwydd* or story-teller. But many of the *dramatis personae* are in origin old gods and goddesses of Celtic mythology, having their counterparts in early Irish saga. The Children of Dôn, so prominent in *Mabinogi Math,* correspond to the *Túatha Dé Danann* ('Peoples of the Goddess Donu') of Irish tradition. Lleu, whose name survives in Nantlleu and Dinas Dinlleu (modern Nantlle and Dinas Dinlle in Caernarfonshire) and incidentally in the European cities of Lyon, Laon and Leyden, has his counterpart in Lugh, and Manawydan fab Llŷr matches the Irish Manannán mac Lir. Above them all towers Brân or Bendigeidfran fab Llŷr, identified by scholars as the prototype of Bron, the Fisher King of the Grail legend.

We do not know who gave these tales their extant form. An eleventh-century bishop of St. David's, Sulien, or his son, or both in collaboration have been suggested, but all scholars are agreed that whoever composed them was an artist of great skill and a master of prose. He was of south Welsh origin, a native probably of Dyfed. His provenance is suggested by the prominence of the Dyfed hero Pryderi, who is present in all the four branches, by the preference shown for Dyfed in the third branch, *Mabinogi Manawydan,* and by the obvious sorrow expressed in the grief of Pryderi's men after his death in combat with Gwydion in *Mabinogi Math.*

As to the author's sources, the most difficult question is how much of his work is directly derived from the narrative tradition, how much is the product of his own creative ability and imagination, and how much comes from other external sources. Obviously, a great deal of his material came from oral tradition. Various other sources, such as the triads and the references of the medieval poets, are evidence of the existence of other independent versions of material found in the Four Branches, but the extent to which the author was indebted to the oral narrative tradition is a matter concerning which scholars differ. We do occasionally, however, have a glimpse of the manner in which he handles material deriving from the oral narrative tradition. Attention has frequently been drawn to the fact that the story-teller has sometimes employed obvious duplicates of the tale he narrates. This duplicating undoubtedly reflects in some instances varying oral versions of the traditions that he drew upon, and *Mabinogi Branwen* offers an interesting and illuminating example of the fusion of two variants of the one tale in the portion of the branch dealing with the story of the feast in Harlech and Gwales.

After the battle in Ireland between Bendigeidfran's men and the Irish, only Branwen and seven men survive to return to Wales, bearing with them Bendigeidfran's severed head. Bendigeidfran had instructed them to take his head with them to Harlech where they were to spend seven years feasting, entertained by the birds of Rhiannon. Then they were to proceed to Gwales (the island of Grassholm) where they could remain on condition that they did not open a forbidden door which faced Cernyw (Cornwall); once they broke the prohibition, they were to leave and bury Bendigeidfran's head in London. The seven duly returned from Ireland and journeyed to Anglesey where Branwen died and was buried on the banks of the river Alaw. They spent seven years feasting in Harlech, as foretold by Bendigeidfran, and then journeyed south to Gwales. There they feasted in joy, with all their sorrow forgotten. One day, one of the seven, Heilyn fab Gwyn Hen, opens the forbidden door and all their sorrows return to them and they must depart and bury Bendigeidfran's head in London.

This complete episode is referred to in the text of the tale as *Yspydawt Urdaul Benn* ('The Feast of the Noble/Wondrous Head'), and *Yspydaut Benn* ('The Feast of the Head'), and also as *Yspadawt Uran* ('The Feasting-Hall of Brân'). It is at once apparent that the accounts of the feasts in Harlech and in Gwales are duplicates of one and the same story. It is the same characters who are present at both feasts, and in the titles referred to above, the form *ysbyddawd* ('feast') is in the singular, so obviously only one feast originally took place. Why, then, does *Mabinogi Branwen* tell us of two feasts? The answer is, that the whole episode in the tale is based upon two variant versions of the story, two versions that are attested elsewhere. The 'Gwales' version is referred to in a poem in the thirteenth-century manuscript known as *Llyfr Taliesin* ('The Book of Taliesin'). It was clearly independent of *Mabinogi Branwen*, from which it differs in many details. The 'Harlech' version is attested by two fifteenth-century poets, whose references are to the feast in Harlech. Evidently that was the version of the tradition known to them. Our author, obviously familiar with both versions, fused the two together by the simple expedient of stating in Bendigeidfran's instructions to the seven survivors, that they were to spend a period in both Harlech and Gwales. He thus neatly side-stepped the difficulty arising from having two different localities for the feast in his sources.

This episode illustrates two aspects of the question of the relationship between the literary tale and its oral antecedents. On the one hand, we see that the basic material is directly derived from the oral narrative tradition. On the other, the fusion is entirely literary, the product of our author's own creative ability and artistry, and the extent to which the details of the story now deviated from its oral sources can only be a matter for surmise.

One cannot leave this particular portion of the Four Branches without reference to its author's artistry, so brilliantly displayed in the account of the feast in Gwales and its sorrowful ending. The whole is a miniature masterpiece. In the words of Professors Gwyn and Thomas Jones, 'he achieved the effect of illumination and extension of time and space which lies beyond the reach of all save the world's greatest writers'. Here is the account:

> And at the end of the seventh year they set out for Gwales in Penfro. And there was for them there a fair royal place overlooking the sea, and a great hall it was. And they went into the hall, and two doors they saw open; the third door was closed, that towards Cornwall. 'See yonder,' said Manawydan, 'the door we must not open.' And that night they were

there without stint, and were joyful. And notwithstanding all the sorrows they had seen before their eyes, and notwithstanding that they had themselves suffered, there came to them no remembrance either of that or of any sorrow in the world. And there they passed the fourscore years so that they were not aware of having ever spent a time more joyous and delightful than that. It was not more irksome than when they came there, nor could any tell by his fellow that it was so long a time. Nor was it more irksome having the head with them alive . . . This is what Heilyn son of Gwyn did one day. 'Shame on my beard,' said he, 'if I do not open the door to know if that is true which is said concerning it.' He opened the door and looked on Cornwall and Aber Henfelen. And when he looked, they were as conscious of every loss they had ever sustained, and of every kinsman and friend they had missed, and of every ill that had come upon them, as if it were even then it had befallen them; and above all else because of their lord. And from that same moment they could not rest, save they set out with the head towards London.

What then of the origin and development of the materials which crystallized into the Four Branches? The late Professor W. J. Gruffydd, whose researches have been an outstanding contribution to the study of these tales, viewed them as an organic whole, which had grown from an original nucleus over a long period of oral development, during which they were passed from one generation of professional story-tellers to another, finally reaching their extant form at the hands of a story-teller of immense literary achievements. Another theory, put forward by Professor K. H. Jackson, argues that they had no such continuity of development, but were rather ill-remembered fragments of older stories, cleverly woven together by a particularly gifted writer of prose. The most serious challenge to Gruffydd's viewpoint is presented in Dr. Proinsias Mac Cana's study of the Second Branch, *Mabinogi Branwen*. Here, it is argued that this branch, at least, had no claim to having a prolonged period of oral development behind it, but was rather the conscious literary creation of its author, a great deal of whose inspiration and material was derived from Irish literature. This theory, therefore, implies a complete rejection of Gruffydd's thesis that all four branches had a simultaneous development over a long period of time in the oral narrative tradition. Like Mac Cana, Gruffydd also laid heavy emphasis on the influence of Irish literature on the content of the Four Branches, but through oral rather than literary channels. Indeed, the doctrine of 'Ireland the donor and Wales the receiver', so prevalent in the field of archaeology, has also applied to studies of the Four Branches. Irish literature, both literary and oral, has been an important source of external influence on the content matter of the Four Branches, especially in the case of *Mabinogi Branwen* as Dr. Mac Cana has shown, and relations between Ireland and Gwynedd, in particular, were very close in the second half of the eleventh century when Gruffudd ap Cynan, who had been reared and had spent many years in exile in Ireland, became king of Gwynedd. Irish influence has however been over-emphasized. Many of the parallels between the two literatures spring from the common Celtic inheritance of the two countries, and there probably existed a body of stories, themes and motifs shared in common by both countries within the unity of the Irish Sea Province.

The theories concerning the origin and development of the Four Branches all have their individual merits, but only W. J. Gruffydd's theories, embracing as they do all four branches, have provided a coherent synthesis which offers a convincing explanation of the genesis and development of the underlying materials. This is not to deny that there are many points in Gruffydd's theories which lack proof and often stretch the bounds of credibility, and that there are many factors capable of a quite different interpretation. Gruffydd's intuition often led him where facts would not.

In their main outline, Gruffydd's theories proceed as follows. The original nucleus or *'mabinogi'* was that of Pryderi, the legendary hero of Dyfed. This saga was divided into four branches, each being a complete tale in itself and based upon one incident in the life of the hero. These four incidents were his birth, his imprisonment, his exploits and his death. This is parallel, Gruffydd claimed, to a pattern frequently found in early Irish saga literature, which classified individual tales dealing with four such incidents as *compert* (conception and birth), *macgnimartha* (exploits), *indarba* (interpreted by Gruffydd as 'imprisonment', but more correctly 'banishment') and finally *aided* (death). In Gruffydd's reconstruction the saga went as follows: Pryderi was the son of Pwyll, king of Annwfn, and Rhiannon, also originally from Annwfn, who had married the mortal king of Dyfed. Pwyll had always loved Rhiannon, and he tricked her husband into changing places with him. As a result, Rhiannon bore him a son Pryderi. So Pryderi, ostensibly son of the king of Dyfed, was in fact the son of the king of Annwfn. That was the original *compert,* and traces of it still survive in *Mabinogi Pwyll.* For example, the exchange story occurs almost intact, but the story of Rhiannon and the king of Dyfed's marriage, and Pryderi's birth, are told later.

The king of Annwfn still showed enmity towards the king of Dyfed, an enmity which he extended to his own son, Pryderi, whom he imprisoned in Annwfn. This was the original *indarba.* There are two versions of this incident in the Four Branches. One, in *Mabinogi Pwyll,* tells of how Pryderi was stolen from his mother's bedside. The second, in *Mabinogi Manawydan,* tells how both Pryderi and Rhiannon were imprisoned in Annwfn. During their imprisonment, desolation fell on Dyfed, prosperity returning only on their release.

Pryderi, as king of Dyfed, himself led an expedition to Annwfn, seeking its greatest treasure, a cauldron which could restore life to those killed in battle. From this expedition only seven men, including Pryderi, returned. This was the original *macgnimartha,* and traces of it still survive in *Mabinogi Branwen,* although the location of the expedition is now Ireland, and the cauldron, though present, is no longer the motive for the attack. Pryderi is named amongst the seven survivors.

Lastly comes the fourth and final incident in the saga, the death of Pryderi, the *aided.* He was killed by the king of Annwfn. This tale survives in *Mabinogi Math,* but the place of the king of Annwfn is now taken by Gwydion.

Thus went the original saga. To this basic material, Gruffydd maintained, became attached two major independent traditions, namely, the tales of the Children of Llŷr, in *Mabinogi Branwen* and *Mabinogi Manawydan,* and the tales of the Children of Dôn, which also contain the complete saga of Lleu Llaw Gyffes, the hero of Gwynedd, in *Mabinogi Math.* To these two groups came further accretions. To the Llŷr group were added various tales, some clearly of Irish provenance. To the Dôn group came the theme of the *King with the Prophesied Death* and that of *The Unfaithful Wife.* Lastly came two popular medieval themes, that of *The Calumniated Wife,* attached to Rhiannon and Branwen, and that of the Eustace Legend, attached to Manawydan fab Llŷr. This was not all, for Gruffydd further argued that the Pryderi saga at an earlier date had itself become confused with material deriving from Celtic mythology.

Fascinating as it is to delve into the possible origin and development of the Four Branches, it is their excellence as literature that is their lasting and enduring feature. They are perhaps the Welsh people's finest contribution to European literature. The artistry of their author is indeed superb. He was a master of his medium, composing easy-flowing, balanced prose. There are no alliterative runs here, no prodigal use of adjectives, no deliberate use of the complex compounds and laborious descriptive passages found in other Welsh tales, such as *Culhwch and Olwen* and *Breuddwyd Rhonabwy* for example. The keynote is restraint and economy. Descriptions and characterisation are clear-cut and decisive, with an unfailing flair for the exact word or phrase. The rapidly approaching ships from Ireland come *'a cherdet rugyl ebrwyd ganthunt'* ('with an easy swift motion'); the deserted court apartments of Dyfed are described as *'yn wac, diffeith, anghyuanhed'* ('empty, desolate, uninhabited'). Two or three adjectives are the most that are employed. Not a word is wasted or a statement expanded. Bendigeidfran's sorrow on reading his sister's letter revealing her plight in Ireland is tersely expressed: 'And when the letter was read he grieved to hear of the plight that was upon Branwen'. And Branwen's death is recorded with brevity and pathos: 'Then she looked on Ireland and the Island of the Mighty, what she might see of them. "Alas, Son of God," said she, "woe is me that ever I was born: two good islands have been laid waste because of me!" And she heaved a great sigh, and with that broke her heart. And a four-sided grave was made for her, and she was buried there on the bank of the Alaw.'

The narrative is liberally broken up with dialogue, which is perfectly matched to the mood and character of the speakers. Note Rhiannon's cutting remark at Pwyll's naïvety when he foolishly granted his boon to Gwawl son of Clud, who turned out to be a suitor for Rhiannon, Pwyll's own future wife, and Gwawl promptly asked for Rhiannon. The narrative relates: 'Pwyll was dumb for there was no answer he might have given. "Be dumb as long as thou wilt," said Rhiannon, "never was there a man made feebler use of his wits than thou hast." "Lady," said he, "I knew not who he was."' Likewise Branwen's spirited retort to her husband's messengers' greetings to her as 'lady' though she had been degraded to the status of a kitchen maid: 'Messengers went to Branwen. "Lady," said they, "what thinkest thou that is?" "Though lady I am not," said she, "I know what that is."' But nowhere is the dialogue more strikingly employed than in the scene where Blodeuwedd seeks the secret of how Lleu might be killed, so that she might then give the secret to her lover, Gronw Bebyr. Her feigned concern and fear for her husband's safety, to hide her true designs, fascinate and repel as she wheedles the secret out of him: 'And that night he (Lleu) came home. They spent the day in talk and song and carousal. And that night they went to sleep together, and he spoke to her, and a second time, but meantime not a word did he get from her. "What has befallen thee?" he asked; "and art thou well?" "I am thinking," said she, "that which thou wouldst not think concerning me. That is," she said, "I am troubled about thy death, if thou were to go sooner than I." "Ah," said he, "God repay thee for thy loving care. But unless God slay me, it is not easy to slay me," said he.

"Wilt thou then, for God's sake and for mine, tell me how thou might be slain? For my memory is a surer safeguard than thine." "I will, gladly," said he.' Lleu then disclosed the secret, and the narrative continues: 'No sooner had she heard this statement than she sent it to Gronw Bebyr.'

The narrative power of the tales is remarkable. The scene is ever changing, cause and event following one another rapidly. The element of surprise, of rapid development and dramatic moments is brilliantly employed. We are held paralysed by the awful deliberateness of Efnisien's savage act in throwing his infant nephew to the flames—the climax to a crescendo of apprehension surrounding the uneasy peace reached between Bendigeidfran's men and those of the king of Ireland, all culminating in a disastrous battle, dramatically brought to an end by Efnisien himself.

The author of the Four Branches evidently possessed a wide range of literary knowledge. There are skilful and pertinent references to the rich and varied background of the narrative tradition with numerous quotations from the Triads. He probably had access to some collection of pedigrees, for such was quite possibly the source of at least one of the seven *cynweisiaid* or overlords named in *Mabinogi Branwen*—Iddig fab Anarawd Walltgrwn, an obscure member of the family from which Rhodri Mawr, the ninth-century king of Gwynedd, was descended. He shows a predilection for place-name speculation and consequently the onomastic element is a marked feature of these tales. There are also one or two instances of incomplete onomastic tales in the text, the significance of which was either unknown to the author or has possibly been lost in the process of transmission. As well as being fully versed in the narrative tradition of his own country, he was also conversant to some degree with contemporary Irish literature and affairs. Most of all, however, he was a consummate artist.

BIBLIOGRAPHY

Editions:
(In Welsh)
Ifor Williams, *Pedeir Keinc y Mabinogi,* Caerdydd, 1930. This is the standard edition.
(In English)
R. L. Thomson, *Pwyll Pendeuic Dyuet,* Dublin, 1957.
Derick S. Thomson, *Branwen Uerch Lyr,* Dublin, 1961.

Translations:
The Mabinogion, translated by Gwyn Jones and Thomas Jones. Everyman's Library edition, 1949. (The quotations in the foregoing pages are from this translation.)

Critical Studies:
W. J. Gruffydd, *Math vab Mathonwy,* Cardiff, 1928.
Idem, *Rhiannon,* Cardiff, 1953.
A. O. H. Jarman, 'Mabinogi Branwen: Crynodeb o Ddadansoddiad W. J. Gruffydd', *Llên Cymru,* IV, 1957, 129-34.
Idem, 'Pedair Cainc y Mabinogi', Chapter 4 in *Y Traddodiad Rhyddiaith yn yr Oesau Canol,* gol. Geraint Bowen, Llandysul, 1974, 33-142.
Proinsias Mac Cana, *Branwen Daughter of Llŷr,* Cardiff, 1958.
Kenneth H. Jackson, *The International Popular Tale and Early Welsh Tradition,* Cardiff, 1961.
T. M. Charles-Edwards, 'The Date of the Four Branches of the Mabinogi', *Transactions of the Honourable Society of Cymmrodorion,* 1970, 263-98.

CHAPTER IX

TALES AND ROMANCES

BRYNLEY F. ROBERTS

That the story-tellers of medieval Wales had a repertoire far more extensive than the group of a mere eleven tales referred to in modern usage as Mabinogion seems obvious from the brief references which remain in collections of traditional material such as the Triads of the Island of Britain, the Stanzas of the Graves, the roll-call of heroes in *Culhwch and Olwen,* and also from the fragments of stories preserved in a few early poems. The evidence, incomplete and allusive as it is, nevertheless reveals that medieval Wales had an oral tradition as rich as that which has been more fully preserved in Irish. Old Irish sources refer to the *ollam,* who spent a period of twelve to fourteen years mastering his craft. He was expected not only to know two hundred and fifty main tales and a hundred subsidiary tales (classified according to their themes, cattle raids, battles, visions, births, wooings, voyages, deaths, etc.), but also to be able to harmonize separate tales with one another. The extant Welsh material, complete tales and a number of fragments and allusions, affords no more than a glimpse of what must have been a similar rich and varied storehouse of story. The conservers of this tradition were the story-tellers, *cyfarwyddiaid* (sing. *cyfarwydd),* who entertained the courts and aristocratic houses with tales of wonder, of heroes and of gods. By the time our stories were written down, much of their deeper significance had been lost and the tales are mainly entertainment, but the nature of the basic themes of Welsh story can be deduced from the Triads, a corpus of allusions to stories and characters listed in groups of three similar episodes or themes, which would seem to be a mnemonic device which enabled story-tellers to recall tales quickly and also provided poets with a quarry for eulogistic references and comparisons in their work. The Triads are by nature cryptic and allusive, but a careful study by Dr. Rachel Bromwich reveals that the body of underlying story dealt with mythological themes, with the traditional history of the Island of Britain and with figures from the Welsh heroic age. These, together with more purely folkloric and fantastic tales, were the main content of medieval Welsh *cyfarwyddyd* or story.

The story-tellers would seem to have been closely related to the bards in their social function. One or two references link the words *bardd a chyfarwydd,* while the classic reference to story-telling is that in the Fourth Branch of the Mabinogi where Gwydion and his companions are described as bards from Glamorgan who are called upon to entertain the court with a *cyfarwyddyd.* Story-telling may have been one of the functions of the poets or of a particular grade of poet. That the poets as a learned class, like their counterparts in Ireland, were expected to be familiar with native tradition (Irish *seanchas)* is shown by the poetic triad which stated that knowledge of histories, poetry and *hengerdd* give amplitude to a poet, and it is no surprise that the works of court poets and later *cywyddwyr* contain many allusions to characters from the tales. Some tales were told in a combination of prose and verse. In most cases, only the verse portions remain, as in the dialogues in the *Black Book of Carmarthen,* the Llywarch Hen and Heledd cycles, and some of the poems in the *Book of Taliesin* which belong to a Taliesin saga. Later copies of this saga, however, retain both prose and verse, as do late copies of the story of Trystan and Esyllt.

No information remains which would show how the story-teller learnt his art, but as with other social crafts, the apprentice would probably be in the company of experienced *cyfarwyddiaid* listening to tales, thereby acquiring a wide repertoire and mastering the art of telling a long narrative without confusing or impairing its structure. The story-teller has a trained retentive memory, but he is usually not a passive bearer of tradition. To remember a tale frequently means the ability to analyse it into its significant features, to recall individual episodes and to relate them to the rest of the story. With the progression of the tale as a sequence of episodes in his mind, the *cyfarwydd* is able to introduce new elements by supplying for them new motivations, and he is enabled to tell his tale fluently by his experience of a traditional style which will supply him with his vocabulary, expressions, sentence structure and comparisons. The master of his craft has an ear for language and an innate gift of expression, but these have a firm foundation in a stock of stereotyped expressions or formulas which he can use, adapting and varying them as the opportunity arises, e.g. the opening and closing sections of a tale, descriptions of battles, fights, storms, journeys, admission to castles, persons or dress, the denoting of love, anger, wonder or passage of time. The tale is told in a syntactically simple style which makes use of co-ordinate rather than complex sentences, linked by conjunctions, but the narrative is enlivened by direct speech, dialogue and rhetorical devices. It is a visual rather than an introspective style. The tale derives its appeal from the interest and wonder it invokes and from the vivacity of the telling, for an oral style affords no opportunity for subtleties of characterization or of inner significance.

This living oral tradition of Welsh story-telling died before more than a few examples could be noted and it can never be re-created. What we have are versions of prose tales written in the medieval period by particular authors. They are in each case literary versions rather than verbatim copies of the oral tales on which they are based. The *cyfarwyddiaid* were probably illiterate and it is very doubtful that they were responsible for the tales as we have them. Our tales would seem to have been written by men who were not *cyfarwyddiaid,* who were not experienced in the art of recalling the tight structure of a story and who were relying on an untrained memory for the content and development of the narrative (though it should be remembered that the memory of medieval man was more retentive than ours). This may mean that the tales were passing out of the hands of a professional class and may not have been as highly regarded as entertainment in their own right as previously. The act of writing implies that the 'authors' of the extant tales were men with a learned literary background who were not as bound to the tradition as the *cyfarwyddiaid*. Some of the faults in the structure of the tales, most marked perhaps in the Four Branches of the Mabinogi, or the differences between our versions and information found in the Triads or the poetry, may be due to the handling of complex material by amateurs who were more accustomed to playing the role of listener than of performer, but by the same token, the virtues of style and expression revealed in the majority of the tales are presumably those of the oral story-teller.

The style is marked by a concise directness which allows only for minor digressions and which permits the narrative to flow smoothly and swiftly. Descriptive passages are cut to a minimum and apart from passages of rhetoric, adjectives are used sparingly. This style is seen at its most economical in the Four Branches, for the authors of the other tales are a little less sparing and show more delight in brightness and colour. But even here, the descriptive details, vivid and colourful but never exhaustive, do not retard the action or dam the narrative flow. The style is at once vivid and suggestive, varying in tempo, careful and almost contrived, so that it has an air of being a literary, rather than an oral, visual or declamatory style. The pace of the narrative is of primary concern to the authors and the emphasis remains on the tale as a succession of actions and adventures. The sentence patterns, simple, co-ordinate, frequently parasyntactic as in speech, and predominantly verbal, reflect this interest in action rather than in personal motivation, and there is little characterization. Personae have almost no individual characteristics, details of description, brief and stereotyped, are restricted to dress, colouring and build. Formulaic commonplace expressions occur in comparisons, descriptions of dress, to denote passage of time, to report greetings and courtesies, to open tales by giving the name and status of the hero and to open subsections or chapters, but the use of formulas is not a conspicuous feature of these stories. The structure of the tales is usually a linear progression of incidents strung together within the framework of the hero's life, a journey or quest. New sections may open with their own formulas ('one day . . .'), so that it is fairly simple to analyse the story into its constituent components. The danger of such a structure, however, is that a tale may progress beyond what seems to us to be its logical and artistic ending as the author inserts irrelevant episodes into his story which contribute nothing to his basic theme though they may add to our conception of the hero. This fault (in our eyes) derives from the authors' desire to make their stories of particular heroes as complete as possible and also perhaps from an attempt to create tension by delaying the fulfilment of the denouement as long as possible. Another method of creating tension is to delay the completing of an episode by splitting it into three similar incidents, each adding a little to the previous one. This stylistic device is skilfully used: the variations in detail, the change in tempo, the choice of significant features and the re-echoing of familiar phrases all convey a sense of mounting tension. Realistic natural dialogue which enlivens the narrative is a feature of all the tales, but in the best of them, the Four Branches and the Romances, it is used more skilfully both as a vehicle for the action and to delineate character, and here, most clearly, we move away from an external world of wondrous adventures typical of the folk-tale, to a personal use of story to express attitudes and an inner significance. All our tales, although reflecting the modes of the *cyfarwyddyd,* in varying and differing degrees are the compositions of individual authors and they are to be viewed not solely as remnants of tradition but as literary works in the modern sense. An examination of their themes and motifs contributes to our understanding of them, but where these do not conform to analogous patterns we should be ready to accept not merely that folklore themes may be corrupt but that they may be adapted for artistic or personal reasons.

The earliest example of a 'Welsh' *cyfarwyddyd* is an account of the arrival of the Saxons in Britain which is found, interspersed with selections from a Life of St. Germanus, in a Latin compilation of historical materials, *Historia Brittonum,* ascribed in its most well-known form to Nennius (Nemnius), a Welsh cleric of the ninth century, who claimed to have drawn both on Latin chronicles and on the 'traditions of our ancestors.' Earlier Gildas, writing in the sixth century, had referred in his *De Excidio Britanniae* to the arrival of the Saxons, invited by a 'proud tyrant' to assist the Britons in their defence against the Picts and Scots, but Nennius reflects the popular, second-stage development of this theme at a time when the English conquest was an historical fact to be explained and portrayed in more imaginative terms. The 'proud tyrant,' now named Guorthigirnus (Gwrtheyrn), fearful of the Picts and Scots and of his compatriot Ambrosius (Emreis, Emrys), receives kindly three shiploads of exiles from Germany, led by the brothers Hors and Hengist, and grants them the Isle of Thanet. The British king, however, is attracted by Hengist's daughter, and in return for her hand bestows Kent on the Saxons. This foolish gift, made as a result of a drunken infatuation, marks Gwrtheyrn's alliance with the Saxons and the beginning of the English conquest. Gwrtheyrn becomes the arch-traitor of Welsh history, from whose act all misfortunes flow. The Saxons turn against the Britons and reveal their deceit in the episode of the Treachery of the Long Knives. Gwrtheyrn, rejected by both Saxons and Britons, becomes a hunted fugitive whose lamentable end is just payment for his sins.

Although this story is found only in its Latin form, stylistic features in the narrative are best explained, as Sir Ifor Williams has argued, as literal translations from Welsh, and stripped of the interwoven narrative of St. Germanus, this account of Gwrtheyrn and the Saxons is a typical *cyfar-*

wyddyd, swiftly moving, graphic, centring on personalities and full of marvellous incidents. The tale has moved away from the political features presented by Gildas and the emphasis is on Gwrtheyrn's love for Hengist's daughter more than on the strategic advantage of hiring Saxon mercenaries. History becomes personalized in Gwrtheyrn, dramatized in the episode of the Long Knives, the exemplar of Saxon treachery, and gains greater effectiveness and relevance by being re-localized in Wales.

The theme of the loss of Britain which gave rise to a Gwrtheyrn saga was balanced in the historical tradition by the place given to vaticinations which revealed the final restoration of British sovereignty. A central episode in Nennius's account is Gwrtheyrn's attempt to flee from his troubles. His druids advise him to build a fortress in the mountains of Eryri, but when the day's work disappears each night, they recommend that the foundations be sprinkled with the blood of a fatherless boy. Such a boy is found, but he confounds the druids by revealing that the true reason for the disappearing foundations is that they are laid upon a pool where two dragons are asleep. The dragons, one red, the other white, awake and begin to fight. The boy explains that their conflict symbolizes prophetically the struggle of Britons and Saxons for supremacy and the ultimate success of the British. The origin of these sleeping dragons is given in the Welsh tale *Cyfranc Lludd a Llefelys*. Like all the other stories of the Mabinogion this is found in the *Red Book of Hergest* (1375-1425), and a fragment is contained in the earlier *White Book of Rhydderch (c.* 1325), but it occurs first as an addition in one of the earliest versions of *Brut y Brenhinedd,* a Welsh translation of *Historia Regum Britanniae,* dated to the first half of the thirteenth century. Both the 'Mabinogion' and the 'Brut' versions derive from a common redaction, though not unnaturally the 'Mabinogion' version has elaborations which place it stylistically more firmly in the *cyfarwydd* tradition. The story describes the defeating of three *gormesoedd* (supernatural oppressors) by Lludd, king of Britain, aided by his brother Llefelys, king of France. Though Llefelys does not play an independent role in Welsh tradition, Lludd, son of Beli Mawr, was well-known. Together with his father and another brother, Caswallawn, whose name corresponds to that of the historical Cassivellaunus who opposed Julius Caesar's landings, he seems to have been a member of a family which played a part in pseudo-historical stories of the defence of Britain against foreign invaders. *Cyfranc Lludd a Llefelys* is a popular re-working of this pseudo-historical theme, where foreign invaders have been replaced by folklore characters, the fairylike race of *Coraniaid,* a mighty man of magic and fighting dragons whose cries devastate the land until they are lulled into a drunken sleep and buried at Dinas Emrys, an episode which has probably been developed from the Nennian *cyfarwyddyd.*

A reference to the tale in a late eleventh century poem suggests that it was known in an oral form by then. This tale was re-told by the translator of the Brut where it takes its place unobtrusively because of its factual tone and unimaginative expression. Even in the 'Mabinogion' version, the *Cyfranc* does not have the descriptive quality or attention to detail which heightens the effect of wonder or the natural realism which are features of the other stories. In its flat, neutral style, conciseness has given place to artless austerity. The repetition of identical incidents reveals no variations, there is an almost complete lack of dialogue and no attempt to dwell upon the wonder of the *gormesoedd.* The Red Book version is not derived directly from a *cyfarwyddyd* but from the Brut which in turn is an historian's re-telling of the gist of a tale. It reflects the usages of the *cyfarwyddyd* in its vocabulary and some of its common expressions, but on the whole it reveals few of the skills or stylistic features of the oral story-teller.

These are better reflected in another tale which derives from the pseudo-historical tradition, *Breuddwyd Maxen Wledig,* probably of the twelfth century. The Maxen of the tale is, in origin, the historical Magnus Maximus, the Spaniard who was proclaimed Emperor by his troops in Britain in 383 A.D. He led his men to the Continent where he ruled as emperor of the western provinces until he was killed at Aquileia by Theodosius in 388. The sixth-century cleric Gildas refers simply to Maximus's departure with his troops 'who never more returned home,' but Nennius again reflects the development of this tradition when he claims that these troops were granted lands on the Continent: 'These are the Armoric Britons (i.e. Bretons) and have never returned hither to this day.' To Gildas Maximus was a rebellious usurper, and even the more nationalistically-minded Nennius criticized him for denuding Britain of her defence, but the event impressed itself on the Welsh mind as providing for the Britons a place within the history of the Empire. They were the heirs of Rome in Britain and 'Maxim' Wledig appears as the founder of a number of Welsh dynastic and ecclesiastical families. Maximus is viewed in a favourable light in the *cyfarwydd* tradition, which may reflect a more popular, native view of him than that of the Latin 'Roman' chronicles used by Gildas and Nennius. He becomes, not the usurper of the imperial purple, but the emperor who wins Britain so that he may win a bride. He crosses to the Continent not to seize a crown but to regain a throne and succeeds only when he leads his British troops to besiege Rome. Some of his troops, led by Cynan, remain to settle in Brittany. These historical speculations regarding Roman Britain and the Breton settlements as viewed by the *cyfarwyddiaid* are the fabric of the *Dream of Maxen*.

Maxen is the Roman emperor who falls in love with a maiden in a distant land seen in a dream. After much searching she is found and he marries her. This is a common enough folk-tale motif which could have been the theme of a complete story. It is made up of three similar sections, the dream journey and awakening, the search which re-enacts the dream with much less detail but where significant features are specifically called to mind by the messengers, and finally Maxen's journey to Caernarfon to meet his love. The dream journey, though vivid and realistic in its description of geographical features, is intentionally vague. The search narrative, however, gives a succession of place-names which serve to localize the adventure in the audience's experience and to contrast it with the unspecified area of the dream. The section closes with the messenger's return to Rome, having found the girl. 'We know her name . . ,' they say, but the author does not reveal it and the tension is retained until the emperor makes the journey himself. The third section, the swiftest of all, told in a few lines, gives a new dimension to the tale by supplying the historical background of a Roman conquest and by providing for the first time the names of characters already encountered in the dream and the messengers' search. The three sections, by stressing different aspects, form a coherent whole, tightly knit and without a single wasted word, which moves gradually from an imprecise dream world to a carefully defined geographical and temporal setting. What could have been a monotonous repetition of incidents becomes a delightful romantic narrative, moving briskly to an inevitable conclusion but glowing with the bright colours of the hall at Caernarfon and vivid in its precise description of landscape.

The love story of the dream maiden, which is perhaps the author's greatest debt to an underlying oral tale, is followed by a series of new and not fully integrated items which open with the normal chapter formula: 'And one day . . .' These episodes, onomastic explanations, the origins of roads, followed by the account of the siege of Rome and of the Breton settlement, reveal the antiquarian interests of the author who has attempted to combine in a single artistic whole the romantic story of Maxen's bride and the historical traditions of the founding of Brittany by Maximus's British soldiers. The attempt is not wholly successful as the emperor ceases to be the central character and the interest of the story inevitably moves away from him to Cynan (Meiriadog), the traditional founder of Brittany. The tale is very brief and the direct conciseness of the telling cannot contain the insertion of additional material.

For modern readers the *Dream* is marred a little by a lack of unified structure as the author progresses beyond what may strike us as the end of his story. This may not be a valid criticism of a medieval tale, but even modern readers will feel that the structural 'fault' is more than outweighed by the flawless perfection of the first 'chapter,' by the imaginative handling of historical tradition and by the balance, warmth and brightness of the narrative style.

The rest of the native Welsh tales are examples of that most dominant and fruitful theme of medieval secular literature, the legend of Arthur. It seems assured that Arthur was an historical leader of Britons in the late fifth century who achieved significant successes against the Saxons, which may have brought about a period of comparative peace and stability. The golden memory of his victories, mulled over, re-told constantly, elaborated and exaggerated, is the seed from which grew the later legend of an heroic figure. His true figure begins to blur as his historical exploits drift into folklore. His name alone evokes an aura of heroism, and he attracts to himself victories he never won, battles that were never fought. In short, Arthur caught the popular imagination and developed into a folklore figure, the hero of fantastic adventures that have, at best, only a vague historical context. His legend draws to itself heroes, themes and tales from other story-cycles, some semi-historical, others wholly imaginary. These stories are hinted at in a few poems in the *Book of Taliesin* and the *Black Book of Carmarthen,* as in the Triads and some saints' Lives, and they afford glimpses, tantalizingly incomplete, of some of the elements of Welsh Arthurian Legend, Arthur's warband, his fights with oppressive monsters, his voyage to the Otherworld to free a captive and win a cauldron, the abduction of his wife Gwenhwyfar, the circumstances of his last battle at Camlan, his death and prophesied return to free his land of her enemies. The legend of Arthur was firmly established among the Brythonic people of Wales, Cornwall and Brittany and was localized by the connection of the hero's name with topographical features. The earliest examples of Arthurian topography occur in the list of the Marvels of Britain included in Nennius's *Historia Brittonum,* though it may well be that the Arthurian features have been grafted on to existing tales told of these stones and tumuli. One of these marvels is *Licat Amr* (Gamber Head, Herefordshire) where, it was said, Arthur killed his son Amr. The other wonder associated with Arthur is *Carn Cabal* (Corn Cafallt, near Rhaeadr) where a stone bears the footprint of Arthur's dog Cafall, made while he was hunting the boar *Troit.* The hunting of this beast, Twrch Trwyth or Trwyd, is a major episode in the earliest Arthurian tale which has been preserved, *Culhwch and Olwen,* dated in its latest redaction about 1050-1100.

Here most clearly we are presented with a native Welsh view of Arthur, rude, rough, and heroic but already displaying some of the virtues of generosity and hospitality characteristic of him in later romance. In his encounters with the Black Witch, with the fearsome Twrch Trwyth, or as he frees the immemorial captive Mabon, he exults in his strength and physical dominance. Nevertheless, his heart warms as he meets his cousin Culhwch and he gently chides the traditionally thin-skinned Cai for his ungraciousness. The admixture of physical heroism and warmth of feeling, of gigantic boars and tiny ants, is one of the elements which, with its humour and gusto, give the tale its particular appeal.

In conception it is the most ambitious of all medieval Welsh stories; in its basic structure it is one of the simplest. Culhwch is fated to marry none other than Olwen, daughter of Ysbaddaden chief giant. He seeks her, finds her, but may not marry her until he has accomplished the tasks which her father has set. The tale recounts the fulfilling of the tasks and ends with the death of the giant and the marriage of Culhwch and Olwen. In this familiar folk-tale motif of the Giant's Daughter, the seemingly impossible tasks have the aim of encompassing the death of the hero, as of all previous suitors. But the hero fulfils all his tasks successfully, sometimes with the aid of the girl, sometimes assisted by helpful companions, e.g. the runner, the marksman, the listener, whose particular abilities enable him to accomplish specific tasks. Though the folk-tale versions of the Giant's Daughter theme progress incident by incident, they have a unified, closely-knit plot, as each task is related to a particular character and as the return of the hero to the giant on the completion of each task puts each one firmly in the context of winning the girl. The author of *Culhwch and Olwen*, however, thought on a grand scale and worked on a large canvas. He has used the Giant's Daughter theme as the framework for a number of separate tales and has elaborated the basic folk-tale so that it becomes the repository of originally independent stories, now explained as the accomplishing of tasks set by the giant. This attempt at a picaresque novel unfolding a series of adventures to delight readers, coupled with the author's prodigal energy, gave rise, however, to structural difficulties which are not fully resolved. Had the attempt succeeded, *Culhwch and Olwen* would have been a remarkable work, but the author's discipline was not commensurate with his design.

His is a tidy mind, fond of order and classification. The first section of the story, up to Culhwch's arrival at Arthur's court, bears the marks of a typical hero-tale. It opens with a traditional formula, followed by an account of the hero's wondrous birth and naming. The motif of the Jealous Stepmother is introduced which in turn becomes the motivation for the main theme. The winning of Olwen has three sections, the listing of helpers, the enumeration of tasks, and the fulfilling of them. Obviously the third section is the core of the story and logically it should contain and use information given in the first two sections. It is here that the story begins to break down, for though the author revealed his skill in constructing a well motivated unified narrative in his opening pages, he was not able to discipline his abundant energy and wide knowledge, and he begins to lose sight of his finished design in its proper proportions. By the time he came to the kernel of his story he had overspent himself, with the result that what should have been the *raison d'être* of the scheme becomes a rather hasty succession of briefly told adventures, sometimes almost in note form, at others better developed, and occasionally revealing what might have been, as in the story of the freeing of Mabon with its skilfully inserted introduction of the quite separate motif of the Oldest Animals or in the buoyant, bouncing story of the hunting of Twrch Trwyth. The original purpose of the tasks was to bring about the death of the hero. By removing this motivation and inserting new tales of his choice, the author has further weakened the structure of his story. Some of these tales, e.g. Twrch Trwyth, Mabon perhaps, were already associated with Arthur who is thus introduced into the story and usurps the place of Culhwch, who becomes a purely nominal hero for the greater part of the tale. He retains the central position and fulfils an heroic role only up to the first encounter with Ysbaddaden, reappearing in the closing sentences to claim Olwen, so that there is full justification for the giant's last words as he bestows his daughter upon him: 'And thou needst not thank me for that, but thank Arthur who has secured her for thee.'

The list of helpful companions, now Arthur's companions rather than Culhwch's helpers, grows from a mere six to a roll-call of scores of heroes and characters from the whole range of Welsh story and the author's fancy. The six remain, buried in the mass, but their powers are barely used. The list functions for its own sake as an extended rhetorical device in which the author deploys his skill and knowledge, and by extolling Arthur's greatness it shifts the emphasis from the hero to the helpers who become the dominant figures. Modern readers find the list interminable and complain that it interrupts the flow of narrative too severely. Medieval audiences would not have shared this view, for many of the names would have been familiar, and the brief allusions to stories found here would have struck an echoing chord in their minds, so that they could supply for themselves a living context for the majority of these characters, giving the flesh of well-remembered tales to the bare bones of personal names. No doubt also, they would have been more prepared than we to accept the sheer nonsense of some names and to applaud the feats of associative memory underlying the list.

The narrative regains its movement as the roll-call ends, and the scene at Ysbaddaden's court is graphic, full of savage comedy. The giant lists the thirty-nine tasks Culhwch is to fulfil, neatly arranged as those necessary to supply food, drink, dress and entertainment for the wedding feast, and those which will enable Ysbaddaden to prepare himself for the occasion. The first group comprises eight primary tasks, e.g. ploughing waste land so that food may be grown or obtaining miraculous food-supplying vessels, and five secondary tasks necessary to complete the ploughing, e.g. seeking the ploughman Amaethon and the smith Gofannon. The second group has a similar division of four primary and nineteen secondary tasks, e.g. the winning of specific hounds and huntsmen to hunt Twrch Trwyth so that the comb and shears between his ears may be obtained. The last task to be mentioned, the sword of the giant Wrnach, does not fit either group. It is unlikely that the author ever intended to write a fulfilment tale for every one of these tasks and it is no surprise that the majority of them are not mentioned again, for most of them are derived from the author's passion for analysing the elements in the tasks and his exuberant spirit. In fact, Culhwch fulfils sixteen, but of these, six form a single episode briefly referred to during the preparations for hunting Twrch Trwyth. The tale therefore resolves itself into the accomplishing of ten tasks, or ten stories which the author hoped to integrate in a single tale by making Ysbaddaden's demands the motivation for them.

Though the tasks are not fulfilled in the order set by Ysbaddaden, there are signs that the author had intended to follow a logical pattern. The sword of Wrnach, the last in the list and the first to be accomplished, is probably an addition to the tale. This is followed by two 'freeing of the captive' stories, the former, told in a very cursory manner, serving as an introduction to the latter. The brief account of the capture of the two whelps of the bitch Rhymi follows, after which the heroes disperse 'one by one, two by two.' Ysbaddaden had named the task of making a leash from the beard of Dillus Farfog to hold two unnamed whelps, and one suspects that the next story should be the adventures of one of the pairs of heroes who dispersed after capturing Rhymi's whelps, namely Cai and Bedwyr's encounter with Dillus. However, the story of the nine hestors of flax seed (which opens: 'And as Gwythyr son of Greidawl was journeying over a mountain one day') has been inserted, but as further information about Gwythyr is given after the episode of Dillus's beard, it may be that his tale of the flax seeds belongs here. Preparations for the first hunt follow and Ysgithrwyn is quickly slain. A second hunt, that of Twrch Trwyth, is now undertaken. The Boar is in Ireland, and while Arthur's men spy out the land, they are able to obtain the cauldron of Diwrnach the Irishman. The stage is now set for the major episode in the tale, which is told with verve and gusto, as the chase moves at a thrilling breathless pace across south Wales. A few comic touches release the tension, and the single remaining task, the slaying of the Black Witch, is told with farcical humour.

Culhwch and Olwen, in outline, is a tidy and simple tale. Its contradictions, gaps and apparent complexity arise, on the one hand, from the author's delight in elaborating his material, and on the other, from his decision to list all the tasks on one occasion rather than to follow each task with its fulfilment tale. Though the stories are the starting-point for the composition of the tale, their recitation must be delayed until the list is complete. The lag between the setting of a task and its fulfilment, together with the loosening of the tie between characters and tasks, weakens the structure and is the main source of contradictions.

The style of the story, with its emphasis on the wondrous, the huge and the physical, is typically oral, appealing to a visual imagination and delighting in its feats of hyperbole and mastery of words. It reveals the rhetorical devices of the storyteller in the formalized descriptions of Culhwch's journey to Arthur's court, his parley with the porter, or the bright picture of Olwen, with their runs, compound adjectives, archaic vocabulary, rhyming names and stylized syntax. But the ornate rhetorical style is found only in stereotyped situations. The author has an equal mastery of other styles, leisurely and detailed in his opening narrative, swift and incisive in his account of Gwythyr and of Mabon. He knows the value of repetition, and when to stop before it becomes tedious, he varies his tempo, slowing the pace of his narrative to a standstill in his lists, the one closing his introductory chapter, the other following the scene of primitive violence at Ysbaddaden's court. The stories themselves alternate between brief condensed accounts and fully narrated self-contained episodes, and it is a measure of the author's skill that the tale, in spite of its length, never flags. There are a few touches of dry humour, but more characteristic of the author is his fondness for broad farce. There are no real characters, but a wide sweep of heroic adventures. The action is everything for this author, and not for him the deep moral view of human relations which inspired the author of the Four Branches or the gemlike discipline which gives the *Dream of Maxen* or *Owain* their special quality.

Nevertheless, *Culhwch* is more literary in concept than the oral *cyfarwyddyd*. Its attempt at a sophisticated structure neatly divided into self-contained elements, the well-classified list of tasks, the disproportionate number of helpers, and some borrowings from written sources, suggest that the author was a literary man, perhaps following a common medieval mode of composition as he used and adapted an existing framework to serve as a vehicle for some favourite folk-tales. Structurally, it is easy to fault the tale for its lack of balance and its overlaying of so much detail that the thread of the plot is lost, but it is as well to recall that even in its literary form, *Culhwch* remains a tale to be heard, and that these faults are not as obvious to the listener as to the silent reader. For the reader who is willing to participate in the story, the movement of the narrative, its wonders, its farce, its heroism, make any deficiencies in structure irrelevant.

Culhwch and Olwen, like some of the Arthurian poems, shows that Arthur had become the centre of Welsh storytelling by the late eleventh century. His retinue includes heroes drawn from other cycles: his court is the setting for new adventures and the destination of young champions seeking fame. This view of Arthur's court and a statement of his preeminence was presented in a literary, historical setting by Geoffrey of Monmouth in his *Historia Regum Britanniae* (1136) where the king was portrayed in terms acceptable to a Norman audience as the emperor of a far-flung domain whose throne had been won and established both by personal bravery and skilful generalship. Although he retains an air of primitiveness, as became a Welshman in the Norman context, his court is essentially chivalric: his knights, emulated the world over, delight in their mock battles, demonstrating their prowess to the ladies of the court who love only men whose skill at arms is proven. Geoffrey is not the source of Arthurian romance, but the first fully worked out example of the development of the Arthurian scene for a non-Welsh audience. Geoffrey indirectly, his contemporary William of Malmesbury overtly, both refer to Welsh stories about Arthur, and it was these tales which other Normans discovered in their encounters with the Welsh, especially perhaps in the southern Marches, Gwent and Morgannwg. Glamorgan itself, Normanized from about 1090, was a province containing both Welsh and Norman lordships. In the second half of the twelfth century many of these Welsh lords were allied to the princes of Deheubarth and to the Lord Rhys, who although an independent prince, yet held high office under the crown and must have provided a channel for French influence in south Wales outside Morgannwg. Bilingualism was probably common among the aristocracy, and there were abundant opportunities for military, political and social contacts between Welsh and Normans. There existed a variety of channels, both formal and informal, for the transmission of Welsh story, and Welsh themes, episodes, characters and tales became an important part of the material used in a sophisticated literary form by the French romance writers of the twelfth century, whose story-cycles were later classified as the Matter of Rome, the Matter of France and the Matter of Britain.

The second of these cycles, that of the Old French epic, frequently linked with Charlemagne, is closest in spirit to the older heroic poetry in its pseudo-historical setting, its battles against uneven odds and death in a hopeless cause. The poems are essentially the literature of a community, or even a nation, the heroes are members of armies and an important theme is the ideal of allegiance. But by the middle years of the century the ethos of society had changed. The defence of Christendom against the heathens had drawn to a close, aristocratic, but landless, fighting men were free to seek employment, the castle became a centre of social intercourse and refinement where feminine graces could flower. As the concept of the war-band and communal war waned, interest in the individual increased. R. W. Southern has shown how this affected the view of life in all its variety. Solitary prayer and meditation, the search for fulfilment in the spiritual life, have their counterpart in the courtly world in the adventures of the solitary knight-errant setting out on his quest. The literary expression of these secular ideals is the chivalric romance, which consists of a series of adventures in which the hero is involved during a journey or quest, undertaken only from a wish to seek the marvellous, or motivated by love for a lady or friend rather than by allegiance to a lord. The hero is no longer simply a warrior. He is a knight, brave, generous, refined, both fighting man and lover, whose prowess engenders love in his lady whose love in turn engenders prowess, the chivalric topos on which Geoffrey of Monmouth based his picture of Arthur's court. The romance takes place in a fictional, barely localized, but conventionalized world in which a central place is given to the magical or fantastic episode which needs only the creation of an otherworldly atmosphere as its motivation. These adventures may be used for their own sakes, but the more developed romances do not simply recount a string of episodes. They are concerned with the development of the knight's virtues; they follow his 'education,' examine his feelings and motives, comment on his actions. The narrative has an inner meaning which the author reveals and which he embellishes with his own thoughts.

Three Old French romances by Chrétien de Troyes bear an obvious similarity to three Welsh stories. *Erec et Enide* and *Yvain (Le Chevalier au Lion)* correspond to *Geraint ac Enid* and to *Owain (Iarlles y Ffynnon)*, *Perceval (Le Conte du Graal)* has a less close similarity to *Peredur*. The nature of this correspondence in personal names, sequence of events, specific details and working out of the plot, is still a matter for debate, and it need not be the same in every case. Significant differences between the Welsh and French texts make it unlikely that the Welsh stories are taken directly from Chrétien, but a popular view has been that both versions derive independently from a common source, defined as French tales used by the poet. It is assumed that Welsh stories of Geraint, Owain and Peredur passed to France and were forgotten in Wales, returning later in a new, less-Welsh guise. Some of these French influences are said to be the minor role assigned to Arthur, some foreign personal names, and the logical structure of the romances or their vague geography contrasted with the 'incoherence and diffusion' and specific topography of native tales. None of these arguments is, however, decisive as they can all be satisfied by the citing of purely Welsh evidence. Recently, this commonly held view has been challenged by critics who stress the improbability of the thesis that these three tales should be forgotten in Wales and re-imported later. Chrétien's sources, they believe, were the Welsh tales essentially as we have them, 'possibly with a few touches added later.' Any

French influences which have been at work, in the vocabulary, forms of personal names, descriptions of dress or custom, can be explained in terms of the Anglo-Norman element in Normanized areas of Wales.

Linguistically and stylistically, the three romances are firmly in the *cyfarwydd* tradition as it appears in written literature. The authors use the same vocabulary and formulas as the other tales, they show the same ability to write concisely and smoothly, varying their syntax and their tempo. They are equally skilled in creating pithy dialogue: like the *Dream of Maxen,* the romances are full of colour and brightness; like *Culhwch,* they have rhetorical flourishes. They are never over-descriptive or tedious, but balanced and symmetrically rhythmic. The authors use the technique of varying an incident repeated three times and they are able to re-tell the same episode twice with subtle changes in tempo and emphasis. Whatever may be their immediate antecedents, the Welsh romances are the work of authors well-versed in the Welsh narrative tradition and intimately familiar with Welsh story-telling. The tale is still viewed as a succession of episodes following one another quickly. The narrative is far more direct than in the French equivalents, as the authors show no interest in the rhetorical or literary examination of the characters' feelings or motives and do not attempt descriptive or 'psychological' digressive elaborations in the French style.

Nevertheless, the romances have novel features. In atmosphere they reveal an unreal fairy-like quality which is not found in the other tales. *Culhwch and Olwen* moves in a never-never world of witches and giants typical of the wonder-tale, but the romances have a real setting where humans live in a world of daydreams, which is at once both familiar and strange. The concept of the lonely knight-errant is a new feature as is the interest in love as a motivation for action. A love element is not lacking in other tales, but neither the *Dream of Maxen* nor *Culhwch* analyses love, though *Math fab Mathonwy* seems to make critical comment on the social dangers of infatuation.

The romances, however, accept the topos of chivalric love and are concerned not only to describe successful wooing but to comment on the meaning of love. They may not follow the conventions of courtly love closely, but neither are they simply stories in which actions derive their complete motivation within the tale. The narrative, rapid and interesting indeed, is the expression of a theme which is revealed by the action. *Peredur* has as its theme the education of a knight. *Geraint* and *Owain* are closely related in their thematic structure, both relating the hero's winning of his bride, her subsequent loss and their final reconciliation. This is more than a 'neat antithesis,' that Geraint is rebuked for his loss of interest in tournaments because of his attachment to his wife while Owain forgets his bride in the delights of courtly life. Taken together, the two romances reflect two aspects of the knight's character as soldier and lover and are portrayals of the fault of immoderation, the overemphasizing of one virtue at the cost of another, which is, as Geoffrey of Monmouth had noted, the tension inherent in the topos of chivalric love. The Welsh romances have the same knightly themes as the French: they differ from them in that the deeper significance of the adventures is implicit in the narrative and never made explicit by the author's comments. If Chrétien's sources were the Welsh tales as we have them, he is indebted to them both for his material and its significance, but if we assume that the literary development of story material to display chivalric themes is more likely to have occurred in French circles than in Welsh, the 'touches added later' to the Welsh romances have to do not with superficialities of vocabulary but with the fabric of the tales. The relationship between the Welsh and French romances is more complex than may be expressed only in terms of borrowing or reworking material. The Welsh authors have rejected the more purely literary features of French verse romance as being too foreign to the native tradition of prose narrative. They follow native stylistic conventions while absorbing and adapting features from foreign fashionable literature. The romances are the fruits of the meeting of two cultures and two narrative forms, perhaps *c.* 1200, and they are the most sophisticated examples of imaginative writing in Middle Welsh prose.

Peredur is a long, incohesive tale which is found in two recensions. Peniarth MSS 7 and 14 contain two sections, *(a)* the hero's upbringing, his arrival at Arthur's court, subsequent adventures which take him to several castles at one of which he sees a bleeding lance and a bloody head in a salver carried in procession, and his return to Arthur's court; *(b)* new adventures apparently unconnected with *(a),* culminating in an alliance with the Empress of Constantinople at whose court he remains for fourteen years. The White Book of Rhydderch has a third section which takes Peredur back to unravel the mystery of the head and lance found in *(a).* In its episodes, though not always in their sequence, Chrétien's poem *Perceval* agrees with the Welsh romance, but it has nothing corresponding to *(b)* and in place of the head it describes a grail (dish, platter) brightly glowing and containing the wafer of the Mass.

The first section reveals an author who is able to keep a tight rein on the several threads of his narrative and to suggest an underlying significance to his hero's adventures. On a superficial level, the story tells of a youth protected from knightly society by his mother lest he be killed as were his father and brothers. Desiring to become a knight, he comes to Arthur's court where his uncouth appearance causes merriment and relief from a challenge newly presented by a strange knight. Peredur vows never to return to the court until he has avenged the injury Cai has caused to a dwarf and his wife who had prophesied great things for the bumpkin. After many adventures, the boy defeats Cai in combat and returns. Peredur's frequently expressed wish to avenge Cai's insults gives cohesion to his adventures, but this is merely an echo of the true theme of his quest, for there is a more mysterious refrain running through the story. The dwarf had greeted Peredur 'Flower of Knighthood' (a chivalric term, *Flos Militiae),* and it becomes apparent that the real purpose of the adventures is to educate the youth in knighthood and to justify this description. He begins by imitating as best he can the outer appearance of a knight: his mother's advice, which he follows innocently, represents an outsider's view of chivalric behaviour. At the court he wins by his own efforts the arms of a knight, and his readiness to defend the weak reveals his innate ideals. At an uncle's castle he learns the courtesies of life and is told: 'You will be the best man that strikes with a sword in this island'; at the castle of a second uncle he is proclaimed: 'You are the best man . . . the third is yet to come.' Subsequent actions justify his uncles' view of him, and after his fight with one of the witches of Gloucester, who further instructs him and who reveals that 'it was fated and foreseen that I should suffer affliction from thee,' Peredur has won his status as a knight. What he lacks is the experience of love as the deepest motivation to refine and temper his martial skills, but the intensity of Peredur's feelings are shown immediately after his encounter with the witch in his love-trance. His education, the drawing-out of his potential and innate knighthood, is complete, and Peredur's adventures are seen to be not a series of chance encounters but a pre-ordained thread woven by powers represented by the dwarfs, the uncles and the witches.

Structurally, the whole section is an interweave of episodes. The mother's advice frameworks the early adventures which are, however, left incomplete to be returned to later. Peredur's abrupt departure from home motivates a later adventure which also explains the appearance of the dwarfs, while the cryptic allusion to Peredur's dead father links with the tale's opening sentences. The author is the master of these threads and writes with dramatic effect and suggestive descriptive power. But though Peredur has avenged Cai's insult and has fulfilled the dwarf's prophecy, the romance is not complete as the significance of the bloody head has not been revealed. Literary convention and narrative expectation demand that the hero returns to the uncle's castle. The purpose of Peredur's education is not yet fulfilled, and the theme of prophecy and revenge is not yet resolved at the deepest level.

Section *(b)* has two episodes. In the first, a simple tale of the winning of a reluctant love is the framework for a number of adventures. The second episode is more contrived as each adventure is motivated by a previous one, and the whole seems to be welded together within the mythological theme of the hero's marriage with the Sovereignty of his land, represented by the Empress of Constantinople in her various guises. This may have been an important element in a Welsh Peredur-saga, too characteristic to be omitted though not forming part of this particular romance. Section *(b)* may thus contain popular Welsh tales associated with Peredur which the author has inserted to enhance the hero's status and to make his story as complete as possible.

The third section opens abruptly when an ugly maiden appears at Arthur's court. She addresses Peredur angrily (though it has not been said why or when he had returned): 'Blind was fate when she bestowed favour and fame upon thee,' and she blames the ills of the land and its king upon his failure to enquire after the meaning of the bleeding lance. Her words link the story with the unfinished episode at the uncle's castle and call attention to the theme of destiny running through section *(a)*, but in addition the maid refers to other exploits worthy of the knights. Gwalchmai undertakes these, but before he can begin he is accused by a strange knight of killing his lord. This new adventure, in turn, is interrupted so that Gwalchmai may free a besieged maid. Thus his adventures begin to form a new romance, structured in an interlace pattern, which would presumably have interwoven with Peredur's quest. But the author leaves Gwalchmai with the words: 'Under that head the story says no more of Gwalchmai than that,' though a trace of the original scheme may remain in the re-uniting of the two knights at the close of the romance. Peredur's quest ends when a youth appears and in a few breathless sentences reveals that in one of his various guises he had carried the bleeding lance: 'And the head was thy cousin's, and it was the witches of

Gloucester that had slain him ... and it is prophesied that thou wilt avenge that.' Peredur defeats the witches, who acknowledge that they were fated to be killed by him, and the tale ends with the theme of destiny which ran through the first section. The vengeance upon Cai is merely an example in human terms of a retribution which the hero, unknown to himself, is fated and prepared by powers not of this world to bring about. But section *(c)*, in comparison with the intricate composition of *(a)*, is banal, being a succession of badly constructed and unexplained episodes (perhaps extracted from an interlaced account of Gwalchmai and Peredur). The central adventure of the killing of the witches is brief, lacking all drama. The source of *Peredur* may itself have been corrupt and section *(c)* may be an attempt to write a conclusion based on confused oral versions combined with details from Chrétien's poem or its source, with which it agrees in some features which are inconsistent with section *(a)*, but which had replaced the vengeance quest (symbolized by the head of Peredur's father, perhaps, not his cousin) by the themes of the Grail and the Waste Land.

Nevertheless, to leave *Peredur* as though it were only a literary puzzle is to ignore its stylistic virtues, wholly within the Welsh tradition of conciseness enlivened by touches of rhetoric, of vivid but sparing description and of realistic dialogue, and is to disregard also the intricate skills of section *(a)* which are new in that tradition. Peredur himself is portrayed with sympathy and humour, and in spite of the unreal atmosphere of the romance, he is, with some of the characters of the Four Branches, the most human and natural of the heroes of the Welsh stories.

Geraint and Enid has three parts, the winning of Enid, introduced by the episode of the hunting of the White Stag; the hero's return to his own kingdom where his dalliance with his wife gives rise to criticism of him; the estrangement from Enid and Geraint's proving of himself, or of his wife, in a series of encounters. The author delays the reconciliation so that he may introduce a number of loosely arranged combats set in the framework of a journey, and even after the reconciliation, a further irrelevant adventure at the Hedge of Mist is included.

The Welsh and French versions are close to each other in their sequence of episodes, but the Welsh seems more reasonable in its explanation of the central episode, the patient Griselda theme of the testing of Enid, and in its more logical motivation for the opening hunt scene. The Welsh author formalizes the stages in his opening narrative ('their story so far'), where Chrétien marks only the end of his first section formally. The French romance is the more obviously literary of the two and follows different conventions from the Welsh. Scenes of chivalry and love are carefully described, the descriptions of the heroine follow a rhetorical pattern and there are analyses of the lovers' feelings. The Welsh story, however, moves more briskly, concentrating on the active elements in the tale and giving place to subjective musings only where they are necessary to explain Geraint's mistrust of his wife. The Welsh romance is conceived of as a written story as the author refers to a previous episode as that which was said *above,* but the narrative conventions are different. Thus the Hedge of Mist is no more than a final adventure, whereas for Chrétien the corresponding episode of the Joy of the Court is an allegory summarizing, with characteristic irony, the meaning of the romance.

Geraint and Enid suffers from a lack of conciseness and loose construction. The author is unable to repeat episodes to bring out different emphases, he uses formulas (some times carelessly), to a greater extent than other authors, and like the author of the Four Branches, he is interested in matters of precedence in seating arrangements and in accounting for every minute of his characters' time. He uses an excess of personal names for unimportant characters and his dependence on traditional conventions is seen in his liberal use of rhetoric. In both style and structure, the romance seems closer to the techniques of the *cyfarwydd* than to the composing of an author.

Owain, however, marks the shift towards a disciplined, carefully formulated style of narration. It is a well constructed, balanced tale, almost wholly free from digressions and told with an economy of words in a lively, slightly rhetorical style. In its colour and movement it is like the *Dream of Maxen* and both authors are masters of the technique of repeating identical episodes that contribute to the development of the story. But the author of *Owain* has an eye for drama, revealed in Luned's wonderfully naturalistic interview with her lady, in the subtly contrived description of the lord's funeral and Luned's fanning of the flames of Owain's love, and in the carefully constructed account of Owain's fight with his friend Gwalchmai.

The tale has two contrasting sections. The first recounts Cynon's unsuccessful quest at the Fountain, told to an audience at Owain's insistence, Owain's successful quest and his marriage to the Lady of the Fountain followed by his forgetting of his wife upon his return to Arthur's court. The second part opens when a maiden rebukes him for his neglect of the Lady, and the rest of the story is an account of the physical and moral rehabilitation which enables him to regain his status as knight and husband of the Lady of the Fountain. The tale ends with the return of Owain and his lady to Arthur's court. The theme of the romance is Owain's discovery of himself and his awareness of the need to hold in balance the ideals of prowess, companionship and duty. The climax of the first part, Owain's return to Arthur, is re-echoed in the second in the true climax and resolving of tensions in the return of Owain with his wife. The story becomes a unified whole when it is realised that the winning of the Lady is a necessary introduction to the theme of loss and rehabilitation which follows. Luned, a well-drawn character in her own right, fulfils a structural role as she is the means of leading Owain to the Lady in both parts of the tale. At the end of the first section, the author, in the space of a few lines, repeats the 'three years' of Owain's stay at court, contrasted with the 'three months'' duration of the feast, no less than four times. These hammer blows define the enormity of

Owain's neglect and are a bridge to the second part. Owain leaves the court, as he had at the beginning of the tale but with his very different feelings briefly suggested, and undergoes physical and moral degradation. His loss not of knighthood simply but of humanity is shown in his literal 'wildness,' an old Celtic theme here used symbolically, and his rehabilitation begins, again symbolically, when he descends from the hills to the inhabited valleys. His eyes are opened, he feels shame *(kewilyd)*. The two episodes which follow restore him to physical health and regain for him his knightly status, so that the way is clear for him to return to the Fountain. The climax is, however, delayed by the insertion of a new adventure, the minor motif of Owain and the grateful lion which, though not part of the main theme, is however well integrated into the romance. The only flaw in the triple-staged structure of the winning of the Lady, and her re-winning separated by Owain's degradation, appears to be the episode of the Du Traws, which seems unnecessary, perhaps because it is misplaced.

In its balanced construction, its tightly-knit structure, its skilful repetition of well-designed episodes and its drama, *Owain* is one of the finest of Welsh tales. Its use of the quest motif and marriage theme, and its allegory, serve to show that it is the work of a conscious literary artist using native conventions to comment on contemporary ideals.

With the *Dream of Rhonabwy* (for which dates have been suggested ranging from the mid twelfth century to the end of the thirteenth) we return to the older traditional view of Arthur as the leader of armies whose duty it is to guard the Island of Britain. This is the active Arthur of *Culhwch and Olwen,* not the benevolent figure-head of the romances, and the heroic undertones of the portrayal are made explicit in the reference to 'the comrades of Rhwawn Bebyr son of Deorthach Wledig; and yonder men have mead and bragget in honour, and they have the wooing of the kings' daughters of the Island of Britain without let; and they have a right thereto, for in every strait they come in his van and in his rear.' The tale reflects the earlier concept of Arthur and the atmosphere is, on the surface, wholly Welsh. Nevertheless, the *Dream* is the most consciously literary of all the Mabinogion stories. The only extant medieval copy, in the Red Book of Hergest, ends with a note:

> And this story is called the Dream of Rhonabwy. And here is the reason why no one, neither bard nor story-teller, knows the Dream without a book—by reason of the number of colours that were on the horses, and all that variety of rare colours both on the arms and their trappings, and on the precious mantles, and the magic stones.

The tale, it is true, has an abundance of colourful descriptions but their formalized patterns and permutations of colour would not have presented a problem to a trained *cyfarwydd*. The note is, as Thomas Parry suggests, a scribe's explanation of why the *Dream* was never recited as were other tales but read, and the correct explanation is surely that the story is a work written by an individual author who has drawn on other literary sources, Geoffrey of Monmouth, *Culhwch,* perhaps *Geraint,* and on traditional elements, Owain's ravens, the cosmic chess game, the ring of memory, the mantle of invisibility, vision-producing sleep, the Battle of Badon. These themes and motifs, however, are not of the essence of the story but are introduced into a new composition.

The story is set during the reign of Madog ap Maredudd, the prince of Powys who died in 1159. Rhonabwy and two companions, on a search for the prince's brother, are billeted for the night at the house of Heilyn Goch son of Cadwgawn ab Iddon in a filthy smoke-filled hall. Rather than spend the night tossing on a flea-infested blanket, Rhonabwy sleeps on a yellow ox skin and the vision he is granted comprises the greater part of the tale. This introductory section is wholly realistic and specific in its geography, it is precisely dated and, so it has been claimed, carefully located in the house of a family well-known in east Powys. Rhonabwy's companions, moreover, have specific localizations, and all the descriptive details are vivid. The author has obviously aimed for, and has attained, an air of complete reality. The incoherence of the vision which follows is in studied contrast to these realistic details and suggests that the chaotic and inconsequential events which are described have been as carefully designed by the author as the first part of his story.

The dream consists of a number of independent but incomplete scenes, vividly and graphically described in a wealth of colourful detail, which follow one another in quick succession but which give almost no sense of progression towards a climax. The tale, therefore, has been criticized as being devoid of action, too static, 'a succession of illuminated pages, deficient in movement and character, but a *tour-de-force* of close observation and description.' The author's delight in colourful description, his rhetorical portrayals of dress and arms, his formalized symmetrical structure, and especially his pride in his mastery of florid prose and rhetoric, and his ability to create noisy confused crowd scenes, have all clogged the flow of whatever narrative he had hoped to write. But though this is a fair description of the tale, it need not be a statement of the author's failure.

He writes with satirical purpose which he expresses on more than one level. He looks with a critical, amused eye on contemporary society, the 'little fellows . . . found away up the road.' Arthur smiles as he sees them, that 'men as mean as these keep this island, after men as fine as those that kept it of yore . . . It will not be easy to defend this Island from this day forth for ever.' But the author's regard for the past is not wholly admiring, for although Arthur's time is portrayed in heroic terms, the king himself has little of the heroic about him. Rhonabwy's dream is an upside-down world where black is often white, where time is reversed and values upset. The heroic atmosphere is consistently suggested, but there is nothing in the dream to justify it. As Dafydd Glyn Jones has pointed out, the author's criticism acts upon the realities of contemporary society and upon the myths of the Arthurian era. It is no surprise that contemporary literary standards are satirized and it is not difficult to see in the reference to incomprehensible praise poems to Arthur a view of the abstruse intricacies of formal court poetry. The irrelevant use of a multitude of personal names devoid of their traditional connotation, and the inconsequentiality of the events in the dream may be a further example of the author's satire. French verse romances of the twelfth century (to some degree), and the prose romances of the following century (to a very large degree and more formally), not only make use of descriptive digressions which elaborate and illuminate the development of the story, but also utilize a narrative technique best described in Eugène Vinaver's words: 'Interweaving a number of separate themes . . . they have to alternate like threads in a woven fabric, one theme interrupting another and again another, and yet all remaining constantly present in the author's and reader's mind'. These methods of controlled digressions and interlacing of themes are obviously traps for the unskilled author, in whose hands a romance may degenerate into a loose collection of episodes, vividly described, but lacking cohesion and fulfilment. Chaucer's *Tale of Sir Topaz,* which was his 'own' contribution to the Canterbury Tales, is a satire on the prolixity of contemporary romance. The author of the *Dream of Rhonabwy* was an equally conscious writer of a satirical turn of mind, who may have contrived the incoherence of the vision as humorous comment on contemporary literary techniques.

The *Dream of Rhonabwy* was the last wholly native tale to be written in the Middle Welsh tradition. Present evidence does not suggest that other oral tales were given a literary form or that new romances based on traditional material were composed. Their place is taken by translations of stories which were popular in England and France, and presumably in bilingual societies in Wales. The *cywyddwyr* of the fourteenth and fifteenth centuries show their familiarity with foreign romance by their liberal use of personal names and story-titles taken from texts which were not translated as from those which are found in Welsh. The choice of stories translated reflects the vogue of Arthurian romance, of the *chansons de geste* of the

Matter of France and of miscellaneous romances; they are evidence of the popularity of foreign material as a source of entertainment among the Welsh aristocracy of south Wales, possibly to the detriment of native tales. Patrons and *littérateurs* were well aware of the contemporary scene in England and it would have been natural for them to direct their energies towards obtaining Welsh versions of popular fiction at the cost of preparing literary versions of more familiar tales. The 'three romances' reveal the adapting to the Welsh tradition of French standards, the *Dream of Rhonabwy* seems to satirize contemporary techniques; by the end of the thirteenth century foreign influences become overt as French romances are translated. The oral story-teller continued to tell his tales (it appears that the tradition was alive in the last century), but his skills and material may have been less highly regarded in sophisticated society and they do not appear again in their full effect until the close of the medieval period.

Evidence of the persistence of a strong prose tradition is, however, that these translations from Old French and Latin follow the linguistic conventions of the native tales. They are translations in the medieval sense, fairly free renderings, sometimes corresponding closely to the original, at others paraphrasing, condensing or adding material. The structure of the tale is not affected but the translator's forms of expression and his narrative ideal are derived from his experience of the prose tradition. The Welsh versions in general tend to be more succint and to present a more rapid narrative than the French. They lack the smooth balance of the native tales, but frequently slip into their vocabulary, collocations and occasional formulas. Traditional rhetoric is not a feature of the translations, but nevertheless the authors are not devoid of the ability to create a string of compound adjectives or achieve a rhetorical effect by using pairs of synonyms to render single words. There is, of course, a strong French influence on the vocabulary, but this never affects the essence of the language. They follow the French in their formal dialogues rather than the naturalistic conversations of Welsh tales, and a new element is the derogatory comparisons common in the *chansons de geste.* Throughout, they succeed in capturing the heroic, blunt forms of expression of the French poems, and in conveying vivid battle scenes, details of dress and the arming of knights. They are, in brief, highly competent translations which convey both the flavour and the details of their originals without causing violence to native standards. Though they represent a new development in Welsh narrative, they are in no way a break with tradition.

Ystorya Bown o Hamtwn (Beves of Hampton) is a typical *roman d'aventure,* a long rambling episodic account of Bown's exploits and tribulations, which was popular throughout Europe. The Welsh version, based on a lost Anglo-Norman poem, has a vigour and a rough humour of its own. The translator has a wealth of vocabulary which he uses to effect in passages of abuse, dialogue and fights, and which may well have derived from the colloquial idiom. The Charlemagne romances are represented in Welsh in a series of texts translated at various times but set in sequence in the manuscripts to form a cycle usually known as *Ystorya de Carolo Magno.* The basis of the compilation is a translation of a Latin chronicle, ascribed to Archbishop Turpin, Charlemagne's chief cleric, but in fact part of a Book of St. James composed about 1140-50 to exalt the shrine of the Apostle at Compostella. It is a militantly Christian work which recounts how Charles wrested Spain from the Saracens and won the grave of St. James as had been foretold to him in a dream. The Welsh version, prepared by one Madog ap Selyf about 1265-1283 for a patron who was a descendant of the Lord Rhys, follows the Latin closely with a few minor alterations and is a fluent rendering, more natural than other translations of Latin originals made in the same period. One episode in the Chronicle (Chapter 27), is the bribing of Charles's knight Ganelon by the Saracens with personal gifts of gold and silver, and similar gifts and a thousand beautiful girls to his men. The heathen are enabled to attack the rearguard of Charles's army, under the command of his nephew Roland, in the narrow valley of Roncesvaux, and inflict dreadful slaughter. Charles returns as he hears the sound of Roland's horn and wreaks retribution upon Ganelon and the Saracens. This episode is the subject of the finest of the *chansons de geste, The Song of Roland,* which not only devotes greater space than the Chronicle to a vivid picture of the battle but which is concerned also with a critical examination of the motives and heroic ideals of the main protagonists. A Welsh translator, familiar with a version of the poem, revealed his artistic feeling when he removed chapter 27 from the Chronicle and inserted in its place his rendering of the events leading up to the battle and the description of the massacre as found in the *Chanson* up to lines 1660-1670. The sounding of the horn, Roland's death and Charles's vengeance, together with the story of the Saracen women and its 'theological' significance, are however retained. The translator has, perhaps, missed the full force of the poem, for though he has conveyed the dramatic clash of characters in the opening scenes, and does not conceal either Oliver's view of Roland as impulsive and proud, or Ganelon's passionate criticism of his zest for war, the omission of the later stages of the battle in its irony and tragedy, its contrast between the sage Oliver and the heroically vain Roland, deletes the large question mark which hangs over the hero's conduct. The translator is more concerned with providing for his readers a pulsating account of a famous battle than with revealing the theme of the poem, and given this aim, we may feel that he has been successful. Two other romances were subsequently inserted to complete the compilation, the strange and ribald story of Charles's Pilgrimage to Jerusalem and Constantinople, and the romance of Otuel, the noble heathen converted by Roland. This cycle has grown in stages but all the translators provided linking passages or edited the closing or opening sentences of existing texts so that the joins might be as unobtrusive as possible. The most ambitious link is seen at the end of the *Song* where the translation moves within a single sentence from the Old French back to the Latin of the Chronicle. The formation of this cycle in stages between the end of the thirteenth century and *c.* 1336 suggests that Welsh *littérateurs* were aware of similar collections of Charlemagne material in Middle English, but the fluency of the renderings and the self-assured unifying handling of diverse originals suggest that these confident skills are the products of a school of translators, working within the Welsh narrative tradition, but eager to develop it by adapting foreign stories.

The *Friendship of Amlyn and Amig* is another popular story on the fringes of the Charlemagne cycle, which was translated into Welsh around the beginning of the fourteenth century. It is a version of the Latin life of the inseparable warrior saints, not of the corresponding French *chanson de geste* of the two friends, which does not contain the religious and pietistic elements of the former. The translator was familiar with the stereotyped phrases of the native tales which he echoes in a brief love scene or in a battle scene which has a typically heroic line, *a'r brein yn greu uch benn y kalaned.*

Arthurian prose romances are represented in Welsh by *Ystoryaeu y Seint Greal,* a fourteenth-century translation of two independent French texts, the *Queste del Saint Graal,* (*c.* 1225), a branch of the Vulgate Cycle of Arthurian romances, and *Perlesvaus* (1191-1212). Both have as their theme the search for the Grail, carried out unsuccessfully by a number of Arthur's men but finally fulfilled by the spiritually perfect knight; both relate the adventures in a Christian ascetic setting. *Perlesvaus,* viewed as a continuation of Chrétien's Grail romance, has as its hero Perceval who fulfils the task he had earlier left undone and wins the Grail Castle, after which a number of other secular adventures, unconnected with the Grail, are undertaken. *The Queste* has greater strength in unity and vision. The Grail is here the vessel of the Last Supper, brought to Britain by Joseph of Arimathea and, enveloped in mystery and hidden from sight, guarded by his descendants. It is a symbol of God's grace, freely offered but attainable in its fullness only by the pure. Arthur's knights attempt the search, but their spiritual inadequacies cause some to fail completely while three are granted partial visions. Only the perfectly chaste Galahad achieves ecstatic union. The Welsh translator abbreviates the original and may be more interested in the adventures than in their allegorical or mystical significance, but the translation brings a new dimension to Welsh narrative, for though scenes of adventures could be expressed by means of an existing vocabulary, Biblical quotations and theological explanations were new elements in a story-context, as was the interlace structure in the narrative tradition. The translation seems to have been done for a member of the Morgannwg aristocracy, as one or more copies in the libraries of noblemen of that province are referred to by poets in the fourteenth and fifteenth centuries. An account of the birth and nurturing of Arthur, and his subsequent winning of the sword from the stone, was also translated in the fourteenth century, and seems to be based ultimately on the Vulgate *Merlin* branch. Though this translator, like that of the *Seint Greal,* linked his foreign material with native tradition by giving Welsh forms of personal names and offices, he does not display the same intimate acquaintance with the story-telling usages.

The fluency, vocabulary and commonplaces of these translations show that the native prose tradition obviously had not died, though foreign romance was in vogue. It is not surprising, therefore, that the native conventions and features of the oral style of the *cyfarwyddiaid* reappear towards the end of the medieval period. *Chwedlau Saith Ddoethon Rhufain* is the Welsh version of a popular collection of stories set within the narrative framework of the defence of a young prince by his mentors, the Seven Sages of Rome. The story, probably of eastern origin, came to Europe towards the middle of the twelfth century and achieved widespread popularity on account of the tales contained in the framework, stories of the *exemplum* and *fabliau* type, humorous stories of old men and young wives, of feminine fickleness and of faithfulness rewarded. The Welsh version does not seem to be a translation. It contains two new stories not found in other versions; stylistically, it is close to the *cyfarwydd* tradition as represented in the native tales. It opens with a traditional formula, at one point it uses a Welsh proverb to elaborate a statement, and it employs dialogue as skilfully as the other tales. Throughout, the style is marked not only by the use of familiar phrases and *clichés* but also by the same traditional syntax, and a number of examples of the rhetoric of compound adjectives. The work is attributed to Llywelyn Offeiriad, about whom nothing is known, but who is probably to be regarded more as the author than simply the translator of the text. He was familiar with the extant tales as is evidenced by his borrowings from and echoes of passages in *Culhwch and Olwen, Owain, Maxen* and perhaps the Dingestow Brut, and he was versed in the conventions of story-telling. His work testifies to the persistence of those conventions throughout the period of the French translations down to his own day, towards the mid fourteenth century.

More striking evidence for the continuity of Welsh oral techniques is provided by the *Areithiau Pros* (Prose Rhetorics), comparatively brief passages written in a highly ornate style. The majority of them are found in manuscripts of the sixteenth century or later, and a number of those edited by the late Dr. Gwenallt Jones appear to be literary exercises in rhetoric consisting of a profusion of compound nouns and adjectives used in a contrived setting, e.g. love letters, lists of likes and dislikes. Many are linked with the names of poets and these flourishes would seem to be an aspect of the traditional verbal skills of the bards possibly influenced in their late forms by Renaissance ideas of 'abundance' of language. Medieval prose authors, however, were more sparing in their use of rhetoric, employing it in conventionalized descriptive passages or as a flash of colour or movement in the narrative. The *Areithiau* which have been termed parodies, *Araith Wgon, Araith Iolo Goch, Breuddwyd Gruffudd ab Adda ap Dafydd,* are close to this tradition and may be regarded as simple folk-tales or anecdotes which reflect the oral style of the story-tellers more faithfully than the literary development of that style found in the tales and romances.

These *Areithiau* have features which link them both with the fully developed tales and with late medieval folk-tales. They are centred around well-attested historical figures, two of them open with the normal introductory formula, and unlike the majority of *Areithiau,* these do not exist in a narrative vacuum. The earliest of them, *Breuddwyd Gruffudd ab Adda* which is found in a fifteenth-century manuscript, uses the motif of the dream-maiden and search, while the other two are simple humorous tales of trickery and one-upmanship which represent the less serious part of the *cyfarwyddiaid*'s repertoire, the brief anecdote or single situation rather than the fully developed hero or wonder tale. *Araith Iolo Goch,* termed a *chwedl* in the manuscripts, is the most sophisticated of the three. It is made up of a number of references to characters drawn from romance, contrasted with jocular allusions to what may be near contemporaries. It is the pairing of incompatibles, within a minimal narrative framework, which gives the composition its point and humour. *Araith Wgon* is written in a simple unadorned style. It is a straightforward story of rival attainments which provide an opportunity to write passages of abuse and boasting well suited to rhetoric. All three *Areithiau* are characterized by the liberal use of compound nouns and adjectives, common collocations and stereotyped expressions, but an equally conspicuous feature, which must derive from an oral style, is their use of formulas (not found in the literary tales), stylized syntax and rhythmic passages made up of balanced clauses and expressions. The clearest debt to an oral style is seen in the *Breuddwyd* which contains a description of a battle expressed not in realistic but in rhetorical terms. This passage, a succession of colourful and connotative expressions, each with two stresses (a rhythmic pattern found in the rhetorics in *Culhwch and Olwen),* rhymes, and alliterations, has a breathtaking quality even on the written page, and is the best, if not the only true example in Welsh, of the rhetorical device called a 'run' in Irish folk-tales. The *Breuddwyd* ends with a conversation in *englynion* between the hero and the dream-maiden, which represents the convention of the prose-verse *cyfarwyddyd* referred to earlier in this essay.

These *Areithiau* are not so much parodies of the literary tradition as examples of the style of oral story-telling which underlies the tales and romances and which comes to the surface briefly at the close of the medieval period.

BIBLIOGRAPHY

Editions:
F. Lot, *Nennius et l'Historia Brittonum*, Paris, 1934.
Ifor Williams, *Cyfranc Lludd a Llevelys*, Bangor, 1922.
Brynley F. Roberts, *Cyfranc Lludd a Llefelys*, Dublin, 1975.
Ifor Williams, *Breuddwyd Maxen*, Bangor, 1928.
Glenys W. Goetinck, *Peredur*, Caerdydd (at the press).
R. L. Thomson, *Owein*, Dublin, 1970.
G. Melville Richards, *Breudwyt Ronabwy*, Caerdydd, 1972.
Morgan Watkin, *Ystorya Bown de Hamtwn*, Caerdydd, 1959.
Stephen J. Williams, *Ystorya de Carolo Magno*, Caerdydd, 1968.
J. Gwenogvryn Evans, *Kymdeithas Amlyn ac Amic*, Llanbedrog, 1909.
Robert Williams, *Y Seint Greal*, London, 1876.
Thomas Jones, *Ystoriau'r Seint Greal*, Caerdydd (at the press).
J. H. Davies, 'A Welsh Version of the Birth of Arthur,' *Y Cymmrodor*, 24 (1913), 247-64.
Henry Lewis, *Chwedleu Seith Doethon Rufein*, Caerdydd, 1967.
D. Gwenallt Jones, *Yr Areithiau Pros*, Caerdydd, 1934.

Translations:
Gwyn Jones and Thomas Jones, *The Mabinogion*, Everyman's Library, 1949.
Robert Williams, *Selections from the Hengwrt Manuscripts*, 2 vols. London, 1876, — contains translations of *Bown, Seith Doethon Rufein* and *Y Seint Greal.*
Robert Williams, '*Ystoria de Carolo Magno,*' *Y Cymmrodor*, 20 (1907).

Critical Studies:
Geraint Bowen (ed.), *Y Traddodiad Rhyddiaith yn yr Oesau Canol,* Llandysul, 1974. Contains chapters on *Culhwch and Olwen, The Dream of Rhonabwy,* Romances.

Rachel Bromwich, *Trioedd Ynys Prydein,* Cardiff, 1961; 'The Character of the Early Welsh Tradition,' *Studies in Early British History* (ed. N. K. Chadwick), Cambridge, 1959, 83-136; 'The Celtic Inheritance of Medieval Literature,' *Mod. Lang. Quarterly,* 26 (1955), 205-27; 'Celtic Dynastic Themes and the Breton Lays,' *Etudes Celtiques,* 9 (1961), 439-74.

Mary Giffin, 'The Date of the Dream of Rhonabwy,' *Trans. Cymmrodorion,* 1958, 33-40.

Glenys W. Goetinck, 'Historia Peredur,' *Llên Cymru,* 6 (1961), 139-53; 'Peredur a Perceval,' ibid. 8 (1964), 58-64.

W. J. Gruffydd, 'Mabon ab Modron,' *Revue Celtique,* 33 (1912), 452-61; 'Mabon vab Modron,' *Y Cymmrodor,* 42 (1931), 129-47.

Kenneth H. Jackson, *The International Popular Tale and Early Welsh Tradition,* Cardiff, 1961.

Gwyn Jones, *Kings, Beasts and Heroes,* London, 1972.

R. M. Jones, 'Y Rhamantau Cymraeg,' *Llên Cymru,* 4 (1957), 208-27.

T. Gwynn Jones, 'Some Arthurian Material in Keltic,' *Aberystwyth Studies,* 8 (1926), 37-93.

R. S. Loomis (ed.), *Arthurian Literature in the Middle Ages,* Oxford, 1959 (contains chapters on *Culhwch and Olwen, Breuddwyd Rhonabwy,* the Romances); *Arthurian Tradition and Chrétien de Troyes,* Columbia, 1949; *Wales and the Arthurian Legend,* Cardiff, 1956.

Jean Marx, *Nouvelles recherches sur la littérature arthurienne,* Paris, 1965.

John Rhys, *Celtic Folklore, Welsh and Manx,* Oxford, 1901.

Ifor Williams, *Hen Chwedlau,* Caerdydd, 1949.

Mary Williams, *Essai sur la composition du roman gallois de Peredur,* Paris, 1909.

Glenys W. Goetinck, *Peredur: A Study of Welsh Tradition in the Grail Legends,* Cardiff, 1975.

CHAPTER X

HISTORICAL WRITING

BRYNLEY F. ROBERTS

Reference has already been made to the duty of the poets as a learned class to conserve and transmit the traditional history of the Welsh, 'the History of the Notable Acts of the Kings and Princes of this land', referred to in a late bardic treatise. Some traces of this history survive in the allusions to the Roman conquest, in the dynastic and heroic associations of the end of Roman rule, and in references to elusive characters like Prydain fab Aedd, probably an eponymous founder of Britain, and Beli and his sons, especially Lludd and Caswallon. The use of the term the 'Island of Britain', and the evidence of the texts themselves, show that traditional learning, both historical and geographical, viewed Britain as a single entity divided into three parts, the North, Wales and Cornwall, later designated in changed political circumstances, the North, Wales and England. The sovereignty of Britain, symbolized by 'the crown of London', was the right of the Britons, or the Welsh, as the descendants of the first settlers and founders of the realm. The unity of Britain and the claim of the Welsh to be sole overlords are a basic concept of medieval Welsh historiography. This overlordship had been threatened throughout history by invading nations, Romans, Picts, Scots, and in more recent times it had been usurped by the Saxons who now bore the crown of London and claimed the sovereignty of Britain. The theme of dispossession which runs through Welsh history is, however, not an irreparable loss, for it is balanced by the sure hope of the restoration of British rule in a future golden age, expressed in prophetic poems describing the banishment of the Saxons.

The loss of Britain theme first appears in Gildas's *De Excidio Britanniae* in the sixth century, and is used again, though tempered with political prophecy and hope, in Nennius's *Historia Brittonum,* where for the first time the Welsh are given a Trojan origin, their descent being traced from Brutus, the grandson of Aeneas who escaped from the sack of Troy. The most influential historian of medieval Wales, however, was Geoffrey of Monmouth whose *Historia Regum Britanniae* appeared about 1136. His aim was to write a narrative of Welsh history from its beginnings after the fall of Troy down to the loss of overlordship to the Saxons in the seventh century. He presents a succession of kings under whose rule the kingdom of Britain is sometimes divided, sometimes lost, and at times enjoys the prosperity and fame which only a just and successful ruler can bring about. The Britons achieve their fullest flowering during the reign of Arthur, although this is but the glow before the sun of British rule finally sets. Central to Geoffrey's view of British history is the concept of a single kingdom ruled by a succession of kings, but though this and many details, both nominal and thematic, are derived from traditional Welsh learning, the most important single factor in his work is his imagination which welded together diverse elements taken from literary sources and tradition to produce a new composition, a fictitious history of Britain. The *Historia* achieved immediate popularity and became the most influential work of medieval British historiography. It has an air of authenticity derived not only from the source Geoffrey claimed for the work, an ancient British book, but also from the author's ability to imitate some of the features of contemporary historians, in his use of 'authorities,' of classical authors and of documents and letters, and in the unified structure of his work. Moreover, the *Historia* filled a gap in British history, providing for Normans a history of their adopted land which seemed to be a precedent for Angevin imperialism, and granting the Welsh their first coherent history of themselves, a glorious view of their past, critical of them in parts perhaps, but suggesting for the reader wishing to find it, the possibility of a new British age.

There exist several Welsh versions of the *Historia,* referred to as *Brut y Brenhinedd, Ystoria Brutus,* etc. The earliest translations, from the thirteenth century, are generally close renderings of the Latin, but later versions, sometimes new translations, at others amalgams of previous ones, tend to condense the original and to add new material. All the translators or 'editors' attempt to combine Geoffrey's history with accepted Welsh tradition. Usually this involves little more than the addition of a sentence or comment, but as has already been noted, one early translator seized the opportunity of inserting into his version his retelling of the tale of Liudd and Llefelys.

The *Historia,* which opens with the flight of Aeneas from Troy, is frequently preceded in the manuscripts by the standard medieval account of the Trojan war, the *De Excidio Troiae* of 'Dares Phrygius' which purported to be the work of an eyewitness with Trojan sympathies. The Welsh versions of the text, *Ystoria Dared,* have no independent value and appear to have been translated solely as an introduction to *Brut y Brenhinedd.* Geoffrey, however, had ended his book with the comment that he was leaving the history of the English to two fellow-historians, William of Malmesbury and Henry of Huntingdon, and the story of the princes who subsequently ruled in Wales he commits to his contemporary Caradog of Llancarfan. There were a number of attempts to continue the *Historia.* In Wales the most important is *Brut y Tywysogion* or the 'Chronicle of the Princes', which opens with an entry designed to link with Geoffrey's closing episodes and which follows the story down to 1282. It was natural that the work should be ascribed to Caradog but modern research has shown that it is based on monastic annals and is to be dated in its final recension after 1286. It is in every respect a very different work from Geoffrey's, in its annalistic structure as opposed to his narrative history, and in its careful dependence on authentic historical material which makes it a major source for medieval Welsh history. Though the original Latin chronicle has not survived, it was twice translated into Welsh and a third version is a combination of the Chronicle with English annals.

Together these three texts, *Ystoria Dared,* the Brut and the Chronicle, present a panorama of Welsh history from the origins of the nation in the mists of the Trojan war, through the period of settlement in Britain, the vicissitudes of fortune under the rule of successive kings, the climax of Arthur's reign, down to the loss of sovereignty. Geoffrey's narrative gives way to the sober factual entries of the Chronicle: the scene shifts to Wales and the gradual development of the Welsh principalities is unfolded and Gwynedd emerges as the dominant power. Two groups of manuscripts present these texts in sequence as a 'majestic compilation' extending over thousands of years of Welsh history and must have been an important element in the sustaining of national consciousness in the years following the Edwardian conquest.

The translations have a certain dignity and sonority, though they frequently seem wooden and unnatural in their style. They have points of contact with the tales both in vocabulary and in some stylistic features, but in general they are influenced by Latin syntax and appear laboured in expression. They do not seem to be the work of writers truly familiar with the *cyfarwydd* tradition as were the translators of the tales. They represent, rather, the attempts of authors with a learned Latin background to treat in Welsh a subject for which the natural medium in the Middle Ages was Latin.

BIBLIOGRAPHY

Texts:
Henry Lewis, *Brut Dingestow,* Caerdydd, 1942.
Thomas Jones, *Brut y Tywysogion or the Chronicle of the Princes: Red Book of Hergest Version,* Cardiff, 1974.

Critical Studies:
Thomas Jones, 'Historical Writing in Medieval Welsh,' *Scottish Studies,* 12 (1968), 15-27.
Brynley F. Roberts, *Brut y Brenhinedd,* Dublin, 1971.
Brynley F. Roberts, 'Testunau Hanes Cymraeg Canol,' *Y Traddodiad Rhyddiaith yn yr Oesau Canol,* (ed. Geraint Bowen), Llandysul, 1974, 274-302.

CHAPTER XI

FUNCTIONAL PROSE: RELIGION, SCIENCE, GRAMMAR, LAW

MORFYDD E. OWEN

The literary tradition of Wales in the Middle Ages, like that of most of the countries of Europe, is marked by a duality which stems from its development from the literary inheritance of its Celtic past, combined with an enormous debt to the general culture of Latin Christendom. Nowhere in Welsh literature is this duality so marked as in the wealth of functional or useful prose which has survived. Nearly all this prose with the notable exception of the law texts is derived from works originally written in Latin. The transmission of these works would in itself make an exciting story. They cannot compete with works of Welsh native genius like the Mabinogion, but their very fluency of language and style testifies to the virility of the literary tradition on to which they were grafted. These works are religious, scientific, grammatical, medical, agricultural and philosophical, and demonstrate the wealth of the heritage available to the cultured Welshman of the high Middle Ages.

Cynddelw Brydydd Mawr knew of the *Imago Mundi*. Soon after his time a translation, *Delw y Byd*, was available in Welsh. Hopcyn ap Tomos, a Glamorgan nobleman, had a copy of the *Elucidarium* in his library:

> Wealth to hand in his Court
> The golden lead of the Lucidarius,
> And the Grail story and Annals,
> And the force of every law and its grace.

References in the Welsh law tracts suggest that the compilers of those books were familiar with medical treatises in the style of the writings of Meddygon Myddfai. The world of medieval Wales was not purely that of Celtic romance and magic, of archaic legalism, heroic praise poetry and love lyrics, but a complex mixture of philosophy, religion, science, music and grammar which underlay and enriched the native literary *genres* traditionally associated with the period. The purpose of this chapter is to indicate the nature of at least some of the material written in Welsh which goes to make up this complexity.

Much of this literature was translation, most of it from Latin but with one or two texts from French, like the agricultural treatise of Walter of Henley, or from English like the version of the *Enfant Sage* legend contained in *Hystoria Adrian ac Ipotis*. In view of this, it is not strange that the problems of translation are referred to in the *incipit* of more than one medieval text. Some unknown Phylip translated a Latin alchemical text *De Corio Serpentis (Deuddeg Rhinwedd Croen Neidr)* into Welsh because he considered it an essential part of the equipment of a medieval doctor. Fully aware of his shortcomings as a translator, he introduced it with the words, 'I Phylip, though I be least in my knowledge of languages, have turned this text from Latin into Welsh.' A more sophisticated and considered approach to the art of translation is revealed in the Introduction to the Welsh translation of the Athanasian Creed where Brother Gruffudd Bola, possibly a Franciscan friar, explained to his patroness, Efa, daughter of Maredudd, how translation should be tackled:

> One must realise from the beginning that, when something is translated from one language to another, one cannot always substitute word for word and at the same time fairly maintain the proper usage and sense of the language. For that reason, I have sometimes translated word by word and other times I have replaced sense for sense according to the manner and nature of our language.

Professor G. J. Williams suggested that there were schools of translators working in Glamorgan from the fifteenth to the seventeenth centuries, especially trained in the art of translation. Certainly the amount and quality of Welsh translation prose would not belie the idea of such professionalism at an earlier date.

The world of the medieval European was essentially a Christian one and much Welsh functional prose is religious or connected with religion. The importance of this religious prose is emphasized by the existence of several manuscripts devoted to collections of religious writings. The most famous of these collections is *Llyfr yr Ancr* ('The Book of the Anchorite') which Gruffudd ap Llywelyn ap Trahaearn of Cantref Mawr caused to be written 'by the hand of a friend, namely a man who was anchorite at that time at Llanddewifrefi,' in the year 1346.

The contents of *Llyfr yr Ancr* give a fair idea of the range of the religious works which were available in Medieval Welsh. Professor Thomas Jones classified them under five headings:

(i)   Scriptural passages with or without a commentary.
(ii)   Apocalyptic texts.
(iii) Texts in dialogue form.
(iv) Miscellaneous Theological Tracts.
(v)   Lives of Saints.

The *Llyfr yr Ancr* list is notable because it has no reference to the Bible as such. Indeed, no substantial part of the Bible was translated into Middle Welsh, as might be expected in a world where more emphasis was put on the offices of the Church than on the substance of the Bible. The so-called *Bibyl Ynghymraec* is really a summary of biblical history translated from the *Promptuarium Bibliae* of Petrus Pictavensis, one of the Paupers' Bibles. Derived from works which originally related the Bible to the medieval concept of world history by a series of genealogies, the *Promptuarium Bibliae* belongs to the tradition of historical writing in Wales as much as to the tradition of religious writing, though the book incorporates certain translated passages of the Bible. The most notable of these is a translation of the story of the Creation from Genesis I and II:

> Pryt nat oedh dim eithyr Duw ehun yn dair person ac yn vn Duw, yna yn y dechrau y creodh Duw nef a daear. Canys y dhaear a oedh orwac a dielw, a thywyllwch a oedh ar wyneb yr eigion. Ac yspryt yr Arglwydh a dhyborthit ar y dyfredh. Ac yna dywedyt a oruc Duw, 'Bit leuuer,' heb

Ef. Ac ef a wnaethpwyt lheuuer. Ac ef a welas Duw bot yn dha lheuer. A gwahanu y lheuuer y wrth y tywylhwc, a galw y lheuuer yn dhydh a'r t(y)wylhwc yn nos. Ac velhy y gwnaethpwyt brynhawn a boreu y dydh cyntaf.

The other parts of Scripture which were directly translated into Welsh are passages which were particularly associated with the liturgy of the Church, such as the *In Principio* of St. John's Gospel. Another example is the story of the Passion, referred to as *Y Groglith* and probably the lesson which was read in Church on Good Friday.

If little of the Bible itself was translated, many texts connected with the Bible are found in Welsh, both apocrypha and midrash. These texts are narrative like the paraphrase of the *History of Susanna and Tobit* or the *History of Adam and Eve his wife,* which tells how Adam and Eve did penance in the waters of Jordan and the Tigris and then journeyed back to the gates of Paradise. Some texts add to the information given in the New Testament, like the story of *How Elen found the true Cross,* or the account of the *Ascent into Heaven of the Blessed Virgin, The Letter of Pilate to Claudius* and *The Story of the Infancy of Jesus Christ.* References in the poetry of the period show that this literature was familiar to the Welsh poets and must have been part of the current idiom of the Church.

In 1284 Archbishop Peckham visited the four Welsh dioceses and, it is thought, preached the need for the Welsh priests to have available in the vernacular texts which were fundamental to forwarding the beliefs of the Church. This visit seems to have stimulated literary activity. Manuscripts which were written in the period following it contain all the texts which a conscientious priest would need to read in order to instruct his flock in the Christian faith. Translations were made of the *Apostles' Creed,* of the *Ten Commandments,* and of a series of instructions on *How the Father, the Son and the Holy Ghost are to be understood as one God,* and on *How a man should believe in God and love God, keep the Ten Commandments, shun the Seven Deadly Sins and receive the Seven*

Sacraments of the Church. Imposing penances for their sins on the faithful was one of the tasks of the priests and a work which gave guidance in this was the *Penityas* as translated from the work of Raymond de Pennafort, *Summa de Poenitentia et Matrimonio.*

These are on the whole instructional texts. *Llyfr yr Ancr* and the other manuscripts of religious prose contain texts which deal at greater length with theological problems. Their contents suggest that the Welsh on the whole were not deeply involved in the *avant-garde* theological disputes of the Middle Ages: they are translations of popular works intended for the ordinary clergyman and layman.

The most famous of Medieval Welsh theological texts is typical of this tendency, namely the *Liwsidarium* or *Hystoria Liwsidar,* a translation of a work of the early twelfth century by Honorius Augustodiensis, a monk of Ratisbon in Germany, *Elucidarium sive Dialogus de Summa Totius Christianae Theologiae,* one of the most popular of all medieval theological texts. The *Elucidarium* attempted to systematize some of the religious questions of the period. The Welsh translation is an abridged version of the three books of the original which are written in typical medieval catechism or dialogue form. Honorius described the three books as dealing with Christ, the Church and the Future Life.

The first book deals with the nature of God and gives an account of the angels, demons, man and other creatures of the earth. The second book, linked with the first by a discussion of the Eucharist, deals with the choice between good and evil and the problem of sin; it discusses the virtues of pilgrimage and the road to salvation open to the various trades and professions:

> 'What hope is there for the minstrels?' 'There is none because they are serving the devil with all their strength. Of those it is said, "They know not God," and for that reason God looked askance at them and God shall mock them. For he who mocks will be mocked.' . . .
> 'What about the labourers of the earth?' 'Many of them are saved because they lead a humble life and feed God's people on their sweat, so is said, "Blessed be he who eats of the toil of his hands."'

FUNCTIONAL PROSE: RELIGION, SCIENCE, GRAMMAR, LAW 253

The third book describes life after death and the medieval concept of paradise.

The number of manuscript copies that have survived and literary references suggest that the *Elucidarium* was as popular in Wales as in other European countries. Iolo Goch in his *Cywydd I'r Llafurwr* made convenient use of it:

> Old lively Lucidarius
> Says with certainty:
> 'Blessed be he, who through his youth
> Yonder holds the plough in both his hands.'

Another question and answer text dealing with theological matters was the *Hystoria Adrian ac Ipotis*. This is a much shorter work. In it, the Emperor Adrian asks the wise wonder child Ipotis questions concerning the nature of God and the World. The work ends with Ipotis revealing himself to be Christ:

> Then the Emperor Adrian said to the boy, 'I demand of you, O child Ipotis, before you leave me, in the name of the Father, the Son and the Holy Ghost and Jesus Christ who suffered in death for the sake of our resurrection: What are you? Are you a good spirit or an evil one?' The boy answered him like this, 'I am the man who made you and bought you dearly.' And then he ascended into the heights of heaven from whence he came. And in this way ends the discussion of the Emperor Adrian and Ipotis, the spiritual son of God.

If the *Elucidarium* is a fairly representative example of a medieval theological text, another text in *Llyfr yr Ancr* is a representative and at the same time an exceptional example of another type of religious literature, namely the literature of mysticism. Professor Caerwyn Williams has suggested that the religious reformation of the thirteenth century produced not only a new awareness of sin, but a new awareness of the emotion of love, and this second awareness found its expression in the wonderful mystic text known as *Cysegrlan Fuchedd* ('Holy Living') or *Ymborth yr Enaid* ('Aid for the Soul'). A book in three parts, the first treats of vices and virtues, the second of the Divine love between God and Man and Man and God, and the third of the ecstatic experiences of mystic union with the Holy Spirit. It has been suggested that this was a book intended for monks or nuns. It refers to the mystical experiences of a Dominican, 'a certain brother of the preaching orders', and contains instructions concerning the way to achieve mystical experience. The climax of the whole work is the section known as *Pryd y Mab* ('the Vision of the Youth'), where a young boy appears before the brother. The passage contains a glorious baroque description of Christ as a child of twelve years, in rhythmic alliterative prose:

> Y Mab, mab melynnwynn adueindwf oed val yn oet deudegmlwyd. Ac yn gymedrawl y dwf a dyat y gorff, o hyt a phraffter vrth y oet. penn gogygrwnn gwedeid idaw. A gwallt penngrychlathyr pefyrloyw eureit velynlliw arnaw yn vnffuryf a phei gellit llunyaw neu vedylyaw dwy yscubell o van adaued neu van gasnad o eur trinawtawd a hynny megys ar voe no rychwant o bop tu yr deu wyneb glaerwynnyon.

> The golden white slender lad was as though he were twelve years old. Moderate in the growth and shape of his body. His height and girth were of his age, he had a shapely rounded head and a golden-yellow bright shining curly head of hair on it of the same form as though you were able to shape or imagine two sheaves of fine thread or fine fleeces of molten-worked gold and as though they were more than a span's width on each side of the two shining white surfaces.

The Dominican monk overwhelmed by his vision fell in a faint before the child, from the impact of the love which swept over him. The child raised him up and ordered the monk to love him as much as he could. The monk replied in words that have scarcely been equalled for their exposition of the reciprocal nature of love:

> 'Oh Lord,' said the brother, 'there is no need to thank me for loving you, for there is no one who sees you that would not love you.' 'Indeed there is,' he said, 'for I should not appear to you unless you loved me, and you do not love me as much as I love you and yet you have not seen the whole of me, and when you see me, your love for me will have greater meaning. Tell the poets, to whom I have given a share of the spirit of my delight, that it is better for them to reciprocate that than to praise the love of empty transient things.'

FUNCTIONAL PROSE: RELIGION, SCIENCE, GRAMMAR, LAW

The last sentence of the quotation brings to mind at once the puritanical criticisms of the poets by Siôn Cent and his condemnation of 'empty flattery and satire', or the words of Dafydd ap Gwilym's friar:

> No good is the praise of the body
> That draws man's soul to the devil.

The *Cysegrlan Fuchedd* marks the climax of Welsh medieval religious experience and is perhaps the most moving piece of religious prose written in the whole history of the language. The experience of such love and ecstasy was hardly the lot of all and it is doubtful whether *Cysegrlan Fuchedd* reached a wide reading public.

Other types of visionary literature were also available in Welsh. Three of the notable vision texts of the period, the *Visio Sancti Pauli*, the *De Purgatorio Sancti Patricii*, and the *De Spiritu Guidonis*, were translated into Welsh. The most notable of these texts is the *Purdan Padrig* or the translation of the *De Purgatorio Sancti Patricii*.

There was on an island in Lough Derg in the north of Ireland a cave which, tradition maintained, God had shown to Saint Patrick, saying,

> Whosoever may go in penance armed with the rightful faith to this cave and remain there for a day and a night, shall be cleansed of all his sins. And after walking through it, he shall see the pains of the evil and if he be constant in his faith, he shall see the joy of the good.

This cave was afterwards known as St. Patrick's Purgatory and became a famous place for penitents and those seeking otherworld visions from the whole of Western Christendom; for visits to the cave seem to have produced visions and experiences comparable with those described by Dante in the *Divine Comedy*. The Welsh *Purdan Padrig* is a version of the story of the visit of Owain the knight to the Purgatory, describing his journey to it and the horrors which he witnessed and experienced there:

And this meadow was full of people, men and women, young and old, lying naked with their faces to the earth, dragged down with pure white nails through their feet and their hands on the earth, and sometimes you would see them biting the earth for pain, and other times crying in complaint and shrieking and clamouring wretchedly and begging like this: 'Save, oh save, Lord,' or 'Take mercy on us.' And there was no one there who knew either mercy or salvation. There were nevertheless devils in their midst and upon them, raising them up without rest and beating them with hard whips. Then the devils said to the knight, 'You must suffer all the pains which you see, unless you obey our advice, that is namely, cease from your intent and go back from here. And if you wish that, we shall take you back peacefully and without harm to the gate from which you came.' The knight refused that and the devils cast him down to pull him on to the nails as were the others, but as he called on the name of Jesus they could not fulfil their intent.

It is difficult today to appreciate the masochistic motives which lay behind descriptions such as these. Doubtless the *Purdan* is much indebted to the early penitential ideals of the Celtic Church but this does not entirely explain its popularity as a literary form until the end of the Middle Ages.

The religious literature which was most familiar to the ordinary Welshman, the labourer and the nobleman who stood with their fellows in the parish church, was that which they heard from the pulpit. Much of this was in the form of stories and prognostications used regularly to cajole and coerce the faithful into a better way of life by threats of the dooms to come, by moralizing anecdote and by holding up as an example the pattern of the Holy Lives of the Saints who had gone before them.

The Fifteen Signs before Doomsday and *The Antichrist and the Day of Judgement* are two works which give some idea of the pictures of Judgement Day which were presented. The first work lists the upheavals which precede the Great Judgement. *Englynion,* ascribed to both Bishop Morudd and Llywelyn Fardd enumerating the signs in metrical form, testify to their popularity:

> Morudd, mighty his manner,
> For God's sake, told
> The measure of the signs which will be
> The fifteenth day before Judgement.

FUNCTIONAL PROSE: RELIGION, SCIENCE, GRAMMAR, LAW 257

The second work describes in a dramatic rhetorical manner the horrors which will come, leading up to a climax in God's speech of reproach at the final hour of Doom:

> Then he said to all of them:
> 'Also wretched accursed people, you have been unmerciful to the cry of those hungry ones seeking food, to the thirsty asking drink, to the naked seeking clothes. Wicked and ungentle have you been in visiting the sick and the prisoners in order to entertain them, for you have always preferred to devote yourselves to evil deeds and sins at the command of the devils yonder, turning and dwelling in your evil living and sins without repenting or confessing them until death or devoting yourselves to knowledge of me and my laws. And because you did not do these things before death and you had no fear, today you are lost.'

These words are echoed in Siôn Cent's poem on the *Great Judgement*, and the *Gogynfardd* poem to Judgement Day:

> Where is he, the man unfortunate in his living
> And the false accuser, and the false usurer,
> And the treacherous deceiver, with the betraying hands,
> And the graceless thief and the two-faced man
> And the gluttonous and the lazy, the avenging frightener?
> The adulterer and the liar, and the false believer?
> Since they have no faith, they fled beforehand,
> Into the midst of the host, to the depths of hell.

These threats must have had great dramatic value on the lips of a skilful preacher, and poems like Dafydd ap Gwilym's *Ymddiddan â'r Brawd Llwyd* suggest that such a note was frequently heard. Other works suggest that there was a gentler side to preaching. This gentler note was to be heard in other kinds of works known to be read in the pulpit, namely, the *exempla* and the saints' lives. *Exempla* were short pithy stories used by the clergy throughout Europe to illustrate the nature of sins and virtues, and were regarded by the Church as a necessary part of the stock-in-trade of any preacher:

> Inasmuch as examples are more effective than words, as Gregory said, and they are accepted more easily into the mind and they cling more deeply in the memory and many are the readier to listen to them, it is worth while for those who have taken to preaching to possess a supply of them ...

A famous collection of *exempla,* that of Odo of Cheriton, an English clergyman of the thirteenth century, was translated into Welsh in 1375. These *exempla* are notable in that, like *Aesop's Fables,* they are all animal stories. The author uses the special characteristics of individual creatures, for example the cunning fox, the bravery of the lion, as examples of the universal qualities which these characteristics represent. Here is the 'story' of *The Cuckoo and the Hedge-sparrow:*

> It is the nature of the cuckoo to lay eggs in the hedge-sparrow's nest. That bird then sits on the eggs as though they were her own and hatches out the bird and rears it until it is strong and big. And when it be fully grown and strong it swallows the one that reared it and thus expresses its thanks.
>
> Thus it is that many people are hostile towards and cause evil and cruelty to those who have reared them and have done good to them in their weakness and poverty. And those people may be compared with the cuckoo.

Saints' lives form an important part of all medieval literatures. Those to be found in Welsh fall into two classes: *(a)* The lives of foreign saints translated from well-known collections such as the *Legenda Aurea* of Jacopo de Voragine or the collection of lives of women saints containing the Lives of Saints Catherine, Margaret, Mary Magdalen and Mary of Egypt, and *(b)* those of the native saints. Only two native saints' lives written in Welsh have been preserved from the medieval period, *Buchedd Dewi* ('Life of Saint David'), and *Buchedd Beuno* ('Life of Saint Beuno').

Medieval saints' lives are never strict history. The *exempla* may be considered the religious counterpart of the *fabliaux;* the saints' lives are the religious counterpart of secular heroic saga with the saint playing the part of the central hero. The lives of Saint Beuno and Saint David are the product of the chief churches connected with the saints' cults, namely Clynnog Fawr and Saint David's. Their chief aim is to exalt the reputation of the patron saints of these churches by accrediting them with miraculous deeds. The lives are based on a nucleus of historical fact but many of the adventures and happenings recorded in the lives belong to a period later than the original age of the saint. *The Life of Saint David,* a translation of a Latin work by Rhigyfarch (1056-99), is supposed to have set a pattern in Welsh hagiography, and a glance at its contents gives an idea of the nature of this kind of literature. The life begins with a genealogy which traces the descent of St. David from the sons of Cunedda,—most early Welsh saints were of royal or noble stock. It then gives a list of the miraculous events which happened to his mother, Non, before his birth and after it, while he was still a babe in arms. Then follows an account of other miracles, a list of the churches which St. David founded, an account of his battles with certain secular rulers, notably the Irish chieftain Boia, and the story of the Synod held at Llanddewibrefi. The life ends with an account of Dewi's death and his final sermon to his followers:

> And after he had laid his blessing on everyone, he uttered these words: 'Lords, brethren and sisters, be joyful and keep your faith and creed and do the small things which you heard and saw me do. And I shall go the way that Our Father went. And fare you well', said Dewi. 'And may your existence on earth be effective, and never more shall we see one another.'

The popularity of the saints' lives is attested by the number of poems by both *Gogynfeirdd* and *cywyddwyr* which use them as their central theme. Rhys Goch Eryri's *cywydd* to Beuno echoes the prose life and Ieuan ap Rhydderch's *cywydd* to Dewi Sant follows minutely the details of Rhigyfarch's story. One of the miraculous happenings recorded in the *Life* as occurring before Dewi's birth is that Non, his mother, while pregnant, attended a sermon by St. Gildas. Gildas was struck dumb because of her presence:

> Gildas then lost his speech,
> Failed to preach a single word
> Because once Non, fair, fine-complexioned,
> Was behind the door, no one saw her.

A work which is not a religious one but which shows the influence of the style of the saints' lives is *Hystoria Gruffudd ap*

Cynan. Gruffudd ap Cynan (1055-1137) was Prince of Gwynedd, and his reign marked a period of great intellectual and cultural activity. The *Hystoria* is the only medieval biography of a native Welsh prince that has survived. Unlike the saints' lives, most of the work represents a reliable historical chronicle. It begins by describing the birth of Gruffudd ap Cynan in exile in Dublin, giving the genealogies of his mother and father. Gruffudd's mother was descended from the Norse princes of Dublin, and the first part of the book deals with the Norse kingdom of Dublin. His father, Cynan, had died a young man and it was from his mother that he heard of his lost inheritance in Gwynedd. The main part of the book deals with his expeditions to try to win back Gwynedd for himself. After a number of futile attacks, and after being captured by the Normans, he eventually succeeded in his aim by using diplomatic means and ruled as Prince of Gwynedd for thirty-seven years until his death. The *Hystoria* as it survives is the translation of a lost Latin life written by an unknown author. It is full of classical touches:

> King Gruffudd had two brothers of the same mother, Kings of Ulster, namely, Raghnall, son of Mathgamhain, who by his valour gained two parts of Ireland in six weeks. He was a wonderful leaper. There was not among all the Irishmen one who could either withstand or match him in leaping. His horse excelled in various feats and swiftness. Islimach was its name. His leap and that of his horse were equal. It was most like Cinnar, the horse of Achilles and Bucephalus, the horse of the Emperor Alexander. Gruffudd's other brother was Aedh Mac Mathgamhain, of Ulster,

mingled with knowledge of native lore:

> O dearly beloved brother Welshmen, very memorable is King Gruffudd, who is commended by the praise of his earthly pedigree and the prophecy of Merddin as above. And since this is finished, let us hasten to his own particular actions as has been promised by us through ancient history. Let Christ be the author and counsellor in this matter, not Diana or Apollo,

and of the Bible and Apocrypha:

Therefore Gruffudd was exalted from that day forth, and was rightfully called King of Gwynedd; and he rejoiced as a strong man to run his course, freeing Gwynedd from the rulers who came to it from another place, who were ruling it without a right; as Judas Maccabeus defended the land of Israel against the kings of the pagans and neighbouring nations who frequently made an inroad among them.

The author, though he himself did not know Gruffudd, derived much of his information from people who had been with the prince. One of his informants, for instance, was a Norseman who had played a prominent part in Gruffudd's early expeditions to Gwynedd. The description of Gruffudd's person is taken from the account of contemporaries:

Intimate friends of Gruffudd say that he was a man of middle height, fair-haired, hot-headed, with a round face of good complexion, large shapely eyes, fine eyebrows, a comely beard, a round neck, white skin, powerful limbs, long fingers, straight shanks, and fine feet. He was skilled and eloquent in several tongues. He was noble and merciful towards his people, cruel towards his enemies, and very gallant in battle.

Although much of the work is concerned with Gruffudd's military activities, there are descriptions at the end of the work eulogizing his qualities as patron of the Church in a style extremely reminiscent of the hagiographers. It was doubtless his generosity to the Church that caused his life to be recorded as in the *Hystoria:*

Then he increased all manner of good in Gwynedd, and the inhabitants began to build churches in every direction therein, and to plant the old woods and to make orchards and gardens, and surround them with walls and ditches and to construct walled buildings and to support themselves from the fruit of the earth after the fashion of the Romans. Gruffudd on his part, made great churches for himself in his chief places, and constructed courts and (gave) banquets constantly and honourably. Wherefore, he also made Gwynedd glitter then with limewashed churches like the firmament with stars.

Preoccupation with things of the spirit did not mean that the Welsh were unconcerned about the wonders of the world around them. One of the most popular of Latin encyclopaedic works dealing with the nature of the universe was the *Imago Mundi* of Honorius Augustodiensis, the author of the *Elucidarium*. This book was translated into Welsh three times under the title *Delw y Byd*. A fellow abbot called Christen had requested Honorius to write the original Latin work:

> Since I know that you are bathed in a great light of wisdom, I, with others, beg of a spark of the blaze of your knowledge, for it will not be thus lessened for you, and ask you to send to me a description of the composition of the world as though it were engraved on a tablet. For everything that we see is wretched, if, like senseless animals, we understand nothing of it.

The book, beginning with an analysis of the story of the Creation, discusses the four elements and the four humours and their all-pervading influence in the natural world, the geography of the known world, the planets, the stars, astrology or the significance of the stars in the plan of the universe and the fate of man, and the signs of the zodiac. In short it summarized into a regularized pattern all that was known or surmised about the world and the universe.

Delw y Byd offered fairly rationalized medieval scientific information to the Welsh reader. His love of the bizarre and curiosity about strange lands were catered for in two notable works, *Ffordd y Brawd Odrig* and *Llythyr Ieuan Fendigaid*. *Llythyr Ieuan Fendigaid* is a translation of the letter of Prester John, which purported to have been written to the Emperor Manuel Cominus by John, Patriarch of India. The letter tells what a mighty Christian potentate John was and describes his marvellous contrivances, the natural marvels, strange beasts and serpents, monstrous races of men, potent herbs and stones to be found in the lands which he rules.

His kingdom not only possesses great natural wonders but is a kind of political Utopia where there is no poverty, crime or falsehood. Most striking of all is the pomp and wealth which surrounds the person of Prester John himself when he goes to war or when he is at home in his palace. The latter is similar to that which the Apostle Thomas built for Gundaphoris, king of India. Its gates are of sardonyx mixed with cerastis which prevent the secret introduction of poison; a couch of sapphire keeps John chaste; the square before the palace is paved with onyx. Near this square is a magic mirror which reveals all hostile plots in provinces subject to Prester John or in adjacent lands. For a work revelling in extravagant wonders, the letter of Prester John—Preutur Siôn or Ieuan Fendigaid as he is called in Welsh sources—has scarcely ever been surpassed. It is not surprising that the wonders and wealth of his kingdom became one of the standard comparisons in Welsh eulogy. Guto'r Glyn referred to William Fychan of Penrhyn as a Preutur Siôn:

> Who owns the three counties? Prester John.

Lewys Morgannwg in a praise poem to Neath Abbey sings of

> The monks' court and the home of Lleision
> And a prester who is greater than Prester John.

The *Ffordd y Brawd Odrig* ('Way of the Brother Odoricus') records the actual journey of a Fransciscan friar to India and Cathay and describes the wonders and horrors of the countries which he visited. These lands included Ceylon and China and he seems to have known of Lhasa the capital of Tibet. Besides treating of the natural wonders of the countries he saw, Odrig tells of the martyrdom of monks in early Christian foundations in the East.

Both *Llythyr Ieuan Fendigaid* and *Ffordd y Brawd Odrig* are of value as showing what ideas prevailed concerning India and the East, in Wales as well as in the rest of Europe, during the Middle Ages.

Some of the other prose works to be found in Welsh are more technical and closely connected with certain crafts or professions, namely agriculture, medicine, poetry, and finally law. One Welsh critic has referred to the *cywydd* poetry, as containing 'furrows of constant praise'. Welsh medieval society was essentially an agricultural one. It is not strange therefore that one of the most important agricultural treatises of the Middle Ages should have been translated into Welsh. An Englishman, Walter of Henley, working on an estate in the Midlands, produced two manuals on estate management. One of these, a 'Book of Husbandry', was translated into Welsh as *Llyfr Hwsmonaeth*. The work is written in the form of a sermon, with a father in old age giving advice to his son, the theme of the sermon being husbandry. It has been suggested that the *Llyfr Hwsmonaeth* was originally written as a lecture addressed to a group of students. The book begins with a prologue containing certain moralistic instructions on how to live wisely; the main body of the work has three sections, on husbandry, corn-farming and stock-farming. It deals with topics like ploughing, sowing, harvest and the care of different kinds of animals.

Part of *Delw y Byd*, as we have seen, was concerned with astrology or the explanation of the natural order of things and men according to the pattern of the stars. Astrology was an important factor in another aspect of medieval science, namely that of medicine. There are some half a dozen medieval manuscripts preserved in Welsh containing medical material. Some of these contain texts prefixed by a colophon or *incipit* claiming the writings as the work of Rhiwallon and his sons, physicians of Rhys Gryg, Lord of Dinefwr:

> Here with the help of God, the almighty Lord, are shown the most important and essential remedies for man's body. And those who caused them to be written down in this manner were Rhiwallon, the doctor, and his sons, Cadwgan, Gruffudd and Einion; for they were the best and leading doctors of their time and of the time of Rhys Gryg, their lord and Lord of Dinefwr, the man who safeguarded their status and privilege completely and honourably as was their due. And the reason they caused the rules of their art to be written down in this way was lest there be no one who knew them as well as they did after their days.

The Welsh Law texts devote a tractate to the rights of the court physician suggesting that this colophon may in fact preserve a true tradition about the court physicians of the Royal

House of Dinefwr. Rhys Gryg, who flourished from 1197 to 1233, was the son of Rhys ap Gruffudd or the Lord Rhys, a member of a family famous for their patronage of all kinds of learning. The family is traditionally connected with a line of hereditary physicians, celebrated in Welsh tradition, who practised medicine in Myddfai in Carmarthenshire for centuries. Myddfai in the Middle Ages was a royal free manor. The material in these medical books is derived from the general medical learning of the Middle Ages. Their contents consist of collections of recipes deriving from herbals and lists of remedies; rules for hygiene deriving from famous collections like the *Regimen Sanitatis:*

> When you rise in the morning, walk a little, then stretch out your limbs, bending your head and your neck; that will strengthen the body, and bending the head will make the spirit rise from the stomach to the head, and from the head, when you sleep, it slips back to the body again. In summer, take a bath in cold water; that will keep the heat in the head and thence cause an appetite. Afterwards, put on fair clothing, because man's mind rejoices in fair things, and the heart will be cheered.

There are instructions for bloodletting; uroscopies or how illness could be diagnosed by examination of the urine; and descriptions of certain operations.

For the student of Welsh literature the texts are of interest in that they show that devices and ornamentation such as alliteration and triads, which are a striking part of Welsh prose style in other fields, are frequent features in medical prose, thus emphasizing the community of culture which linked the different Welsh professional classes:

> Llyma y tri thew anesgor: auu, ac aren, a challon; a llyna yr achaws y gelwir wynt uelly. Dilis yw y lle y keyrdo clwyf ar un or tri, na ellir gwaret udunt namyn marw yn ehegyr.
> Tri theneu anescor ynt: pilyonen yr emennyd, a glas golud a chwyssigen; achaws or un achaws y maent anescor ar rei ereill.

> Here are the three thick indispensables: liver and kidney and heart; and this is why they are so called. It is certain that whenever a disease attacks one of these three, there is no escape and death comes quickly.

> The three thin indispensables are: the membrane of the brain, the small intestine and the bladder; for they are indispensable for the same reason as the others.

From the point of view of the history of ideas the medical books are important in that they suggest that there were in Wales, during the Middle Ages, professional doctors who had received the kind of training in orthodox practical medicine that was available in some of the great medical teaching centres of Europe, like Bologna and Salerno. These men practised their craft and preserved knowledge of it in writing in the vernacular.

Though doctors are indispensable in most societies, the most noteworthy class of professional learned men throughout the whole of Welsh history has, without doubt, been that of the poets. Others will have shown how they performed an important social function by producing panegyric and by preserving traditional knowledge of the past. Their grammar books reveal them in another light and suggest that the Welsh poets were in touch with some of the important philosophical and intellectual ideas of the twelfth and thirteenth centuries. The earliest versions of *Gramadegau'r Penceirddiaid* or the Bardic Grammars have been connected with the names of Einion Offeiriad and Dafydd Ddu Hiraddug, two thirteenth century clerics. These grammar books treat of topics concerning the language and craft of poetry such as orthography, the nature of syllables and diphthongs, syntax and the parts of speech, metrics, rules for praise poetry and its subject-matter, and they contain lists of poetic triads. Parts of the books are adaptations of Latin treatises on grammar into Welsh. The study of grammar, as Mr. Saunders Lewis has shown, was regarded as a branch of dialectic by the schoolman. The Welsh grammars contain analyses of grammar according to the rules of dialectic, some of which ignore very largely the realities of the nature of the language. For instance in Welsh the numerals are regularly followed by singular forms of the noun, thus *tri dyn*, 'three man', etc., yet the grammar books say:

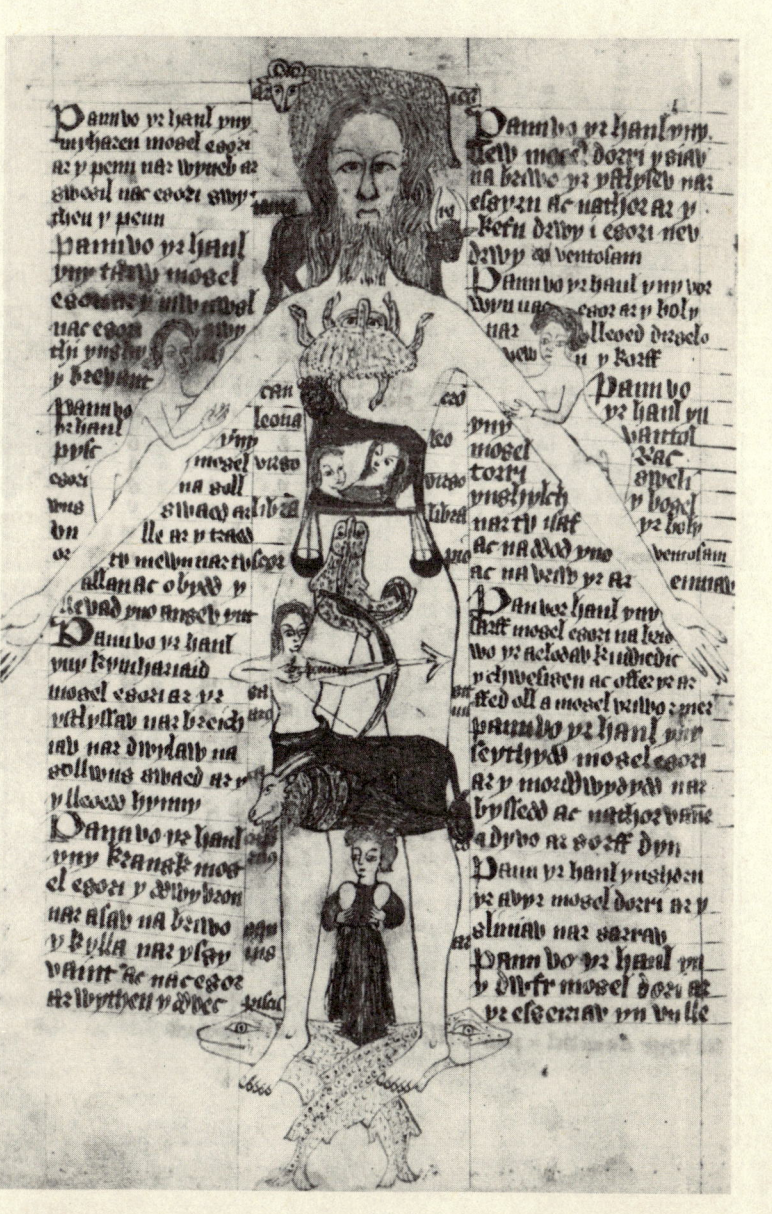

Mostyn 88, p. 26, The Human Figure with signs of the Zodiac drawn on it.

Peniarth 28, four court officials.

One fault to be found in a poem is that singular and plural are brought together as when one finds *pedwar gwr*, 'four man', when *pedwar gwyr*, 'four men', should be used.

The last sections of the books deal with the subject and method of poetry and Mr. Saunders Lewis has suggested that they are based on an Aristotelian classification of Plato's concept of the nature of the universe and society.

Influenced by the teaching of the schools, the grammars possibly demonstrate that there was a philosophic basis to the praise poetry of the Welsh professional poets from the time of Einion Offeiriad. I quote a passage from the section dealing with the subject-matter and style of poetry in illustration:

> This is how the three branches of poetry are spoken of and their metres and aims and the faults and the mistakes which should be avoided in every noteworthy piece of strict poetry. One must further know in what manner everything, to which poetry is sung, should be praised and what things should be praised. There are two kinds of things to which poetry should be sung, namely heavenly spiritual things and earthly corporeal things. Heavenly, spiritual things like God, Mary, the Saints and the Angels; earthly corporeal things like man, beast or place.
> The function of the poet is to praise and to extol and to entertain, and to make praise, glory and amusement, and poetry itself can be classified and can be criticized.

Mr. Saunders Lewis has argued that this passage contains the key to the whole ethic of the Welsh poet in subsequent generations.

If the bardic grammars contain an analysis of the craft of the most important intellectual professional class in medieval Wales, the Welsh laws, which represent by far the most important body of functional prose in Welsh, are the product of another native Welsh professional learned class. The Welsh law texts, unlike all the other works of useful prose, are fundamentally native in their origin. They are the handbooks of practising professional lawyers, who pursued their calling through the centuries in different parts of Wales, and as such are of key importance for the understanding of the composition of the Welsh society which formed the audience for all medieval Welsh literature. They testify more than any other pieces of Welsh to the capacity of the language for the expression of technical ideas.

About forty medieval manuscripts survive containing versions of the so-called 'Law of Hywel Dda.' These manuscripts are written both in Latin and in Welsh but the preponderance of Welsh words in the Latin texts is strong reason for believing that the original language of the laws was Welsh. The texts of the law-books are preceded by a prologue which, together with the pre-eminent position given to the king in the laws, suggest that in their present form the material of the law derives from a legal reorganization brought about by Hywel ap Cadell, a tenth-century king, who held overlordship over the greater part of Wales:

> Hywel Dda, son of Cadell, prince of Wales, summoned to him six men from every cantref in Wales to Whitland, and those men were of the wisest in the kingdom; four of them were laymen and two clerics ... and with the joint efforts of the wise men who came there, they examined the old laws and they let some of them run, and others they amended and some they deleted completely and some they made anew.

Fragments like the 'Surexit Memorandum', which is a document sealing the peace between two kins feuding over a parcel of land, suggest that Welsh was used for legal documents centuries before the time of Hywel and indeed historical comparative studies show that much of the material in the laws derives from an earlier period than the tenth century. Conversely, although some of their contents are very old, the lawbooks as they stand represent the work of lawyers of the twelfth, thirteenth, fourteenth and fifteenth centuries, and side by side with the archaisms are legal innovations which are indebted to the work of foreign legalists like Bracton and Glanville. We know that there existed in Wales hereditary families of lawyers. Iorwerth ap Madog, a relative of Gruffudd ab yr

Ynad Coch, belonged to one of them and the different recensions of the law-books were probably edited by these men.

The books are generally regarded as falling into three classes, known as *Llyfr Iorwerth* ('Book of Iorwerth'), *Llyfr Blegywryd* ('Book of Blegywryd'), and *Llyfr Cyfnerth* ('Book of Cyfnerth'), associated with different parts of Wales, Gwynedd, Deheubarth and possibly Powys. The first part of each book is devoted to a long section on the laws of the court, describing the rights and privileges of the king and his entourage of twenty-four officials. It has been suggested that in its form this section is much indebted to the pattern of Carolingian and Norman documents. The list of officials corresponds closely with texts like the *Constitutio Domus Regis* of Henry I. On the other hand the legal concepts dealt with in the texts, like those of *galanas* ('life-price'), *sarhad* ('honour-price'), *ebediw* ('heriot'), *amobr* ('bride-price') are basically Welsh or Celtic. For the native Welsh law has a great deal in common with the law of Ireland and derives ultimately from a common Celtic heritage. The rest of the law-books deal with subjects like homicide, theft, arson, women and marriage (a section which contains many pre-Christian rules or principles), the training of judges, the rules of co-tillage and lists of the values of animals and property. The rules give a picture of a society where blood-ties *(carennydd)* and the patrilineal kin *(cenedl)* are all-important. Responsibility for an individual's actions in many instances falls on his kin rather than his own person and failure to fulfil this responsibility led to blood-feud. The kin could extend as far as second, sixth or even eighth cousins. For instance, the kin as far as second cousins were responsible for bestowing someone in marriage. Inheritance of land was generally confined to relatives belonging to the same circle. A man's legal value depended on his status or *braint;* society was hierarchical and the status could be that of a king, a nobleman with land or without, or that of an unfree person. Status was equated with a money value which determined wergild or life-price *(galanas)* and insult-price *(sarhad).* Emphasis was also put on a man's Welsh blood and legal status was also determined by that factor. 'The innate freeman is a Welshman both through his father and his mother.' The status of the foreigner *(alltud)* was, in the eyes of the law, almost negligible. Lists of legal values in the laws illustrate what material possessions were prized and were essential to life, in the house, in the field, in hunting and in fishing, things like cauldrons, buckets, blankets, churns, different kinds of ploughs and fishing nets. These lists are among the most important evidences for material culture that have survived from the period.

Echoes of the laws are to be heard constantly in the tales and the poetry. For instance the compensation paid to Matholwch in the story of *Branwen* echoes a passage in the laws of the court. The story of the thieving mouse in *Manawydan* is better understood by reference to the law tract on the Law of Theft, and references to vendetta in the poetry are only to be fully appreciated after a reading of the tractates on *galanas*.

It is not only as a background to the content of story and poetry that the law-books are important for the student of Welsh literature, but also as a key to style and expression. Many years ago Mr. Saunders Lewis suggested that the whole tenor of the medieval Welsh prose tradition was indebted to the style and pattern of the law-books. In Wales, as in most of the countries of Western Europe, prose composition became articulate and written in the first instance in legal documents. In Welsh, besides the primary function of its content, namely the recording of rules and laws, expounding them and giving instructions for their execution, the legal prose is distinguished by the wealth of its technical vocabulary, and by a variety of expression. This variety far exceeds what is normally found in early legal literature. The law-books by the very nature of their contents were in close contact with an active oral tradition, that of pleadings in the law courts. One therefore expects to find in the law-books devices which are closely connected with an oral rhetorical tradition, such as triads, lists and alliteration. It is perhaps worth while to cast a cursory glance at the use made by the lawyers of various devices and figures of speech like dialogue, numerical phrases, alliteration and compound adjectives in an attempt to analyse some of the elements which not only contribute to the wealth and value of the legal prose but which also hold the secret of the excellences of the entire medieval prose tradition.

The first tractate in the Laws of the Court deals with the rights and privileges of the king. It is worth considering the first two paragraphs from the tract in the Book of Iorwerth:

> The king should give the queen a third of whatever wealth he may have from land and soil, and so the king's officials should reward the queen's officials. The life-price of a king is three times his insult-price. There are three ways in which the king may be insulted, one is when his protection is violated, when he grants protection to a man and that man is killed; the second is, when two kings come to their joint boundary in order to confer, and in the presence of the two kings a vassal of the one kills a vassal of the other; the third is to abuse his wife (and the insult-price for that is augmented by a half.)
>
> The honour-price of the king of Aberffraw is paid in this manner, a hundred cows for each cantref which he may possess and a white red-eared bull for every hundred head of cattle and a gold rod as tall as he is and as broad as his small finger, and a gold plate as broad as his face and as thick as the nail of a farmer who has farmed for nine years. No gold is paid except in the case of the king of Aberffraw.

This passage, compared with certain technical tracts, is fairly straightforward both in content and mode of expression. The content of the paragraph is paralleled by a section in *Branwen* describing the *sarhad* of Matholwch. It contains a summary of the rights, privileges and dues of the king. Each sentence is a self-contained statement, yet the balance and rhythm of the whole suggest that it is not a haphazard composition.

'There are three ways in which the king may be insulted'. Triads are one of the favourite devices used in Welsh literature to classify information tersely, dramatically and in a memorable manner. The poets summarized the rules of their craft in the poetic triads, the Triads of the Island of Britain contain a long index to the mythology, history and lore of the Brittonic past, and the doctors used medical triads for classifying illness and remedy. The law tracts, particularly those belonging to the Blegywryd tradition, show that lawyers made ample use of the device. Apart from single triads embodied in technical tractates there are series distinguished by the use of ornament like alliteration, compound words and repetition:

> Tri lleidyr camlyryus yssyd: lleidyr ki, a lleidyr llysseu yn y tyfhont o'r dayar, a lleidyr a tyster arnaw yn gwadu lletrat, ony llyssa.
> Tri lleidyr dirwyus yssyd: lleidyr hyd brenhin, gwedy as llatho y gwn; a lleidyr y pallo y reith idaw; a lleidyr a latho llwdyn y dyn arall yn y ty, neu yn y vuarth, yn lletrat.
>
> There are three thieves liable for a minor fine: a man who steals a dog, a man who steals plants when they grow from the earth, and a thief against whom witness is brought denying theft unless an objection is raised.
> There are three thieves liable for a major fine: a man who steals the king's stag after the dogs kill it; and a thief for whom compurgation fails; and a thief who kills another man's beast in the house or in his yard, stealthily.

It is almost impossible to convey the alliterative rhythm of these triads in translation. Learning them would have been a considerable feat of the tongue and once learned they would be hard to forget. Some of the triads seem to pay considerable attention to producing a dramatic climax as this one referring to *galanas* or feud:

> The three things that arouse revenge are the wailing of relatives, the sight of the kinsman's bier and the sight of his grave unavenged.

Sometimes the odd reference to a triad is included in a technical section. These references have an evocative effect as do references to mythological triads in the Mabinogion. When Matholwch asked for the hand of Branwen, 'one of the three chief progenitors of this island,' the audience who heard the tale was reminded of the other two. In the section of the laws referring to the rights of the court judge it is said of him that 'he is one of the three indispensables of the king', although there is at that juncture no enlargement on the two other indispensables. Numerical classification is not confined to triads but there are groupings of eights, nines and even twenty-fours, the eight pack-horses of the king, the nine credible men, and the twenty-four officers of the court. These groupings were doubtless primarily mnemonic devices but they owe something too to the medieval concept of number symbolism. Another device used by lawyers and showing a liking for terse economy of language is the proverb or gnome, collections of which are found in a number of the law manuscripts and also embodied in the tractates. Proverbs occur such as 'Better an old claim than an old feud.' Such terseness is to be found elsewhere in Welsh prose.

Certain parts of the law-books reveal the use of a style which is the very opposite of terse, that is they contain paragraphs of alliterative, rhythmical prose containing many adjectives and compound words. This kind of prose is generally referred to as *araith* or 'rhetoric', and is found in the later *Areithiau Pros, Breuddwyd Rhonabwy* and *Cysegrlan Fuchedd*. 'Runs' of this prose are found in the sections of the law-books known as *Cynghawsedd* ('Procedure') and in the Model Plaints which are preserved, suggesting that it was from an oral milieu, possibly that of the law courts, that this peculiar style derived:

> O deruyd y wr bonhedic sarhau gwr bonhedic arall, ar neill yn hawlwr ac yn cwynwr, ar llall yn wadwr ac yn amddiffynwr, a roi or arglwyd wir a kyfreith udunt, y cwynwr a dyly holi uel hyn y sarhaet ae kewilyd:
> Y gwr racco ae enwi ac eno y dat ti am kyrcheist kyrch kyhoedawc y ar y teu di, hyt ar y meu inheu hep achos heb defnyd ac ar tir uy arglwyd ac ar y hedwch; sef kyrch a kyrcheist kyrch kyhoedawc a godefawc trwy lit a bar a gwenwyndra ac aghyfreith ac aghyuarch ac amharch ar yr arglwyd ae arglwydiaeth ac yr godef diuur a distryw, ac estwng arnaf uinheu, trwy ryn a gosgryn a dyrchaf a gossot a bonclust, a briw, a chleis ac yssic, a chnith a gwallt bonwyn, a gwalltrwch a thwn ar croen ac ar kic ac asgwrn, a gweli agoret, a gwaet ellygedic o dyrnawt ar pen hyt lawr, a hwnnw a elwir gwaet hyt ran, gwaet hyt len, gwaet hyt lawr a gwaetledu tir yr arglwyd trwy amharch ac aghyfreith ar yr arglwyd, a meuel a chewilyd a sarhaet a chyhoed a chollet ac eisseu y minheu. Ac os amheuy mi ae prouaf arnat, ac os gwedy mi nys gadaf it o uynet yryghot ath wat hyt y gatto kyfreith oreu.
> If one Welshman do insult to another Welshman, and the one a

claimant and plaintiff, and the other a denier and defendant, and the lord grant justice and law to them, the plaintiff is to claim in this manner for his insult and shame:

'The man yonder,' and naming him, and naming his father, 'thou hast assaulted me by a public assault, in thine own person, even upon my person, without cause, without pretence; and that upon the land of my lord, and against his peace; the assault wherewith thou didst assault me was a public assault and unresisted, with wrath, and rage, and malignity, and illegality, and surreption, and disrespect to the lord and his lordship, and to the causing of pain, and injury, and abasement to me, through perturbation, and agitation, and onset, and striking, and a box on the ear, and a wound, and a mark, and a bruise, and a pinch, and uprooted hair, and tearing of hair, and breaking of skin and of flesh and of bone, and open wound, and spilling of blood upon the ground by a blow, and that is called blood to cheek, blood to the waist, blood to the ground, and bloodying the land of the lord through disrespect and illegality towards the lord, and disgrace, and shame, and insult, and publicity, and loss, and want to me. And, if thou doubtest it, I will prove it against thee; and, if thou shalt deny it, I will prevent thee, by interposing between thee and thy denial, as far as the law will best suffer it.'

One of the excellences of Welsh narrative prose is the skilful way in which the story-tellers use dialogue. Notable examples are to be found in the *Enfances* at the beginning of the *Historia Peredur*. Dialogue is used extensively as a means of exposition in the Welsh law tracts. An excerpt from a highly technical passage concerning suretyship illustrates the terse skill of the lawyers' dialogue:

Concerning the right of surety and debtor. If a man gave surety for something to another man, it is right for him to release the surety either by paying him or by giving a gage instead of him, or by denying the surety. If he wishes to deny it, this is how it is to be denied. The two parties and the surety should come before a justice and the justice should ask the two parties to acknowledge whether the man be a surety or not. 'Surety', says the claimant. 'No', says the debtor. Then it is right for the justice to ask the surety, 'Are you a surety?' 'Yes', says the surety. 'Complete denial', says the debtor. 'You are not a surety for me in this matter nor in any other.' 'God knows', says the surety, 'as it is best that a surety should insist that he is a surety, so I insist that I am a surety.' 'God knows', says the debtor, 'as a debtor may best deny a surety, so I deny you.'

Reading the sharp bite of this legal exchange it is significant that some of the finest dialogue passages in medieval story contain echoes of legal contention. There is a notable example in the tale of *Manawydan,* where Manawydan threatens to hang the mouse in punishment for theft.

Dramatic tension, rhetoric, dialogue are thus all part of the style of the law-books. They are devices too, that contribute to the varied wealth of the whole corpus of medieval Welsh prose. It is possible, as Mr. Saunders Lewis has suggested, that this wealth is due to the long tradition of functional prose that the lawyers produced. Gutun Owain, describing the learning of one of his patrons, Elisau ap Gruffudd, said:

> He carried the language of the secular law
> To the root of every story-telling.

One might add that not only the language of the story-tellers but also the wealth of the whole prose tradition is indebted to this legal heritage. It has not been possible to do justice to the wealth, complexity and content of the functional prose within the limits of this chapter. Many works have been omitted from the discussion, horoscopes, charms, a treatise on heraldry, prognostications and even tales. They are all, however, like the religious tracts, the scientific and medical works, threads in the complex weave of the fabric which represents the culture and literature of the Welsh Middle Ages.

BIBLIOGRAPHY

Texts:
  J. Morris Jones and John Rhŷs: *The Elucidarium and Other Tracts in Welsh from Llyvyr Agkyr Llanddewivrevi,* Oxford, 1894.
  Thomas Jones: *Y Bibyl Ynghymraec,* Cardiff, 1940.
  J. E. Caerwyn Williams: 'Purdan Padrig', *National Library of Wales Journal,* iii, 102-6.
  Idem: 'Welsh Versions of *Purgatorium S Patricii', Studia Celtica,* viii/ix, 121-94.
  Ifor Williams: *Chwedlau Odo,* Cardiff, 1957.
  D. Simon Evans: *Buched Dewi,* Cardiff, 1959.

Arthur Jones: *The History of Gruffydd ap Cynan* (including translation), Liverpool, 1910.

Stephen J. Williams: *Ffordd y Brawd Odrig,* Cardiff, 1929.

Henry Lewis and P. Diverres: *Delw y Byd,* Cardiff, 1928.

Ifor Williams and Gwilym Peredur Jones: 'Hen Draethawd ar Hwsmonaeth,' *Bulletin of the Board of Celtic Studies,* ii, 8-16, 132-34.

P. Diverres: *Le Plus Ancien Texte des Meddygon Myddveu,* Paris, 1913.

G. J. Williams and E. J. Jones: *Gramadegau'r Penceirddiaid,* Cardiff, 1934.

Aneurin Owen: *The Ancient Laws and Institutes of Wales* (including translation), London, 1841.

A. W. Wade-Evans: *Welsh Medieval Law* (including translation), Oxford, 1909.

Stephen J. Williams and J. Enoch Powell: *Llyfr Blegywryd,* Cardiff, 1942.

Aled Rh. Wiliam: *Llyfr Iorwerth,* Cardiff, 1960.

Dafydd Jenkins: *Llyfr Colan,* Cardiff, 1963.

Translation:

G. Melville Richards: *The Laws of Hywel Dda,* Cardiff, 1954.

Critical Studies:

J. E. Caerwyn Williams: 'Medieval Welsh Religious Prose,' *Proceedings of the International Congress of Celtic Studies, 1963,* 65-100.

Idem: 'Rhyddiaith Grefyddol Cymraeg Canol,' Chapter 13 in *Y Traddodiad Rhyddiaith yn yr Oesau Canol,* gol. Geraint Bowen, Llandysul, 1974, 360-408.

Idris Ll. Foster: *The Book of the Anchorite,* Sir John Rhŷs Memorial Lecture, British Academy, 1949.

Thomas Jones: 'The Book of the Anchorite of Llanddewibrefi,' *Transactions of the Cardiganshire Antiquarian Society,* xii, 63-82.

Saunders Lewis: *Gramadegau'r Penceirddiaid,* G. J. Williams Memorial Lecture, Cardiff, 1967.

Glanmor Williams: *The Welsh Church from Conquest to Reformation,* Cardiff, 1962.

Dorothy Oschinsky: *Walter of Henley,* Oxford, 1971.

John Cule: 'The Court Mediciner and Medicine in the Laws', *Journal of the History of Medicine,* Vol. 21, 213-36.

Hywel D. Emanuel: *Studies in the Welsh Laws,* Cardiff, 1963.

Dafydd Jenkins: *Cyfraith Hywel,* Llandysul, 1970.

J. E. Goronwy Edwards: *Hywel Dda and the Welsh Lawbooks,* Bangor, 1929.

Geraint Bowen (ed.): *Y Traddodiad Rhyddiaith yn yr Oesau Canol,* Llandysul, 1974; chapters on 'Y Cyfreithiau' and 'Y Bucheddau' by Morfydd E. Owen and D. Simon Evans.

INDEX

A

Abercuawg, 111.
Aberffraw, 43, 135, 152, 162, 178-9, 271.
Aber Henfelen, 196.
Aberlleiniog, 128.
Aber Lleu, 83.
Aber Taradr, 175.
Aberystwyth, 108.
Achilles, 260.
Adam, 186, 251.
adventus Saxonum, the, 27.
Aeddan, 76.
Aeddon, 114-5.
Aedh Mac Mathgamhain, 260.
Aeneas, 245-6; see also Eneas.
Aesop's Fables, 258.
Afagddu, 107.
Afallennau, the, 103-4, 106, 117-8.
Afan Ferddig, 42, 100, 141.
agricultural treatise, 249.
'Aid for the Soul', 253; see also *Cysegrlan Fuchedd*.
Aisling poetry, 16.
Alaw (river), 194, 200.
Alexander, 171.
Alexander legend, the, 119.
alliteration, 66, 141, 147-9, 159-60, 170, 242, 265, 270-3.
alltud, 270.
Alps, the, 181.
Alun, 100.
Amaethon, 217.
Ambrosius Aurelianus, 27, 208.
Ammianus Marcellinus, 17.
amobr, 269.
Amr, 214.
analytic languages, 21, 26.
ancwyn Mynyddog, 69.
Aneirin, 11, 18, 26, 32-7, 41, 43-4, 46, 52-5, 68, 70, 75, 79, 81, 145-6, 158, 161.
Angels, 267.
Angles, 54, 58, 68.
Anglesey, 28, 56, 114-5, 152, 164, 173, 175, 194; see also Mona:

Anglo-Saxons, the, 25.
Anjou, 176.
Annales Cambriae, the, 42.
Annals, 248.
Annwfn, 119, 191-2, 198.
Annwfn, the Head of, 119.
Antichrist and the Day of Judgement, The, 256.
Antonine Wall, the, 12, 35.
Apocalyptic texts, 250.
Apocrypha, the, 260.
Apollo, 260.
Apostle (James), the, 236.
Apostles' Creed, the, 251.
'Apple-trees', 103; see also *Afallennau*.
Aquileia, 211.
araith, 273.
Araith Iolo Goch, 240-1.
Araith Wgon, 240-1.
Arberth, 192.
Areithiau Pros, the, 240-2, 273.
Arfderydd, the battle of, 42, 103-4, 153.
Arfynydd, 60.
Argoed Llwyfain, 60-1.
Argyll, 12.
Armes Prydain, 46-8, 115-7.
Armorican peninsula, the, 20.
Armoric Britons, the, 211.
Arofan, 141.
Arthur, 27, 61, 106, 119, 154, 161, 171, 213-6, 218, 220-2, 225, 227, 230-4, 238-9, 245, 247.
Arthuret, 42, 103.
Arthurian Legend, see Legend, Arthurian.
Arthurian poems, 220.
Arthurian prose romances, 238.
Arthurian romance, 105, 234.
Arthurian topography, 214.
Arthur's court, 219-21, 225-7, 230.
Arthur's warband, 213.
Arwystli, 173.
Ascent into Heaven of the Blessed Virgin, the, 251.

INDEX

Astrology, 264.
Athanasian Creed, the, 249.
Athelstan, 47-8, 116.
athro, 143.
aura, 147.
Auxerre, 27.
awdl(au), 147-8, 159, 166, 169, 180, 182-3, 185.
awdl-gywydd, 66.
awdl to Gwenlliant (Prydydd y Moch), 137.
awen, 16, 158.
awenyddion, 16, 136.

B

Babel, 182.
Bagendon, 13.
baird, 15, 18.
Bala Lake, 107.
Baldwin, Archbishop, 169.
Bamburgh, 34.
bardd, 15, 158, 204.
bardd teulu, 135-6, 138, 148, 158.
bardi, 14, 17.
bardic contests, 134, 144.
bardic families, 135.
bardic grammar(s), the, 130-1, 140, 266-7.
bardic order, the, 142-4, 158, 160.
bardic schools, 132, 138-40, 143, 147-8, 150.
bards, Celtic, 147.
Bardsey, the isle of, 163, 181.
Baschurch, 94.
Bath, 40.
'Battle of Argoed Llwyfain, The', 60; see also *Gwaith Argoed Llwyfain*.
Battle of Badon, the, 232.
'Battle of Gwên Ystrad, The', 59; see also *Gwaith Gwên Ystrad*.
Bede, 34, 37.
Bedwyr, 218.
'*Bedydd*', 161.
beirdd, 15, 18.
beirdd ysbyddaid, 158.
Belgium, 12.

Beli Mawr, 210, 244.
Bendigeidfran, 191, 193-5, 199, 201; see also Brân.
Berddig, 126.
Bernicia, 31, 33-4, 41-2, 68, 146, 161.
Bernicians, the, 100, 161, 184.
Beves of Hampton, 236.
Bible, the, 250-1, 260.
Biblical heroes, 161.
Bibyl Ynghymraec, 250.
Birds of Rhiannon, the 194.
Black Book of Carmarthen, The, 42-3, 45, 81, 98, 103, 160, 204, 213.
Black Witch, the, 214, 218.
Blaen, 71, 73.
Bleddyn Fardd, 136, 185-6.
bleeding lance, the, 225, 227.
Blegywryd, 272.
Bleiddudd, 114.
Blodeuwedd, 192, 200.
blood-feud, 269, 272.
bloody head, the, 225-6, 228.
Bluchbard, 31, 52.
boasting poems, 163; see also *Gorhoffedd*.
Bodleian Library, the 160.
Boia, 259.
Bola, Brother Gruffudd, 249.
Bologna, 266.
Bonedd Gwŷr y Gogledd, 44.
Book of Aneirin, the, 78.
'Book of Blegywryd', 269.
'Book of Cyfnerth', 269.
'Book of Husbandry', 264.
'Book of Iorwerth', 269, 271.
Book of Kells, the, 159.
'Book of Llandaf, The', 190.
Book of St. Chad, the, 189.
Book of St. James, 236.
Book of Taliesin, The, 32, 48, 55, 98, 109, 113, 115, 120, 195, 204, 213.
'Book of the Anchorite, The', 250; see also *Llyfr yr Ancr*.
Bosworth Field, 48, 115.
Bown, 236.
Bracton, 268.
braint, 269.

Braint Teilo, 190.
Brân, 110, 171, 193; *see also* Bendigeidfran.
Branwen, 191, 194, 199, 200, 272.
Brecon, 134, 179.
Breconshire, 134.
Breichiol, 74, 77.
Breton (language), 20-2, 26.
Breton, Primitive, 20, 25.
Bretons, 116, 211.
Breton settlement, the, 211-2.
Breuddwyd Gruffudd ab Adda ap Dafydd, 240-2.
Breuddwyd Maxen Wledig, 210, 240.
Breuddwyd Rhonabwy, 142, 199, 273.
bride-price, 269.
Britain, 12-3, 17-21, 23-5, 27-8, 32, 34-6, 38, 40-1, 43-8, 54-6, 84, 101, 116, 133, 161, 177, 208-11, 238, 244-5, 247.
Britain, the Island of, 204, 231, 233, 244.
'Britain, writing of', 114.
British Isles, the, 46.
British (or Brittonic) language, 11-2, 20-6, 34, 51, 126.
Britons, the, 11, 22, 27, 41 2, 44, 48, 79, 99, 116, 126, 139, 208-9, 211, 213, 245.
Brittany, 46, 102, 211-3.
Brochfael, king of Powys, 110, 169.
Bromwich, Mrs. Rachel, 18, 61, 204.
Bron, the Fisher King, 193.
Bronze Age, the, 13.
Bructeri, the, 16.
Brunanburh, 47-8, 116.
Brutus, 245.
Brut y Brenhinedd, 209-10, 246-7; see also *Historia Regum Britanniae.*
Brut y Tywysogion, 144, 246.
Brycheiniog, 56.
Brynaich, 146, 161.
Bucephalus, 260.
Buchedd Beuno, 258.
Buchedd Dewi, 258.

C
Cadwaladr, 116.
Cadwallon ap Cadfan, 41-2, 100.
Cadwgan son of Rhiwallon, 264.

Cadwgawn ab Iddon, 232.
Caernarfon, 179, 211-2.
Caernarfonshire, 193.
Caer Seon, 114.
Caer Wynt, 117.
Caerwys, 164.
Caesar, Julius, 13, 17-9, 171, 210.
Cafall, 214.
Cai, 214, 218, 225-6, 228.
Cain, 166.
cainc o'r mabinogi, 190-1.
Caledonia, the Forest of, 103.
Calumniated Wife, The, 192, 199.
Cambridge University Library, the, 189-90.
Camlan, 187, 213.
Camulodunum, 13.
Canterbury, the see of, 133.
Canterbury Tales, the, 234.
Cantref Mawr, 250.
Cantscaul, the battle of, 42.
Canu Bychan (Llywarch ap Llywelyn), 179, 184.
canu darogan, 115.
Caradog, 76.
Caradog of Llancarfan, 246.
Caranfael, 95.
Cardigan, 144, 179.
carennydd, 152, 162, 269.
Carlisle, 54.
Carmarthen, 179.
Carmarthenshire, 189, 265.
Carn Brea, 12.
Carn Cabal, 214.
Casnodyn, 150.
Cassivellaunus, 210.
Caswallawn, -on, 210, 244.
Cataracto, 68.
Cataractonium, 68.
Cathay, 263.
Catraeth, 34, 42-3, 68, 70, 73, 75, 77, 79, 86, 99, 100.
Catterick, 32, 34, 68.
Catuvellauni, the, 12.
cauldron, magic, 191-2, 198, 213, 218.
'Cauldron of Inspiration and Knowledge', 107.

INDEX

Cedifor, 180.
Cedifor the Irishman, 174.
Cegin (river), 164.
Celain Urien, 83-4.
Celtic, Common, 21, 23.
Celtic art, 159.
Celtic bards, 147.
Celtic Church, the, 39, 133, 256.
Celtic dialects, 12.
Celtic myth(-ology), 119, 193, 199.
Celtic Otherworld, the, 119, 191, 213.
Celtic saints, 132.
Celts, 14-7, 46-7, 78.
Celyddon, the Forest of, 104.
cenedl, 269.
cerddorion, 135.
Ceridwen, 107-8.
Cernyw, 194.
Ceylon, 263.
chansons de geste, 234, 236-8.
Charlemagne, 221, 236, 238.
Charles (Charlemagne), 236-7.
Charles-Edwards, Dr. T. M., 191.
Chaucer, 31, 52, 234.
Chepstow, 162.
Cheshire, 45.
chess game, the cosmic, 232.
Chester, 41, 161-2, 164, 179.
Chevalier au Lion, Le, 222.
'Chieftainship of Britain, The', 135.
China, 263.
chivalric romance, the, 221, 224, 229.
Chrétien de Troyes, 222, 224-5, 228-9, 238.
Christ, 28, 52, 112, 132, 172, 177-8, 184, 186, 252-4, 260.
Christen, 262.
Christendom, 161, 221, 248, 255.
Christianity, 17-8, 37-9.
Chronicle of the Princes, the, 158, 246-7.
Chronicle of Turpin, the, 236-8.
Church, the, 250-2, 257, 261.
'Churches of Bassa', the, 94.
Church in Wales, the, 40.
chwedl, 241.
Chwedlau Saith Ddoethon Rhufain, 239.
Cian, 31, 52.

Cinnar, 260.
Cistercians, the, 175, 181, 185.
Clancy, Joseph, 59, 63, 65-6, 113, 116, 120, 154.
clas, 40, 133, 169, 180, 182.
Clawedog (river), 164.
Clyde, the, 11, 20, 54.
Clynnog Fawr, 258.
Coed Celyddon, 103.
Coel Hen, 45, 60.
coinage, inscribed, 13, 21.
Collingwood, R. G., 27.
'Colloquy of Myrddin and his Sister Gwenddydd, The', 103.
'Columcille's Greeting to Ireland', 137.
compert, 198.
Compostella, 236.
Computus Fragment, the, 190.
Conran, Anthony, 60-1, 101.
Constantinople, 225, 227, 237.
Constitutio Domus Regis, 269.
Conte du Graal, Le, 222.
contests, bardic and musical, 144.
Continent, the, 12, 21, 138, 211.
Conwy, 114.
Coraniaid, race of, 210.
Corn Cafallt, 214.
Cornish (language), 20-2, 26.
Cornish, Primitive, 20, 25.
Cornishmen, 116.
Cornwall, 12, 20, 27, 38-9, 46, 54, 56, 154, 194-5, 213, 244.
cowardice, theme of, 90, 111-2.
cradle-song, 79, 101-2.
Creation, story of the, 250, 262.
Creator, praise to the, 172.
Cristina, 175.
Cuckoo and the Hedge-sparrow, The, 258.
Culhwch, 214-7, 219.
Culhwch and Olwen, 199, 203, 214-5, 218-20, 223, 231-2, 240-1.
Cumberland, 32, 41-2, 103.
Cumbria, 20, 37.
Cumbric, Primitive, 20, 25.
Cunedda Wledig, 29, 30, 43, 54, 100, 259.
Cunningham, 43.

INDEX

cyfarwydd, -iaid, 141-2, 189, 193, 203, 205-6, 209-11, 223, 229, 232, 239-41, 247.
cyfarwyddyd, 204, 207-10, 219, 242.
Cyfeiliog, 173.
Cyfoesi Myrddin a Gwenddydd ei Chwaer, 103.
Cyfranc Lludd a Llefelys, 209-10, 246.
cymeriad, -au, 148, 150, 159-60.
Cyminawd, 118.
Cymro, Cymry, 41, 154.
Cynan (father of Gruffudd), 260.
Cynan ('son of prophecy'), 116.
Cynan ap Brochfael (Cynan Garwyn), 19, 32, 56-7, 64-5, 110.
Cynan Meiriadog, 211-2.
Cynddelw Brydydd Mawr, 132, 134-40, 146, 148, 157-8, 166-72, 174, 183-4, 248.
Cynddilig (son of Llywarch), 90.
Cynddylan ap Cyndrwyn, 42-3, 45, 93-5, 100-1.
Cynfael, 171.
Cynfan, 76.
Cynfeirdd, the, 35, 67, 98, 113, 119, 123, 162, 169.
Cynfelyn, 173.
Cyngen, 45.
cynghanedd, 66, 147, 149-50.
Cynghawsedd, 273.
Cynon son of Clydno Eidyn, 77, 230.
cynweisiaid, 201.
Cynwyd, 167.
Cysegrlan Fuchedd, 253, 255, 273.
cywydd, 159, 263.
Cywydd i'r Llafurwr (Iolo Goch), 253.
cywydd to Beuno (Rhys Goch Eryri), 259.
cywydd to Dewi Sant (Ieuan ap Rhydderch), 259.
cywydd to the Wind (Dafydd ap Gwilym), 120.
cywyddwyr, 204, 234, 259.

D

dadanhudd, 153, 184.
dadolwch, 163.

Dadolwch Urien, 64-6, 146.
Dafydd ab Owain Gwynedd, 152, 166, 175, 177-8.
Dafydd ap Gwilym, 120, 138-9, 168, 174, 255, 257.
Dafydd ap Llywelyn ab Iorwerth, 183
Dafydd Benfras, 145, 153, 183-4.
Dafydd Ddu Hiraddug, 130-1, 266.
Dálriada, Scottish, 12, 44, 79, 99.
Danes, the, 46-7.
Dante, 255.
'Dares Phrygius', 246.
Dark Ages, the, 34, 38.
David (brother of Llywelyn), 154.
David, Prophet and King, 158, 165.
Day of Judgement, the, 119, 131-2, 256-7.
death-bed (-couch) poem, 131-2, 137, 163, 172, 186.
'Death-Song of Cynddylan, The', 99.
'Death-Song of Owain, The', 61-2, 66.
De Corio Serpentis, 249.
Dee (river), 39, 108, 157, 175.
De Excidio et Conquestu Britanniae, 28, 52-3, 208, 244.
De Excidio Troiae, 246.
Degannwy, 28, 108, 110, 179.
Deheubarth, 119, 126-8, 153, 220, 269.
Deira, 31, 34, 68.
Deity, the, 169, 171, 179.
Delw y Byd, 248, 262, 264.
Deodric, 60; *see also* Theodric.
Deorham, 40.
Deorthach Wledig, 231.
De Purgatorio Sancti Patricii, 255.
Derwent, 101-2.
'Descent of the Men of the North, The', 44-5.
De Spiritu Guidonis, 255.
Deuddeg Rhinwedd Croen Neidr, 249.
'Devasted Hearth of Rheged, The', 83.
Devon, 12, 20, 38.
Dewi Sant, 176, 259; *see also* St. David.
dialectic, 266.
dialects, British, 20-1, 26.
dialogue, 200, 274-5.
Diana, 260.
Diffaith Aelwyd Rheged, 83-4.

INDEX

Dillus Farfog, 218.
Dinas Dinlle(u), 193.
Dinas Emrys, 210.
Dinefwr, the Royal House of, 264-5.
Din Eidyn (Dineidyn), 33, 69.
Dingestow Brut, the, 240.
Dinogad, 101.
Diodorus Siculus, 17, 147.
disgybl disgyblaidd, 143.
disgybl pencerddaidd, 143.
disgybl ysbâs, 143.
Divine Comedy, the, 255.
Diwrnach the Irishman, 218.
Domesday, 126.
Domhnall Brecc, 44, 99.
Dominican, 254.
Dôn, 199.
Dôn, the Children of, 193, 199.
Donatus, 30.
Doom, the hour of, 257.
dragon, the red, 115.
dragon, the white, 115.
dragons, 209-10.
dramatic dialogue, 85.
dramatic monologues, 110.
dream journey, 211.
dream maiden, 211, 241-2.
'Dream of Gwalchmai', the, 165.
Dream of Maxen, the, 211, 213, 219, 223, 230.
Dream of Rhonabwy, the, 231-5.
druides, druids, 17-8, 209.
Dryden, 52.
Drystan, 44.
Dublin, 46, 47, 117, 260.
Duke of Britain, 30.
Dumbarton, 32, 43, 79, 103.
Durham, County, 102.
Du Traws, the, 231.
dwarf(s), 225-6.
dyfalu, 168.
Dyfed, 39, 46, 56, 113, 116, 191-3, 197-9.
Dyfi (river), 108.
Dyfnwal Frych, 44, 99.
Dygen Freiddin, 163.
Dygynnelw, 172.
Dyrham, 40.

E

Eagle of Eli, the, 94.
Eagle of Pengwern, the, 94.
East, the, 263.
ebediw, 269.
Ebyr Henfelen, 110.
Edeirnion, 168, 182, 185.
Eden (river), 59.
Edinburgh, 11, 29, 33, 54, 68, 79.
edling, 134.
Edmyg Dinbych, 113.
Ednyfed, 173.
Ednyfed Fychan, 178, 184.
Edward I, 154.
Edwin, 42, 100.
Efa, daughter of Madog ap Maredudd, 137; *see also* Eve.
Efa, daughter of Maredudd, 249.
Efnisien, 191, 201.
Egypt, the plagues of, 119.
Einion ap Gwalchmai, 181-2.
Einion Offeiriad, 130, 266-7.
Einion, son of Rhiwallon, 264.
eisteddfod, -au, 128, 143-5.
Eithinyn, 73.
elegiac verse, elegies, 11, 18, 32, 61, 70, 75, 83, 88, 93-4, 100, 114, 129-30, 136, 139, 149, 154, 160-2, 167, 177, 180-1, 184, 186-7.
Elegy of Gwên, 87-8, 92, 96.
Elegy for Llywelyn ap Gruffudd (Gruffudd ab yr Ynad Coch), 149, 154-5, 187.
elegy to Cynddylan, 42-3.
elegy to Gruffudd ap Cynan (Meilyr Brydydd), 160-2.
elegy to Llywelyn ap Gruffudd (Bleddyn Fardd), 186.
elegy to Madog ap Maredudd (Gwalchmai), 165.
elegy to Nest (Einion ap Gwalchmai), 181.
elegy to Rhodri ab Owain Gwynedd (Elidir Sais), 177.
Elfael, 118.
Elffin son of Gwyddno, 108.
Elfoddw, 30.
Elidir Sais, 146, 177-9.

Elisau ap Gruffudd, 275.
Ellesmere, 179.
Elmet (Elfed), kingdom of, 32, 41, 57, 65.
Elucidarium, 248, 252-3, 262.
Emperor Adrian, the, 253.
Emperor Alexander, the, 260.
Emperor Manuel Cominus, the, 262.
Empire, the (Roman), 211.
Empress of Constantinople, the, 225, 227.
Emreis, Emrys, 208; *see also* Ambrosius Aurelianus.
enchanted fortress, 192.
Eneas, 164; *see also* Aeneas.
Enerys, 174.
Enfances (Peredur), the, 274.
Enfant Sage, legend of the, 249.
England, 11, 25, 34, 46-7, 54, 62, 66, 87, 115, 123-4, 128, 144, 146, 161-2, 177, 192, 234, 244.
English (language), 145, 249.
English, the, 34, 37, 40-1, 45-7, 57, 68, 75, 79, 83, 85, 93, 100, 115, 118, 146, 161, 164, 246.
English conquest, the, 208.
englyn, -ion, 45-6, 79, 82-4, 93, 96, 101-2, 111-2, 129, 131, 148, 159, 166-7, 169, 172-3, 175, 180, 182-3, 189, 242, 256.
englyn unodl union, 159, 166-7.
Enid, 228-9.
epic, Old French, 221.
Epynt, 168.
equites, 13.
Erec et Enide, 222.
Erechwydd, 60.
Erthgi, 71.
Eryri, 114, 209.
Ethelfrith, 34, 41, 56.
Eucharist, the, 252.
Eudeyrn, 31.
eulogy, -ies, 15, 130-2, 136, 158, 164-6, 169, 172, 175, 179-80, 263.
Europe, 11, 36, 131, 163, 175, 236, 239, 248, 257, 263, 266, 270.
Eustace Legend, the, 199.
Eve, daughter of Madog ap Maredudd, 168; *see also* Efa.

Eve (wife of Adam), 186, 251.
exemplum, -la, 239, 257-8.
Exeter, 23.

F

fabliau, 239, 258.
Faery Fortress, the, 120.
Falkirk, 44.
fatherless boy, 209.
'Feasting-Hall of Brân, The', 194.
'Feast of the Head, The', 194.
'Feast of the Noble/Wondrous Head, The', 194.
Ffordd y Brawd Odrig, 262-3.
Freuer, 94-6.
Fifteen Signs before Doomsday, The, 256.
fili, filid, 15, 18, 142.
Flamborough Head, 23.
Fflamddwyn, 60-2.
Flos Militiae, 225.
'Flower of Knighthood', 225.
The Forbidden Door, motif of, 191-2, 194.
Forden, 173.
Forth, the 11, 13, 20, 29, 38.
'Fortress of Glass', the, 119.
fosterage, 174.
Fountain, Lady of the, 230-1.
Fountain, quest at the, 230-1.
France, 11, 123, 210, 222, 234.
Franciscans, 182-3, 249, 263.
French (language), 249.
French, Old. 235, 238.
French influence, 220, 222-3, 235.
Friendship of Amlyn and Amig, the, 238.
Future Life, the, 252.

G

Galahad, 239.
galanas, 269-70, 272.
Galloway, 37.
Gamber Head, 214.
Ganelon, 236-7.
Gate of Glory, the, 112.
Gaul, 17-8, 35, 38-9.
Gaulish (language), 12.

INDEX

Gauls, the, 12, 14, 78.
gavelkind, 174.
Gellan, 128.
genealogy, -ies, 16-9, 30, 42, 44-5, 54, 83, 142, 250, 259-60.
Genealogy of the Saxon Kings, 30.
Genesis, 250.
Genilles, 165.
Geoffrey of Monmouth, 105-6, 109, 220-1, 224, 232, 245-7.
Geraint, 222, 224, 228-9.
Geraint ac Enid, 222, 224, 228-9, 232.
Germany, 208, 252.
Giant's Daughter, motif of, 214-5.
Gildas, 28-9, 33, 52-3, 183, 208-9, 211, 244, 259.
Gilfaethwy, Son of Dôn, 192.
Giraldus Cambrensis, 16, 19, 133-4, 136, 158, 161, 169, 173, 175, 178.
Glamorgan, 39, 126, 150, 204, 220, 248-9.
Glanville, 268.
Glasgow, 11, 79.
glosses, Old Welsh, 190.
Gloucester, 226, 228.
Glyndŵr, Owain, 115, 154.
gnomic statements, gnomes, 111, 177, 273.
God, 28, 37, 53, 62, 66, 112-3, 116, 129-31, 134, 155, 158, 165, 168, 170-2, 176-7, 181-3, 185, 187, 200-1, 238, 251-7, 264, 267.
Gododdin, 29, 37, 40, 54-5, 68-9, 72-3, 79, 92, 102.
Gododdin, the, 33, 36-7, 42-4, 68-9, 70-1, 74-80, 82, 86, 89, 91-2, 95, 98-101, 129, 145-6, 148, 162, 173, 180.
Goddau, 60.
Goewin, 192.
Gofannon, 217.
gofeirdd, 134.
Gogynfeirdd, the, 98, 113, 119, 123, 127-8, 130-2, 135, 137-8, 141-51, 159, 162, 164, 169, 171, 257, 259.
Goidels, 54, 79, 99.
Good Friday, 251.
Gorhoffedd, 137.
Gorhoffedd Gwalchmai, 137, 163.

Gorhoffedd Hywel ab Owain Gwynedd, 137, 174.
gormesoedd, 209-10.
Goronwy, 173.
Goronwy, son of Gwalchmai, 165.
Gorsedd Arberth, 191-2.
gosgordd (Mynyddog), 69.
Gospel, St. John's, 251.
'Gospel of Nicodemus', the, 132.
Grail, the, 193, 228, 238, 248.
grail (dish), 225.
Grail Castle, the, 238.
Gramadegau'r Penceirddiaid, 266; *see also* bardic grammars.
Grassholm, 194.
grateful lion, the, 231.
Great Judgement, Siôn Cent's poem on the, 257.
Greek (language), 22.
Greeks, the, 11.
'Greetings', 103; see also *Oianau*.
Gregory, 257.
Groglith, Y, 251.
Gronw Bebyr, 200-1.
Gruffudd ab yr Ynad Coch, 149, 154-5, 187, 268-9.
Gruffudd ap Cynan, 126-8, 131, 135, 137, 160-2, 164, 185, 197, 260-1.
Gruffudd ap Cynan ab Owain Gwynedd, 152, 180.
Gruffudd ap Gwrgenau, 180.
Gruffudd ap Llywelyn, 126.
Gruffudd ap Llywelyn ap Trahaearn, 250.
Gruffudd, son of Ednyfed Fychan, 184.
Gruffudd, son of Llywelyn ab Iorwerth, 184, 186.
Gruffudd, son of Rhiwallon, 264.
Gruffudd, son of the Lord Rhys, 118.
Gruffydd, Professor W. J., 196-9.
'*Gueinth Guaut*', 31-2.
Guest, Lady Charlotte, 190.
Gundaphoris, 263.
Guorthigirnus, 208; *see also* Gwrtheyrn, Vortigern.
Guto'r Glyn, 263.
Gutun Owain, 275.

INDEX

Gwaith Argoed Llwyfain, 60-2, 66.
Gwaith Gwên Ystrad, 59, 66.
Gwalchmai, 227-8, 230.
Gwalchmai ap Meilyr, 135-7, 163-6, 181.
Gwales, 191, 194-5.
Gwallawg ap Lleennawg, 32, 57, 63, 65.
Gwasawg, 104-5.
Gwawl son of Clud, 200.
Gwawrddur, 76.
gwelygorddau, 168.
Gwên, son of Llywarch, 85-9, 111.
Gwenabwy son of Gwenn, 77.
Gwenddolau, 103-5.
Gwenddydd, 104-5.
Gwenhwyfar, 213.
Gwenllïan, 174.
Gwenllïan, daughter of Cynan, 150.
Gwenllïant, daughter of Hywel of Gwynllŵg, 137.
Gwent, 56, 126, 164, 175, 192, 220.
Gwenwynwyn, Prince of Powys, 118-9.
Gwên Ystrad, 59.
Gwerfyl, 174.
Gwern Gwygid, 162.
Gwgon, 76.
Gwion, 76.
Gwion Bach, 107-8.
Gwladys, 174.
Gwrtheyrn, 117, 208-9; *see also* Guorthigirnus, Vortigern.
Gwydion, son of Dôn, 141-2, 192-3, 198, 204.
Gwyddno Garanhir, 44, 108.
Gwyn, 76.
Gwynedd, 28-30, 39, 42-3, 52-4, 100, 126-8, 131, 144, 152-4, 160-1, 168, 176-8, 185, 192, 197, 199, 201, 247, 260-1, 269.
Gwynfardd Brycheiniog, 132, 175-6.
Gwynllŵg, Cantref of, 126.
Gwynllyw, 126.
Gwŷr y Gogledd, 32.
Gwythyr son of Greidawl, 218-9.

H

Hadrian's Wall, 24, 30.
hagiography, Welsh, 259.
'Hall of Cynddylan, The', 93.

Hanes Taliesin, 106-10.
Harlech, 191, 194-5.
harp, the, 136, 166.
Hastings, 123.
Haverfordwest, 179.
Hawis, 174.
Heathfield, the battle of, 42.
Heaven, 74, 169.
Hebrides, the, 12.
Hedge of Mist, the, 229.
Hefenfelth, 42.
Heilyn fab Gwyn Hen, 194, 196.
Heilyn Goch, 232.
Heledd, 45, 93-6, 100, 102, 204.
Hell, 132.
Hell, the Harrowing of, 132, 184.
helpers, 215-6, 219.
Hembury, 12.
hen chwedlau, 141.
Hendregadredd MS., the, 160.
Hendwr, 185.
Henfynyw, 176.
Hengerdd, 114, 141, 148-9, 158, 183, 204.
Hengist, 208-9.
Henry I, 124, 269.
Henry II, 152, 175.
Henry VII, 48.
Henry of Huntingdon, 246.
herbals, 265.
Hercules, 171.
Hereford, 47-8.
Herefordshire, 214.
heriot, 269.
Heroic Age, the, 27, 36-7, 40, 43, 54, 70, 91, 158, 161, 164, 204.
heroic ideal, the, 86, 89, 91-2, 95, 237.
heroic verse, 15, 36, 62, 81, 89, 221.
hero's marriage, the, 227.
hero-tale, 215.
Hexham, 42, 100.
Highland Zone, the 24, 26, 28, 36, 38.
hill fortresses, 13.
Hirlas Owain, 146, 173.
Historia Brittonum, 19, 30-2, 34-5, 52, 56, 83, 106, 115, 208, 214, 245.
Historia Peredur, 274; see also *Peredur.*
Historia Regum Britanniae, 105-6, 109,

INDEX

209, 220, 245-6; see also *Brut y Brenhinedd*.
History of Adam and Eve his wife, the, 251.
History of Gruffudd ap Cynan, The, 128; see also *Hystoria Gruffudd ap Cynan*.
History of Susanna and Tobit, the, 251.
'History of the Kings of Britain', 105; see also *Historia Regum Britanniae*.
'*History of the Notable Acts, the*', 244.
Hoan, 99; *see also* Ywain son of Beli son of Nwython.
Holy Land, the, 181.
'Holy Living', 253.
Holy Spirit, the, 254.
Honorius Augustodiensis 252, 262.
honour-price, 269.
Hopcyn ap Thomas, 248.
Hors, 208.
House of Gwynedd, the, 178, 185.
How a man should believe in God, 251.
How Elen found the true Cross, 251.
How the Father, the Son and the Holy Ghost are to be understood as one God, 251.
Huail mab Caw, 44.
hubris, 184.
Hunydd, 174.
Hussa, 32-3.
Hystoria Adrian ac Ipotis, 249, 253.
Hystoria Gruffudd ap Cynan, 259-61; see also *History of Gruffudd ap Cynan, The*.
Hystoria Liwsidar, 252.
Hywel ab Owain Gwynedd, 137, 143, 170, 174, 181.
Hywel Dda, Law of, 124, 134-5, 138, 140, 144, 158, 160, 268-75.
Hywel Dda (ap Cadell), 46, 113, 116, 268.
Hywel Foel ap Griffri, 185.
Hywel of Gwynllŵg, 137.

I

Iarlles y Ffynnon, 222; see also *Owain*.
Ida, 30, 34.
Iddig fab Anarawd Walltgrwn, 201.
Idon (river), 59, 74.
Ieuan, 76.
Ieuan ap Rhydderch, 259.
Ieuan Fendigaid, 263.
Imago Mundi, 248, 262.
indarba, 198.
India, 263.
Indo-European, 21-2.
In Principio, 251.
inscribed stones, 37-9.
insult-price, 269, 271.
internal rhyme, 147-9, 159-60, 163.
Iolo Goch, 253.
Iona, 37.
Iorwerth ap Madog, 268.
Ipotis, 253.
Ireland, 15, 17-9, 29, 35, 54, 81, 102, 110, 112, 116, 127, 130, 134, 136-7, 141, 144, 160, 191, 194, 197-201, 204, 218, 255, 260, 269.
Irish (language), 38, 132, 203.
Irish, Primitive, 38.
Irish, the, 29, 46, 117, 160, 164, 194, 260.
Irish influence, 113, 196-7, 199, 201.
Irish poetry, 127, 173.
'Irish' rhyme, 149.
Irish saga, 193.
Irish Sea, the, 41, 139.
Irish Sea Province, the 197.
Iron-Age Britain, 12.
Isag, 71.
Island of Britain, the, 204, 231, 233, 244.
Island of the Mighty, the, 200.
Isle of Man, the, 38-9.
Isle of Thanet, the, 208.
Islimach, 260.
Israel, 261.
Italy, 123.
Iwys, 46.

J

Jackson, Professor Kenneth H., 25-6, 41, 43, 70, 99, 101, 112, 196.
Jacopo de Voragine, 258.
jealous husband, the, 174.
Jealous Stepmother, motif of the, 215.
Jerusalem, 177, 237.
Jesus, 256.

INDEX

joculatores, 135.
John, Patriarch of India, 262; *see also* Prester John.
Jones, Dafydd Glyn, 233.
Jones, Dr. Gwenallt, 240.
Jones, Professor Gwyn, 195.
Jones, Professor Thomas, 195, 250.
jongleurs, 135.
Jordan (river), 251.
Joseph of Arimathea, 238.
Joy of the Court, the, 229.
Judas Maccabeus, 261.
Juvencus *Englynion*, the, 82, 189.

K

Kent, 208.
Kerry, 173, 179.
Kidwelly, 179.
King with the Prophesied Death, theme of the, 199.
Kintyre, 99.
knight-errant, 223.

L

Lailoken, 102-3.
'Lament in Old Age', 92.
Lancashire, 32, 41.
Laon, 193.
Last Supper, the, 238.
'La Tène', 12.
Latin, 22, 25, 27, 38-9, 55, 105, 189, 208, 235-6, 238, 246-9, 268.
Latin loan-words, 21, 26.
Law of Theft, the, 270.
Laws of the Court, the, 269-71.
Welsh law texts, the, 248, 264, 267-75.
Leeds, 32.
Legend, the Arthurian, 105, 119, 213-4, 220, 234.
Legenda Aurea, the, 258.
Lent, 165.
'Leper of Abercuawg, The', 90, 111.
Letter of Pilate to Claudius, The, 251.
Lewis, Saunders, 58, 60, 62, 147, 266-7, 270, 275.

Lewys Morgannwg, 263.
Leyden, 193.
Lhasa, 263.
Liber Landavensis, 126; see also *Llyfr Llandaf*.
Licat Amr, 214.
Lichfield, 43, 189.
life-price, 269, 271.
Lindisfarne, 33-4, 57, 83.
Liwsidarium, 252.
llallogan, 102.
llan(nau), 40.
Llanbadarn Fawr, 40, 183.
Llancarfan, 40, 246.
Llandaf, 190.
Llanddewi, 133.
Llanddewibrefi, 250, 259.
Llandeilo (Fawr), 40, 189.
Llanfair Caereinion, 107.
Llanfihangel Glyn Myfyr, 182.
Llangwm, 157.
Llanilltud Fawr, 40.
Llannerch, 173.
Llawen (river), 88.
Llefelys, 210, 246.
Lleision, 263.
Lleucu, 174.
Lleu Llaw Gyffes, 192-3, 199-201.
Lloegr, 66; see also England.
Lloegrians, the, 58; *see also* English, the.
Lloyd, Sir J. E., 45, 127, 135.
Lloyd, Mr. Myrddin, 153.
Lloyd-Jones, Professor J., 148.
Lludd, 210, 244, 246.
Llwyfenydd, 62, 65.
Llyfr Blegywryd, 269.
Llyfr Coch Hergest, 190; see also *Red Book of Hergest, The*.
Llyfr Cyfnerth, 269.
Llyfr Gwyn Rhydderch, 190; see also *White Book of Rhydderch, The*.
Llyfr Hwsmonaeth, 264.
Llyfr Iorwerth, 269.
Llyfr Llandaf, 190; see also *Liber Landavensis*.
Llyfr Taliesin, 195; see also *Book of Taliesin, The*.

INDEX

Llyfr yr Ancr, 250, 252-3.
Llygad Gŵr, 140, 153-4, 185.
Llŷr, 110, 191, 193, 199.
Llŷr, the Children of, 199.
Llythyr Ieuan Fendigaid, 262-3.
'Llywarch and his Sons', 84.
'Llywarch and Urien', 83.
Llywarch ap Llywelyn, 131, 152-3, 178-9, 184; *see also* Prydydd y Moch.
Llywarch Hen, 44-6, 79, 82-96, 98, 102, 111, 204.
Llywelyn ab Iorwerth (Llywelyn the Great), 125, 131, 145-6, 152-3, 176-7, 179, 181, 183-5.
Llywelyn ap Gruffudd (Llywelyn the Last), 125, 149, 153-4, 176, 183-6.
Llywelyn ap Madog ap Maredudd, 157, 167.
Llywelyn Fardd, 132, 180, 256.
Llywelyn Offeiriad, 240.
Llywy, 115, 164.
Loch Lomond, 43.
London, 169, 191, 194, 196, 244.
London, the crown of, 244.
Long Hill, the, 169, 173.
Longtown, 42.
Lord of Hosts, the, 104.
Lothian, 29.
Lough Derg, 255.
love lyrics, 138, 248.
love poetry, 137-9.
Lowland Zone, the, 24-5.
Lucidarius, 248, 253.
Lugh, 193.
Luned, 230.
Lyon, 38, 193.
lyres, 15, 147.

M

mab darogan, y, 48; *see also meibion darogan*.
mabinogi, 190, 197.
Mabinogi, Four Branches of the, 190-201, 206-7, 219, 228-9.
Mabinogi, Fourth Branch of the, 141, 204.
Mabinogi, Pedair Cainc y, 190.
Mabinogi, Second Branch of the, 196.
Mabinogi Branwen, 190-1, 194-9, 201, 270-1.
Mabinogi Manawydan, 190-3, 198-9, 270, 275.
Mabinogi Math, 142, 190, 192-3, 198-9, 223.
Mabinogion, the, 158, 183, 190, 203, 209-10, 232, 248, 272.
Mabinogi Pwyll, 190-1, 198.
Mabon, 214, 216, 219.
Mac Cana, Dr. Proinsias, 196-7.
macgnimartha, 198.
Machafwy, 118-9.
Machrau, 118.
Madog, 74, 76.
Madog ap Gwallter, 182-3.
Madog ap Maredudd, 125, 134, 137, 157, 165-8, 176, 232.
Madog ap Selyf, 236.
Maelgwn Gwynedd, 28-9, 33, 41, 52-4, 58, 100, 108, 110, 158, 183.
Maen, 89.
Maescarnedd, 170.
Maestref, 167.
Maes y Croesau, 167.
Maglocunus, 28; *see also* Maelgwn Gwynedd.
Magnus Maximus, 210-2.
Maiden Castle, 12.
Manannan mac Lir, 193.
Manaw Gododdin, 29, 30, 43, 54.
Manawydan fab Llŷr, 191-3, 195, 199, 275.
manfeirdd, 162.
mantle of invisibility, the, 232.
March(es), the, 13, 125, 220.
Marianus, 30.
Marvels of Britain, the, 214.
Marwnad Cynddylan, 99, 100.
Marwnad Owain, 61; *see also* 'Death-Song of Owain, The'.
marwysgafn, 132, 137, 163; *see also* death-bed (-couch) poem.
Mary (the Virgin), 163, 177, 267; *see also* Virgin Mary, the.
Maserfeld, 43.

INDEX 289

Mass, the, 176, 225.
Mathgamhain, 260.
Math, lord of Gwynedd, 192.
Matholwch, 191-2, 270-2.
Mathrafal, 166-8.
matière de France, the, 221.
Matilda, 124.
Matter of Britain, the, 221.
Matter of France, the, 221, 235.
Matter of Rome, the, 221.
Maxen, 210-2.
Maximus, 211-2.
Maxim Wledig, 211.
mechteyrn, 48.
Mechydd ap Llywarch, 90, 112.
Mechydd, son of Llywarch, 90.
Meddygon Myddfai, 248; *see also* physicians of Myddfai, the.
medical prose, 265-6.
medical triads, 265-6, 271.
medicine, 264-6.
Medlan, 96.
meibion darogan, 116; *see also mab darogan, y.*
Meifod, 168-9.
Meigant, 43, 100.
Meigen, 42, 168.
Meilyr ap Gwalchmai, 181-2.
Meilyr Brydydd, 135, 160-3, 166, 172.
Menai, 164-5.
'Men of the North', 32.
Mercia, 42-3, 47, 100.
Merddin, 260; *see also* Merlin, Myrddin.
Merfyn Frych, 113.
Merioneth, 174, 180.
Merlin, 102, 105, 109, 186; *see also* Merddin, Myrddin.
Merlin (Vulgate romance), 239.
Merlinus, 105-6.
'Metcaud', the island of, 33.
metre(s), 42, 66, 141, 148, 150, 159, 177, 179, 183.
metrics, 266.
Michael, the Archangel, 182.
Middle Ages, the, 29, 53, 58, 61, 66, 75, 80, 106-7, 132, 247-8, 252, 256, 263-6.
Middle English, 238.

Middle Welsh, 250.
Midlands, the, 264.
minstrels, the, 252.
Miraculous Harvest, the, 119.
Model Plaints, 273.
Moelfre, 164.
Mold, 179.
Moliant Cadwallon, 42, 99, 100.
Mona, 164, 169-70.
Monmouth, 152.
Montgomery, 179.
Moreiddig, 173.
Morfran, abbot, 180.
Morfran (poet), 141.
Morfran (son of Ceridwen and Tegid), 107.
Morgannwg, 220, 239.
Morgan(t), 32-3, 57.
Morris-Jones, Sir John, 35.
Morudd, Bishop, 256.
Myddfai, 265.
Mynydd Bodafon, 114.
Mynydd Carn, battle of, 126, 160.
Mynyddog Mwynfawr, 33, 42, 68-72, 76, 91, 100.
Myrddin, 44, 102-6, 117-8, 145, 153, 160, 181, 186; *see also* Merddin, Merlin.

N

Nantcarfan, 40.
Nantlle(u), 193.
Narberth, 192.
National Library of Wales, the, 160.
Nativity poem (Madog ap Gwallter), 182.
nature poetry, 111-3, 181, 186.
Neath Abbey, poem to (Lewys Morgannwg), 263.
Neirin, 31, 52; *see also* Aneirin.
Neirthiad, 74.
Nennius, 19, 30, 32, 34, 43, 52, 55, 57, 61, 83, 103, 106, 115, 142, 208-9, 211, 214, 245.
Nest, 174.
Nest, elegy to (Einion ap Gwalchmai), 181.
Nether Went, 126.
New Testament, the, 251.

New Year Feast, 167.
Non, 259.
Norman Conquest, the, 103, 128.
Norman England, 161.
Normans, the, 123-6, 164, 220-1, 245, 260.
Norse kingdom of Dublin, the, 260.
Norsemen, the, 41, 46-7, 116, 260-1.
North, the, 41, 54, 57, 83, 100, 105, 161, 244.
North Sea, the, 139.
Northern Isles, the, 12.
Northumbria, 34, 39, 41, 42-3, 100, 146, 161.
Nwython, 76, 99.

O·

odl, 148.
Odo of Cheriton, 258.
Odrig, 263.
Offa's Dyke, 45, 184.
Ogam(s), 38-9.
Ogfanw (river), 164.
Oianau, the, 103, 105, 117.
Oldest Animals, motif of the, 216.
Oliver, 237.
ollam, 129, 142, 203.
Olwen, 214-6, 219.
onomastic tales, 201.
oppida, Brythonic, 12,
Oswald, 42-3, 100.
Oswestry, 43.
Otuel, the romance of, 237.
Owain, 219, 222, 224, 230-1, 240.
Owain ab Urien, 32, 57, 60-3, 66, 106, 170, 222, 224, 230-2, 255.
Owain ap Hywel Dda, 44.
Owain ap Madog, 139.
Owain Cyfeiliog, 143, 146, 169, 173.
Owain Goch, 185-6.
Owain Gwynedd, 125, 131, 135, 146, 163-5, 169-70, 176.
Owain son of Marro, 73.
Owain's ravens, 170, 232.
Owen, Goronwy, 180.
Owen, Wilfred, 167.

P

pair dadeni, y, 192; *see also* cauldron, magic.
panegyric verse, 11, 14, 17-8, 29, 32, 35-6, 42, 44, 53, 57-8, 113-4, 128-31, 139, 147, 150-1, 154, 157, 171, 266.
Paradise, 251.
Parry, Dr. Thomas, 139, 149, 232.
Passion, story of the, 251.
patient Griselda, theme of, 229.
Paupers' Bibles, the, 250.
Peckham, Archbishop, 251.
pedigrees, 201; *see also* genealogies.
Peebles, 43.
Pelagian heresy, the, 27.
Pembroke, 125, 170; *see also* Penfro.
Pembrokeshire, 192.
pencerdd, 129, 131, 134-6, 140, 142-4, 148, 158-9, 162, 167, 178, 183.
Penda, 42-3, 100.
Penfro, 195; *see also* Pembroke.
Pengwern, 93-4, 96.
Peniarth MS. 2, 32.
Peniarth MS. 3, 160.
Peniarth MS. 6, 190.
Peniarth MS. 7, 225.
Peniarth MS. 14, 225.
penitential lyric, the Middle English, 132.
Penityas, the, 252.
Pennardd, 170.
Pennines, the, 34, 41.
Pentraeth, 174.
Pentre'r-beirdd, 135.
Pen Urien, 83.
Penweddig, 173.
'Peoples of the Goddess Donu', 193.
Perceval, 222, 225.
Perceval, 238.
Peredur, 222, 224-5, 228; see also *Historia Peredur.*
Peredur, 222, 225-8.
Peredur (in *Gododdin*), 76.
peregrini, 39.
Perlesvaus, 238.
Peryf ap Cedifor, 136, 175.
Peter (St.), 163.
Petrus Pictavensis, 250.

Pharaoh, 109.
Phylip (translator), 249.
Phylip Brydydd, 129, 134, 136, 146, 158, 183.
physicians of Myddfai, the, 265; *see also* Meddygon Myddfai.
Pictish (language), 12.
Pictland, 37.
Picts, the, 12, 27, 30, 54, 59, 113, 208, 244.
Pilgrimage to Jerusalem and Constantinople, Charles's, 237.
Plantagenet, 176.
Plato, 267.
Porth Wygyr, 175.
Port Skewet, 162, 175.
Powys, 19, 32, 45-6, 56-7, 81, 83-5, 92-3, 100, 110, 118-9, 126, 128, 134, 153, 157, 165-9, 176, 179, 232, 269.
'Praise of Cadwallon, The', 42, 99.
'Praise of Dewi, In' (Gwynfardd Brycheiniog), 176.
'Praise of Tenby, The', 113.
praise-poems, 14, 130-1, 134, 138, 184-5, 234, 248, 263, 266-7.
Preiddau Annwfn, 119.
Prester John, 262-3.
Preutur Siôn, 263.
Priam, 186.
primogeniture, 124.
'Princeps Wallie', 176, 185.
Procopius, 27.
proest-rhyme, 149, 159, 180.
Promptuarium Bibliae, 250.
prophecies, political, 103-5, 115-9, 245; *see also* vaticinations.
'prophecy, sons of', 116.
prophecy, the gift of, 104, 106-7.
'Prophecy of Britain, The', 46-8, 115-7.
prophecy of Merddin, the, 260.
Prophetiae Merlini, the, 106.
Prose Rhetorics, 240; *see also Areithiau Pros,* the.
prose-verse sagas, 45, 81, 189, 204, 242.
prosody, 18.
proverbs, 273.
'*Prydain briawd',* 161.
Prydain fab Aedd, 244.

Pryderi, 141, 181, 191-3, 197-9.
Prydwen, 119-20.
prydydd, 158.
Prydydd Bychan, Y, 183.
Pryd y Mab, 254.
Prydydd y Moch, 131, 136-7, 139, 152, 178; *see also* Llywarch ap Llywelyn.
Ptolemy, 29.
Pura Wallia, 125.
Purdan Padrig, 255-6.
Pwll, 100.
Pwyll, lord of Dyfed, 191-2, 198, 200.
Pyll, 76.

Q

Queste del Saint Graal, the, 238.

R

Raghnall, son of Mathgamhain, 260.
Ratisbon, 252.
Raymond de Pennafort, 252.
Red Book of Hergest, The, 45, 81, 98, 103, 131, 160, 190, 209-10, 232.
Regimen Sanitatis, 265.
religious prose, 132, 250-9.
religious verse, 112, 131-2, 176-7, 180-3, 187.
Rhaeadr, 214.
Rheged, 32, 34, 40, 54-8, 60-2, 64, 68, 83-4, 87.
rhetoric, 273, 275.
Rhiannon, 191-2, 194, 198-200.
rhieingerddi (Hywel ab Owain Gwynedd), 138.
Rhieingerdd to Efa (Cynddelw), 137, 168.
Rhigyfarch, 259.
Rhiryd Flaidd, 184.
Rhiwallon (physician), 264.
Rhodri ab Owain Gwynedd, 139, 152, 166, 175, 177, 179.
Rhodri Mawr, 44, 113, 161, 164, 201.
Rhonabwy, 232.
Rhuddlan, 170, 179.
Rhufawn, 71.
Rhun (son of Maelgwn Gwynedd), 164.
Rhun (king of Strathclyde), 44.

292 INDEX

rhupunt, 182.
Rhwawn Bebyr, 231.
Rhyd Forlas, 88.
Rhydderch Hen (Hael), 32, 57, 103-5.
Rhymi, the bitch, 218.
Rhys, 173.
Rhys ap Tewdwr, 126.
Rhys Goch Eryri, 259.
Rhys Gryg, 146, 179, 264-5.
Rhys Ieuanc, 129, 134.
Rhys of Deheubarth, the Lord, 118, 125, 144, 146, 158, 171, 175-6, 220, 236, 265.
Ribble, the (river), 41.
Richmond, 68.
ring of memory, the, 232.
Roland, 237.
Roman Britain, 211.
romances, Old French, 221-2, 224, 229, 234-5, 237.
romances, the Welsh, 207, 223-4, 229, 231, 235.
Roman Conquest, the 12-3, 20, 212, 244.
roman d'aventure, 236.
Romans, the, 11, 23, 27, 35, 244, 261.
Rome, 24, 28, 45, 169, 211-2.
Roncesvaux, 237.
Ross Low, 83.
'runs(s)', 242, 273.

S

saga poetry, 81-3, 85, 102, 111, 113.
saga(s), 18, 44, 81, 83, 85, 92-3, 95-6, 101, 103, 107, 189, 197-9, 204, 209, 227, 258.
saints, 39, 40, 130-3, 169, 176, 258-9, 267.
saints, Lives of, 213, 238, 250, 256-60.
Salaün, 102.
Salerno, 266.
Saracens, the, 236-7.
sarhad, 269, 271.
satire, 15, 130-1, 147, 235, 255.
Saxon England, 161.
Saxons, the, 27, 48, 116-7, 208-9, 213, 244-5.
Scandinavians, the, 47.
scélaige, 142.
scop, the Anglo-Saxon, 14.

Scotland, 11-3, 24, 27, 35, 37, 44, 46-7, 54, 102, 116, 144.
Scots, the, 27, 30, 116, 160, 208, 244.
Scripture, 172, 250-1.
seanchas, 204.
Seisyll(t) Bryffwrch, 134, 139, 167.
Selyf, son of Cynan, 56.
Seven Deadly Sins, the, 251.
Seven Sacraments, the, 251-2.
Seven Sages of Rome, the, 239.
Severn, the, 40, 42, 47, 164, 169, 173, 175.
shaman, 15.
Shrewsbury, 179.
Shropshire, 45, 175, 184.
Sicily, 123.
'Signs before Doomsday', 180.
Siôn Cent, 255, 257.
skald, the Icelandic, 14, 131.
Skye, 37.
sleep, vision-producing, 232.
Snowdonia, 162, 186.
Solway Firth, the, 32, 54.
Song of Roland, The, 237.
'Son of God', 200.
South, the, 168, 176, 178-9.
Southern, R. W., 221.
Sovereignty, theme of the hero's marriage with the, 227.
Spain, 123, 236.
'Spoils of Annwfn, The', 119.
Spring, 112.
Stafell Gynddylan, 93.
St. Albans, 12.
Stanzas of the Graves, the, 119, 203.
'Statute of Gruffudd ap Cynan, The', 128, 158, 160.
St. Beuno, 40, 258-9.
'St. Beuno, *Life* of', 258.
St. Cadfan, 132, 169, 180-1.
St. Carannoc, 37.
St. Catherine, 258.
St. Clears, 179.
St. Columba, 37.
St. David, 40, 116-7, 132-3, 169, 175, 258-9; *see also* Dewi Sant.
'St. David, *Life* of', 133, 258-9.
St. David's, 134, 175-6, 180, 193, 258.

INDEX

St. Donnan the Great, 37.
Stephen, 124, 126.
St. Germanus, 27, 208.
St. Germanus, Life of, 208.
St. Gildas, 259; see Gildas.
St. James, 236.
St. Margaret, 258.
St. Martin of Tours, 39.
St. Mary Magdalen, 258.
St. Mary of Egypt, 258.
St. Ninian of Whithorn, 37.
'Story of Taliesin, The', 106.
Story of the Infancy of Jesus Christ, The, 251.
St. Patrick, 255.
St. Patrick's Purgatory, 255.
Strabo, 17.
Strathcarron, the battle of, 44, 99.
Strathclyde, 32, 41, 43-4, 46-7, 54, 79, 81, 99, 101.
Strathclyde Britons, 116.
St. Tysilio, 132.
St. Walloch, 37.
Subhne Geilt, 102.
Sulien, bishop of St. David's, 193.
Summa de Poenitentia et Matrimonio, 252.
Surexit-Memorandum, the, 189, 268.
Sussex, 13.
Swale (river), 68.
Swansea, 179.
'Syladin', 177.
Synod at Llanddewibrefi, the, 259.
synthetic language, 22, 26-7.
Syria, 123.
Sywno 76.

T

Tacitus, 16.
Tale of Sir Topaz, 234.
Talhaearn Tad Awen, 31, 52, 66.
Taliesin, 11, 18-9, 26, 31-5, 37, 41, 44, 46, 52-66, 70, 74, 78, 80-3, 98, 102, 106-11, 113, 116, 118, 141, 146, 158, 161-2, 166, 181, 183, 204.
talu medd, 69.
tasks, 214, 216-9.

Tegeingl, 179.
Tegid Foel, 107.
Teifi (river), 179.
Tenby, 113.
Ten Commandments, the, 251.
Tern, 175, 184; see also Tren.
teulu (family), 182.
   teulu (war-band), 135, 165, 173.
Theodosius, 211.
Theodric, 33-4; see also Deodric.
Theological Tracts, 250.
Third Crusade, the, 169.
Thomas, the Apostle, 263.
Thor, 161.
Tibet, 263.
Tigris, 251.
Trahaearn ap Caradog, 126.
translators, schools of, 249.
Treachery of the Long Knives, the, 208-9.
Tren, 175; see also Tern.
Tre'r-beirdd, 135.
triads, 193, 265-6, 270-3.
Triads of the Island of Britain, The, 141, 158, 201, 203-4, 206, 213, 271.
Trinity, the, 131, 170, 182.
Trioedd Ynys Prydain, 141-2; see also Triads of the Island of Britain, The.
Troit, the boar, 214; see also Twrch Trwyth.
Trojan legend, the, 164, 186.
Trojan War, the, 161, 246-7.
troubadour, the, 138.
trouvère, the, 138.
Troy, 245-6.
Trystan and Esyllt, 204.
Túatha Dé Danann, the, 193.
Tudfwlch, 77.
Tudor monarchs, the, 48.
Tudor victory, the, 115.
Tudur, 173.
Turpin, Archbishop, 236.
Tweed, the, 43.
Twrch Trwyth (Trwyd), 214, 216-8.
Tyne, the, 38.
tyranni, 13.
Tysilio, poem to, 168-9.
Tywyn, 180.

U

ugly maiden, the, 227.
Ulster, Kings of, 260.
Unbeiniaeth Prydain, 135.
Unfaithful Wife, The, 192, 199.
Urien Rheged, 32-4, 42, 44-5, 57-65, 83-5, 87-8, 92, 95, 106, 110, 146, 161.
'Urien's Corpse', 83.
'Urien's Head', 83.
Urien Yrechwydd, 58, 66.
Usk, 39.
Utopia, 262.
uwch cyntedd, 134.

V

Vale of Wye, the, 186.
vates, 17-8.
vaticinations,-atory verse, 16, 46, 48, 103, 106, 117, 136, 160, 185, 209; *see also* prophecies, political.
Veleda, 16.
vendetta, 270.
vengeance quest, the, 228.
Vergil, 107.
Verulamium, 12-3.
Vienne, 38.
Vikings, 164.
Vinaver, Eugène, 234.
Virgin Mary, the, 132; *see also* Mary (the Virgin).
'Vision of the Youth, the', 254.
Visio Sancti Pauli, 255.
Vita Merlini, 106.
Vitae Sanctorum Wallensium, 133-4.
Vita Sancti Gundleii, 126.
Vortigern, 27, 106, 109, 115; *see also* Guorthigirnus, Gwrtheyrn.
Vulgate Cycle of Arthurian romances, the, 238-9.

W

Waelest Edwy, 157.
Wales, 11, 13, 15, 19, 24, 27, 29, 30, 32, 35, 38-48, 52-4, 56, 64, 79, 81, 83, 92, 99, 100, 102-3, 114, 116-7, 123-7, 130, 134, 136, 141, 144, 152-3, 157, 161, 164, 168-9, 171, 173, 175-6, 178-9, 184, 189, 194, 197, 203, 209, 213, 218, 220, 222-3, 234-5, 244-8, 250, 253, 263, 266-70.
Walter of Henley, 249, 264.
'War-band's Return, The', 63-4, 66.
Waste Land, theme of the, 228.
'Way of the Brother Odoricus', 263.
Wear (river), 29.
Welsh, Medieval (Middle), 190, 250.
Welsh, Modern, 11.
Welsh, Old, 189-90.
Welsh Primitive, 20, 25.
Welsh, the, 11, 41, 48, 83, 115, 117-8, 123-4, 133, 153, 161, 163, 178, 185, 220-1, 244-5, 252, 261.
Welsh Church, the, 133.
Welsh Language, the, 11, 20-3, 26-9, 31, 34-5, 51, 53-5, 114, 145-6, 171, 174-6, 189, 208, 234, 238, 242, 247, 249, 251, 255, 258, 262, 264, 266-8, 270.
Welshmen, 116, 179, 185, 220, 248, 256, 260, 270, 273.
wergild, 269.
Wessex, 46-7.
Westmorland, 41.
West Saxons, the, 116.
'White Book of Rhydderch, The', 190, 209, 225.
White Stag, hunting of the, 228.
'White Township', the, 94.
Whithorn, 37.
Whitland, 268.
Wild Man of the Woods, theme of the, 102, 106.
'wildness' (of Owain), 231.
William Fychan of Penrhyn, 263.
William of Malmesbury, 220, 246.
Williams, Professor Caerwyn, 253.
Williams, Professor, G. J., 249.
Williams, Sir Ifor, 43, 45-6, 48, 55-6, 63, 82, 107, 109-10, 112, 148, 191, 208.
William the Conqueror, 123.
Wiltshire, 12.
Wind, *cywydd* to the (Dafydd ap Gwilym), 120.
Winwaed Field, 41.

witches of Gloucester, the, 226, 228.
Woden, 161.
wonder-child, 106, 109, 253.
wonder-tale, 223, 241.
World, nature of the, 253.
writing, 13, 15, 19, 55, 206.
Wrnach, 217.
Wye, the, 47.

Y

Yago, 164.
Yarnbury, 12.
Y Dref Wen, 94.
Yellow Plague, the, 28.
Ymborth yr Enaid, 253.
Ymddiddan â'r Brawd Llwyd, Dafydd ap Gwilym's, 257.
York, 47.
York, Vale of, 34.
Yorkshire, 34, 57, 68.
Yorkshire Wolds, 34.
Yrechwydd, 58.
Ysbaddaden, 214, 216-9.
Ysgithrwyn, 218.
Ysgrifen Brydain, 114.
Yspadaut Uran, 194.
Yspadaut Urdaul Benn, 194.
Ystoria Bown o Hamtwn, 236.
Ystoria Brutus, 246.
Ystoria Dared, 246-7.
Ystoria de Carolo Magno, 236.
Ystoriaeu y Seint Greal, 238-9.
Ystrad Glud, 54.
Yvain, 222.
Ywain, 173.
Ywain son of Beli son of Nwython, 44, 99.

THE LIBRARY
ST. MARY'S COLLEGE OF MARYLAND
ST. MARY'S CITY, MARYLAND 20686

089736